JINGO

JINGO

James B. Lamb

Macmillan Canada
Toronto

Canadian Cataloguing in Publication Data

Lamb, James B., 1919–
    Jingo : the buckskin brigadier who opened up the Canadian West

ISBN 0-7715-9181-0

1. Strange, T. Bland (Thomas Bland), 1831-1925.
2. Canadian – History, Military – To 1900.
3. Riel Rebellion, 1885.   4. Canada.   Canadian
Army – Biography.   5. Great Britain.   Army –
Biography.   6. Soldiers – Canada – Biography.
I. Title

U55.S88L34 1992   971.05′ 092   C92-094316-0

Macmillan Canada wishes to thank the Canada Council for supporting its publishing program.

Macmillan Canada
A Division of Canada Publishing Corporation
Toronto, Canada

1 2 3 4 5   JD   96 95 94 93 92

Printed in Canada

*To Jack Orton, who started it all,
this book is affectionately dedicated*

CONTENTS

AUTHOR'S FOREWORD

One of the difficulties in preparing this book has been that many of the incidents in the life of Thomas Bland Strange, especially during his boyhood years, are described only in his autobiography, *Gunner Jingo's Jubilee*. This book is written throughout in the third person—"young Tommy" becomes "Tom" and ultimately "old Jingo," and nowhere is any touch of personal feeling allowed to intrude in a surprisingly dispassionate and impersonal account of a long life. There is no mention of the personal details of married and family life; we are not told so much as the names of his wife and daughters!

Partly, of course, this was the reticence required of a Victorian officer and gentleman, who did not bandy details of his personal life about in public, but it reflects also Strange's extremely private personality. He maintained the traditional "stiff upper lip" of the British gentleman in adversity and the stoical code of the "what can't be altered must be borne" school, and only very occasionally does any hint of bitterness concerning ungrateful governments and incompetent superiors emerge. However admirable such restraint, it imposes real hardship on a biographer desperate for quotable expressions of feeling on the part of his subject.

Canadian historians, too, have left notable gaps in recording Strange's career; there is no single account covering the various phases of his Canadian experience. What has been written chiefly concerns his campaign during the Northwest Rebellion of 1885, but even here there are curious omissions. Pierre Berton writes of the Alberta Field Force without once mentioning the name of its commander;

indeed, he implies that it was raised, trained, and led by Sam Steele. Desmond Morton acknowledges the many difficulties overcome and hardships borne by Strange, but is content to accept an admittedly jealous Middleton's portrayal of his "fire-eating" subordinate as an unreliable eccentric. Professor R.C. Macleod, in his foreword to Jingo's book, gives him his due as a British soldier without mention of his Canadian context:

> Strange was no brutal, unthinking soldier. He had a very good mind and was widely read in the philosophy and science of his time. His world view, distasteful as it may seem to the modern reader, was reasoned and coherent. Anyone who wishes to understand the phenomenon of British world dominance in the nineteenth century could do worse than to read his memoirs.

Perhaps the best account of Strange's role in the Northwest is in Earl McCourt's *The Buckskin Brigadier*. Sam Steele's *Forty Years in Canada* gives a unique view of Strange as seen by his gifted subordinate.

For the story of Strange's role in organizing and training Canada's first professional army, there is only Colonel G. Mitchell's superb regimental history, *RCHA—Right of the Line*.

The author hopes that the following account may help in some measure to fill the gap in the Canadian record of this remarkable man.

James B. Lamb
Big Harbour, N.S.

ACKNOWLEDGMENTS

The author is indebted to many people for the research on which this book is based, and their efforts on his behalf are hereby gratefully acknowledged. They include Len Gottselig, chief librarian of the Glenbow Museum, Calgary; John Charles, special collections librarian of the University of Alberta, Edmonton; Jane Hall of the information bureau of the *Daily Telegraph*, London; Dr. P.B. Boyden of the National Army Museum, London; and the staffs of the Westminster Central Library, London; the Dalhousie University library, Halifax; the circulating department, public library, Sydney, N.S.; the Robarts Library, University of Toronto; Camberley public library, Camberley, England; and "The News," Camberley, England.

Special thanks go to Mrs. Ann Melvin, librarian at the Royal Canadian Military Institute in Toronto for her invaluable assistance and for access to the Institute's collection of soldiers' diaries, official reports, and other military publications. Thanks also to Mrs. P.E. Bendall, deputy librarian of the Royal Military Academy, Sandhurst, in Camberley, England, for her advice and suggestions.

This book could not have been written without constant reference to General Strange's autobiography, *Gunner Jingo's Jubilee*, third edition, published in London, 1896, by J. MacQueen. This remarkable book was recently reprinted by the University of Alberta Press, 1988, with an erudite introduction by R.C. Macleod.

As this is a book for the general reader, footnotes and references have been omitted, but the interested reader will find a list of books on the subject in the bibliography appended.

JINGO

PROLOGUE

The Prisoner

The little Mounted Police post basked in the pale Saskatchewan sunshine, a huddle of whitewashed frame buildings inside a log rampart. The Union Jack, bright against the blue prairie sky, flapped lazily in the afternoon breeze above the dusty parade ground. At the river's edge below the fort, a paddle steamer lay at the landing stage, the hiss of escaping steam from her funnel emphasizing the serenity of the scene.

On the veranda of the hut that served as a lock-up, an old Indian drowsed, leaning back against the wall to enjoy the benefit of shade on this warm afternoon. A slight, shrunken figure, he had an unusually large head. His tangled hair, falling to his shoulders, framed a shrewd, wrinkled face, its eyes narrowed against the sunshine. From the barred window above his head came the cheerful whistling of his jailer, a young constable, stripped to the waist, who was whitewashing the cells inside.

The sound of approaching footsteps roused the slouching Indian; someone was walking towards him from the open riverside gate—a stranger, and a figure of unusual appearance. He was tall, and carried himself with an exaggerated erectness that made him appear taller still. A beaked nose jutted out above a black beard that cascaded to his chest,

and two piercing dark eyes viewed their surroundings with a
quick and lively interest.

The new arrival moved with an assured step, and his
bearing reflected a commanding, and perhaps autocratic,
personality. His dress, too, was distinctive. His blue trousers with a wide gold stripe down the sides were tucked into
a pair of high cowboy boots, and his fringed buckskin jacket
was topped by a wide-brimmed hat with one side pinned up
by a crest of some sort.

Following the instructions of the sergeant at the gate, the
stranger strode briskly up to the little jail, and the Indian
rose slowly to his feet to meet him, drawing his striped
Hudson's Bay Company blanket about his shoulders with
the impassive dignity of a Roman senator adjusting his toga.
He was, after all, a person of consequence, despite his bleak
surroundings and his present humiliating status as a prisoner of these policemen, and there was no hint of servility in
manner or bearing as he faced his visitor. For he was Big
Bear, chief of the Plains Crees, the most intransigent of the
Canadian Indian tribes, and the man he faced was the
remorseless General Strange, who had pursued him for
months through trackless wilderness and driven him at last,
abandoned and alone, to this white man's jail.

What these two men said to one another in the minutes
that followed is not known. All that Strange would say
afterwards was that he could feel no animosity towards this
man who had led him so long and wearying a chase and cost
him so dearly in both health and wealth. But this confrontation at the tiny Battleford police post in September 1885 was
the most dramatic in the history of the young nation of
Canada, a confrontation both significant and symbolic.

Big Bear was the chief of the tribe that had massacred,
looted, and burned on Canada's remote frontier; his name
had become a byword in the settled and civilized east. No
matter that he was to be proven more sinned against than

sinning, that he had not been present at the Frog Lake murders, that his principal crime had been simply his inability to control his young braves, a fatal weakness in a tribal chief.

More than any man alive, he represented the old plains way of life, when tribes were free to roam wherever they wished, living off the vast buffalo herds. Alone among the tribal chiefs, he had refused to accept the white man's rule, or to live within the confines of a tribal reservation and the edicts of bureaucrats in a remote Ottawa. He had made his tribe a focal point for native unrest and had swelled its ranks with every malcontent and restless renegade from more tractable tribes. But when matters came to a head and Riel preached rebellion among Indians and Métis alarmed at the incursion of surveyors for a railroad across their land, he had been unable to restrain his warriors and had been borne along on the tide of events beyond his control. It was a tide that had carried him through misery and privation and cast him up at last, abandoned by his people, in the confinement of this Mounted Police jail, where he had endured the final reproach of his scattered tribesmen: "the chief with the big head and the small heart."

The farouche figure conversing with the captive chieftain could hardly have presented a greater contrast, but he shared with Big Bear a distrust and dislike of bureaucrats in general and Ottawa bureaucrats in particular, and he sympathized with the plight of the Plains Indians. Indeed, he had gone on record as predicting, before the rebellion, that federal policies designed to convert the heirs of countless generations of hunters and wanderers into settled farmers, grubbing a meagre living from thin prairie soil, could only lead to trouble.

Yet in every other way Strange was the antithesis of the captive Indian he had pursued for so long. Where Big Bear represented the old way of life on the plains, Strange stood for the new. His ranch in southern Alberta was the forerunner of countless others soon to follow. As "Cowboy Tom," in leather chaps and jacket, he was the patriarch of the footloose cowboys already jingling onto the western scene. He was also the father of Canada's professional regular army. The Royal Canadian Artillery gunners he had organized and led had just been bloodied in their country's first shooting war. Canada's first truly bilingual general officer, he had insisted that French-Canadian and Anglo-Canadian must fight side by side in the new Canadian army, and he had made an unwanted, untrained French-Canadian militia regiment a welcome and effective part of his little Alberta Field Force. Above all, he had single handedly raised, trained, and led a sort of private army of Montana cowboys, Alberta ranch hands, North West Mounted Policemen, and green militiamen; had armed, outfitted, and supplied them despite official dilatoriness and downright obstruction; and had taken them on an unbelievable march of more than a thousand miles through a bog-ridden wilderness, the most difficult terrain in the country. In a campaign marked elsewhere by botch and bungle, his achievement shone all the brighter, as the most remarkable military effort in the young nation's history.

He was to receive nothing for his achievement but trouble and endless litigation from bureaucrats far away in Ottawa; no thanks, orders, or medals, no recognition of any sort.

He had been inspired throughout by an exaggerated sense of patriotism, a quality which had won him the nickname of "Jingo," for this India-born Scot had developed an intense love of Canada and all things Canadian, and was as much at home in a habitant cottage or a cowpony's saddle as in the viceregal drawing room.

A born leader of men and one of the last of the great Victorian eccentrics, Thomas Bland "Jingo" Strange was the most colourful Canadian of his time. This is his story.

ONE

As the Twig Is Bent

Thomas Bland Strange—the family name was Strang but army clerks always added an "e," and in the end this anglicization had been reluctantly accepted—was born in the garrison town of Meerut, India, on September 15, 1831. His father was Colonel Harry Francis Strange, a Scotsman; his mother was Mary Letitia Bland of Anglo-Irish descent and he was born to be a soldier. His father was commanding officer of the 26th Cameronians, now stationed in Meerut, and he was the son, grandson, great-grandson, and nephew of countless martial ancestors, most of whom had met their end in various parts of the world while serving King and Country, a tradition of which young Thomas was intensely proud and which, from his earliest days, he intended to emulate.

He could not have been born under more favourable circumstances for following the ancient and honourable profession of arms. Besides inheriting a long family tradition, he was to come of age at a time when the British Empire was approaching the zenith of its power and influence, with responsibilities in every part of the globe. The high noon of Empire brought peace at home at the price of endless skirmishing on far-flung frontiers; there would be scarcely a year in Strange's long lifetime when the British

Army was not campaigning against some warlike tribe in some faraway place, and soldiering was the order of the day.

Nothing better illustrates the proliferation of colonial wars in Victorian times than an exhibit prepared for the Royal Canadian Military Institute in Toronto, showing the campaign medals issued to the British Army in the period between Waterloo and the present day. There are dozens of them, and apart from the handful awarded during the two world wars, they represent colonial campaigns in virtually every quarter of the world and, except for those representing World War II, all were issued during Strange's long career as a soldier.

Thomas's boyhood memories, recorded in his journal years later, were of playing soldiers with other youngsters of similar age in the hot and dusty ditch under the ramparts of the fort at Meerut, and of watching his father's regiment, a Scots unit with a distinguished record of service in the British Army, at their various drills and exercises, wearing the traditional high, plumed shakos and scarlet tunics of the time. The doll he played with as an infant was dressed as a soldier, and he had cut off its left arm (prudently re-attached later by his mother) so that it might resemble Colonel Oglander, the fierce old former commanding officer of the regiment, who had lost an arm with Wellington in Spain. With his mother and older brother, young Thomas was bundled off, while still a very small boy, to the healthier environment of a Himalayan hill town and then, a few years later, was moved with his family back to England and the new base of the Cameronians at Chatham, on the Thames estuary.

It was here that young Tommy, for the first and last time, was able to enjoy life with his father. The two would spend their evenings together on walks about the Chatham lines, the earthwork fortifications that protected the base, while his father explained the functions of ravelin, rampart, and redoubt. It was the beginning of the boy's military education, and these regular and, for Tommy's short legs, exhausting rambles were to become memories cherished throughout a long and eventful life and recorded later in his journal.

The Cameronians had no sooner settled into the routine of home garrison duty than the regiment was posted to the Far East for service in the first China War, and its commanding officer was forced to leave his family for what would be the first of a series of prolonged absences. The two boys and their mother went to stay with her family in Ireland for a summer, and a few months later, when his mother returned to Chatham and his brother went off to school, young Thomas was left with his grandparents. This unusual couple were to have a profound influence on the growing boy. Grandfather Bland, a fierce old ex-dragoon, had fought at Waterloo, and was full of stories about campaigns in India and service with the Duke of Wellington. His Waterloo medal, worn each June on the anniversary of that famous battle, made a deep impression on young Tom, who determined somehow to secure one like it for himself one day.

But it was his Irish grandmother, a tall, white-haired woman once renowned for her beauty, whom Tom loved above all and whose stories, filled with Irish myth and Scottish folklore, captured his youthful imagination. When the time came eventually for Tom to go off to boarding school, she gave him a small pocket-book which had belonged to a favourite son, Tom's uncle, who had lost an arm while serving with the 42nd Highlanders, the renowned Black Watch. It contained a list of the uncle's battles, together with details of laundry lists and mess wine bills—the writing notably crabbed after the loss of the owner's arm— but it was entrusted to young Tom as a sort of sacred relic, and was accepted as such.

The old lady made an even greater impression on the wide-eyed youngster with her romantic tales of his ancient Scots and Irish forebears, for she was determined that he should not forget his proud Celtic lineage even though forced to live among mere Englishmen. Tom was especially impressed by her account of an ancestor who had served with Bonnie Prince Charlie, and was fleeing for his life after the shattering defeat at Culloden. Pursued by English dragoons to the home of his lady-love, he had taken that lady's advice and hidden under her sweeping hoop skirts just before the dragoon officer entered her room. The lady invited the officer to search her house, then turned back to her harpsichord and began playing a series of Jacobite tunes, ending with a sad Highland lament.

The officer noticed a third, and larger, foot beneath the hem of the lady's dress, but he was a true British gentleman. Treading heavily upon this third foot, he bowed and kissed the lady's hand as his dragoons made their departure, whispering, as he did so: "I too would fain be a rebel to secure such a hiding place!" He then withdrew in the wake of his men, while the lady, not to be outdone in these courtesies, played "God Save the King."

This story and a dozen others like it were his grandmother's lasting legacy to young Tom. They left him with an abiding pride in his family heritage, a taste for romance, and a streak of stubborn Scots rebelliousness against established authority which was to play a large part in his subsequent career.

All too soon Tom was packed off to a prep school for Eton, rather than the school he would have preferred where his brother was preparing for entry to Sandhurst and a military career in his father's footsteps. It was a lonely ordeal for a sensitive youngster who was also something of a solitary, but the school terms were punctuated by wonderful holiday sessions filled with sailing, swimming, and rambling, with Irish cousins who lived in a crumbling old castle on the wild west coast of Kerry in Ireland.

It was, on the whole, a well-rounded boyhood, but sterner times lay ahead. After a few years in the Far East, the Cameronians came home to be posted to Edinburgh Castle, and their commandant was able to secure lodging nearby for his family. Tom was taken out of prep school at the end of the term and was entered with his brother at Edinburgh Academy. This was an institution designed specifically to give young Scots of good family the sort of public-school education available elsewhere only in England, and thus to enable them to compete on equal terms with their English contemporaries for places in government services. Great stress was placed on accent, manners, and usage of speech, for such things were important to applicants for commissions in the armed forces or positions in the civil service.

Tom found it a tough school, academically and physically. Because he already spoke with something of an English accent, he was thought by his Scots schoolmates to be guilty of "swank," and was accordingly the butt of much bullying and hazing by older boys. This all came to an end when Tom, goaded past endurance, challenged his most persistent tormentor. In a battle fought before the entire school gathered in a sort of natural amphitheatre on the sports grounds, Tom established himself as a student celebrity. Though given a severe thrashing by his bigger and stronger opponent and knocked to the ground four times, with his eye blacked, his nose bloodied, and his ear torn, he flew into a sort of frenzy, and began raining blows on his rival. One blow got home, breaking his opponent's nose, and when the bigger boy flinched he received Tom's luckiest punch, a blow on the left ear that dropped him senseless to the ground.

Years later, as a major-general, Strange would recall this battle as a turning point in his life, giving him a confidence he would never lose. Together with a natural aptitude for sports, it won Tom a secure place in the school hierarchy, and the spartan routine at the academy soon imparted a toughness that would stand him in good stead in the years ahead.

While Tom was still at the Academy, his father transferred to the Kings Own Scottish Borderers and returned with that regiment to India, a move dictated largely by economic factors. Without a private income of his own, it was difficult for an officer to maintain the expensive living style expected of the colonel commandant of a regiment in garrison on a home station like Edinburgh. Service in India, on the other hand, resulted in both higher pay and lower expenses, as well as a more active service career in a country seething with regional conflict. Since his brother entered Sandhurst at the same time, Tom was left on his own at school, save for occasional visits from his mother, and he quickly matured into something of a student leader at the Academy.

He matured in other ways, too. The realization of his father's sacrifice in giving up family life in order to finance his elder son's entry into Sandhurst and Tom's continuing expensive education brought out a strong sense of duty in the younger son's character and filled him with a determination to succeed. He assumed the role of head of the family, becoming increasingly protective and concerned about his mother, and a friend and confidant as well as a son. "All that was best [in me] was due to her influence," he was to write in later years.

Certainly, she instilled in her son a strong sense of piety, and when he left home to begin his service career she presented him with a Bible, in which she had written these lines:

> Remember, love, who gave thee this
> When other days shall come;
> When she, who had thy earliest kiss,

Sleeps in her narrow home.
Remember, 'twas a mother gave
The gift to one she'd die to save.
And when the scoffer, in his pride
Shall bid thee cast the gift aside,
Which thou from youth hast borne;
She bids thee pause, and ask thy breast
If he or she has loved thee best.

No scoffer was ever to persuade young Tom to cast his Bible aside; he carried it with him till the day he died.

Tom's professional goal was now clear; he intended to enter the artillery, the one branch of the army in which talent and merit counted for more than good family and bravery towards career advancement. It required a rigorous technical training to secure a commission in the artillery, which was granted only after cadets had successfully completed an intensive course at the gunnery school at Woolwich, an institution located in a London suburb close to the huge national arsenal that produced, tested, and stored Britain's artillery.

Tom was determined to gain entry to Woolwich and accordingly his mother, in the absence of his father, took him to London to an interview with the Master-General of the Ordnance, the celebrated Waterloo hero Lord Fitzroy Somerset.

The old veteran, who had lost an arm in the battle, looked over the tall young man with an approving eye.

"Can you pass the entry exam?" he asked.

Tom, who had little idea of what was required but every confidence in his own ability, promptly replied: "Yes, sir."

"Then you shall go up in three months," was the equally prompt response.

Not until he had seen a synopsis of the requirements for entry did Tom realize how unprepared he was. Mathematics,

especially geometry, algebra, and trigonometry were the
chief stumbling blocks. Tom's education at Edinburgh Academy had been in languages and the classics; he knew nothing
of mathematics beyond simple arithmetic. His only chance
lay in an intensive course with a tutor, and accordingly he
presented himself at the home of an established crammer, a
man who specialized in preparing applicants for entry into
the services and universities. But the learned man was appalled at Tom's lack of any mathematical knowledge and
refused to take him as a pupil. He had no hope of passing the
exam in a mere three months, he assured Tom, and his
inevitable failure would bring discredit on his tutor. Tom got
up, went outside, and returned carrying his portmanteau,
which he put down in the hall.

"I mean to stay," he declared.

Impressed by his determination, the mathematics coach
took him on as a pupil and was amazed at the young man's
zeal and ability to learn. At the end of the three months he
told Tom: "You may go up; you will pass."

And he did.

The Royal Military Academy at Woolwich was a unique
and curious institution still dominated by the precepts of
General Borghardt, the eighteenth-century Danish father of
the Royal Artillery. A sort of purgatory through which all
candidates for commissions in the Royal Artillery and the
Royal Engineers had to pass, it had the usual collection of
traditions, typical of such institutions, pertaining to dress
and behaviour of new cadets, so that lanky Long Tom, as he
soon found himself called, had to present himself on his first
day in top hat and tailcoat. It was also burdened with more
than its share of the hazings and humiliations by which
senior students at service schools everywhere attempt to
keep their juniors in their proper and subordinate place. In
addition to "fagging" for their elders and betters—brushing
clothes, cleaning rooms, making toast and coffee, running

errands, and so forth—they were expected to learn to "take a blow" like a gentleman, and woe betide the junior who dared to strike back.

Thus Tom found himself in trouble when, at the top of a flight of stairs, he was kicked painfully from behind and sent sprawling headfirst down the stairs. Turning to confront his tormentor, he found himself facing the smallest and mean-est-tempered of the senior cadets, and one who took advantage of a brutal system to indulge a taste for sadism.

"If you weren't a mere junior you would like to strike me back, wouldn't you?" the little senior taunted, and Tom, getting to his feet, could not resist blurting out that, indeed, he would. For this "insubordination" he was ceremonially beaten by four senior cadets with their broad leather belts, one of them, the little accuser, using the buckle end. As school tradition required, Tom accepted his punishment, standing with feet braced and arms folded, gazing stoically to his front.

But these painful absurdities apart, the Academy proved to be a surprisingly pleasant and interesting experience for the gangling Scot. For one thing, it provided an outlet for his artistic and imaginative temperament, something he had not expected in a service academy. There was extensive art training; artillery officers were expected, in the days before photography, to make quick and accurate sketches of the terrain in which they were campaigning and a surprising number developed into accomplished artists, painting and sketching with rare sensitivity. Tom revelled in this field and quickly developed into the best, as well as the most enthusiastic, artist in his class. For the rest of his life he made a habit of sketching, and often painting, the people and places about him.

As the most "scientific" of the military branches, artillery officers were encouraged to make a variety of magnetic readings and astronomical observations wherever they might happen to be stationed, and as part of their training cadets at Woolwich spent considerable time at the nearby observatory. The marvels of the heavens, as seen through the observatory telescope, fascinated Tom, and he spent much of his off-duty time there. After graduation he would join the observatory staff for a few months, and throughout his long career he habitually made magnetic and other readings at each station to which he was posted.

Always an omnivorous reader, Tom began to take an interest in poetry and even tried his hand at writing verse, although he was careful to hide his work from fellow cadets who would have ragged him mercilessly. But he found a fellow romantic in a senior classman, Charles Gordon, who was later to distinguish himself in the Far East and become known to the public, first as "Chinese Gordon," and later, after his death at the hands of the Mahdi's forces, as "Gordon of Khartoum." Despite their disparity in size, Gordon being short and slight of build, the two became fast friends and often took long walks together. Gordon was obsessed with Africa, the vast and still largely unknown continent just being opened up to European exploration and development, and was determined to go there.

It is difficult today to realize the obsessive fascination which Africa and all things African exercised over the Victorians, a fascination not unlike that felt today for outer space—and for much the same reason. Little more than a century ago, much of the interior of Africa south of the Sahara was as unexplored as the face of the moon. No one, African or European, knew the source of the Nile, one of the world's mightiest rivers. It would be Gordon himself who would play a definitive part in establishing its whereabouts, and so would add his name to those of Speke, Burton, Baker, Stanley, and Livingstone as men who helped resolve the continent's oldest riddle.

Both Gordon and Strange were fascinated with the mystery of Africa. Long before Dart and Broome and Leakey unlocked the secrets of the Olduvai gorge and revealed Africa as the birthplace of the human race, it was apparent that the continent was a sort of time capsule, in which all manner of living things that elsewhere had been altered or eliminated by severe climatic change had survived untouched by the glaciations of the Ice Ages. Scientists were fascinated by races of giants and pygmies, and by people with physical features unknown in Europe since Palaeolithic times, living in primitive tribal societies without the use of metal tools, the wheel, writing, or even a numbering system. To Victorians it was all a sort of Lost World, an irresistible attraction to every romantic and adventurer, as well as to serious botanists, zoologists, and anthropologists. No one was more fascinated than Gordon, and he quickly imbued Strange with his enthusiasm. The two planned an African expedition, to be taken during their first long leave, and they organized their expedition down to the smallest detail.

The fortunes of war were to intervene and prevent the trip, and both men were destined to pursue their careers a world apart, with Gordon dying a hero's death in Khartoum as Strange was organizing his march against Big Bear in the Canadian wilderness, but throughout their lives the two friends would remain in touch with one another.

They had a good deal in common, including a certain intellectual freedom that set them apart from fellow students. They shared, among other things, a deep interest in religious philosophy, a finicky faddism in what they ate and drank, and an abiding concern with physical fitness. Each would prove to be a born leader of men, with extraordinary organizational ability, and each was utterly fearless. But Gordon had an underlying quality of austerity amounting almost to asceticism, whereas Strange enjoyed the good things of life to the full and was a better "mixer" socially than his reclusive companion.

Cocky and assertive, the tall Strange tended to look upon his diminutive friend, who spoke with a pronounced lisp, with a certain protective condescension. Writing in later life about their Academy years together, Jingo admitted that if he had been told then that his impulsive little comrade was to be a great soldier, his self-conceit would have led him to think: "More likely me than him!"

The last letter Strange was to receive from his old friend was addressed simply to "Colonel Jingo, R.A., Quebec" and was dated from Massowah, May 18, 1878.

My Dear Jingo:

I never forgot you or the R.M.A., or our ideas so much in common as they were.—I received your letter on my arrival here from Berbush, Zeyle, and Harar, which is some 235 miles inland. It was very interesting to see Harar, which for years had bullied Abyssinia. It is a walled town of 20,000 inhabitants, founded in the seventh century. Egypt occupied it in 1874 and it is now under my Government.

I have written to (my nephew) to tell him to consult with you about his future. It would be absolute ruin for him, with no profession, to be out here; what can he do; look at him yourself, is he an engineer, a carpenter, a botanist? It is the one great mistake our class of life makes, in educating their children with no trade. Put our birth, our energy, and our determination into shoe-making, carpentering, etc., we could beat the tradesmen out of the field, but now we pay hundreds of pounds for a miserable education of which more than two-thirds is useless. How often during my life I have regretted I could not braze metals, could not solder, etc.—You and I have had different lives, but yours is the safer and smoother; you at any rate are not dependant on a man (H. Highness) having dyspepsia or not; this I am dependant on. Kind regards to Mrs. Strange.

Yours sincerely,

C.E. Gordon

Somewhat to his own surprise, Tom proved an excellent student, leading his class in a range of subjects as varied as painting and sketching, military topography, and astronomy. As an athlete he excelled in most team sports and was such an enthusiastic swimmer that he and Gordon became college celebrities by continuing to swim in the Academy pond throughout the winter, even breaking the ice on occasion to do so.

Holiday breaks were spent in such pursuits as beagling with the commandant's pack—a dozen cadets running after the dogs on foot over the roughest of country—or boating on the Thames. Sometimes they ventured far upstream and slept in the boat overnight before returning. There were the usual pranks and student high jinks, some of which involved signs "borrowed" from the neighbouring High Street. As a result of one such prank, the Academy commandant, Eardley Wilmot, affectionately known as "Ramrod" by his cadets, emerged from his house one morning to find that a sign above his door proclaimed him to be "Licensed to be drunk on the premises."

Tom's only setback was the result of the Academy's spartan routine, which required cadets to take their morning bath under the courtyard pump out in the open. While en route there, Tom stepped on a piece of broken glass and cut his foot so badly that he was forced to spend time in hospital, thereby missing an important examination and several places in the list of the Academy's best qualified cadets.

Nonetheless, in 1851 at the age of twenty Tom passed out near the top of his class and was awarded a commission in the First Artillery regiment. To their mutual regret, his friend Charles Gordon was commissioned into the Royal Engineers and posted to China. Yet this Academy friendship, however brief, was to have a profound and lasting effect on Tom, shaping both his future career and his personal philosophy. For Gordon was one of the new breed of imperial thinkers who were already changing British attitudes towards their scattered colonies and dependencies.

The British Empire had begun more by accident than as the result of established policy. For more than a century British merchants and, after Waterloo, British manufacturers had been seeking new markets and sources of supply in every quarter of the globe. A worldwide carrying trade had grown up, as ship owners took advantage of the nation's command of the seas won so convincingly at Trafalgar. For trade to flourish, law and order had first to be established; peace was the prerequisite of prosperity. In the more barbarous regions, insurrections would interrupt trade and had to be suppressed by British force. Afterwards, garrisons and civil administrations were often established to maintain peace. Military posts were set up in strategic locations to protect newly established trade routes. A heterogeneous collection of colonies, protectorates, naval bases, and trading posts had gradually sorted itself out into a sort of colonial empire controlled from Whitehall and under British law, but encompassing a wide variety of administrative arrangements in order to suit local conditions. India, for example, was a hodge-podge of princely fiefdoms, governed—more often misgoverned—by native despots, together with an ever-growing commercial kingdom under the sway of the Honourable East India Company, maintained by its own private army. Elsewhere, empty lands were colonized by Britain's surplus population. Australia was a convenient dumping ground for convicts, and other colonies were acquired simply because they might prove useful.

But although conceived in greed, the British Empire by the mid-nineteenth century had become an imperial mission, infused by the young Queen Victoria with high moral purpose and administered with remarkable dedication and integrity by the cream of Britain's young men, chosen by a rigorous selection process. The Royal Navy had become the world's police force, suppressing the slave trade here, quelling civil riot there. An American historian might dismiss the British as "a piratical, warrior race," and President Monroe might proclaim his doctrine of non-interference in the Americas by European powers, but it was British naval might that would enforce the President's decree.

Nowhere was the sense of imperial mission displayed more dramatically than in Africa. To bring this vast, unknown land into the realm of the known, and to extend the sometimes dubious blessings of nineteenth-century civilization, had become something of a crusade for middle-class Englishmen. Explorers, missionaries, engineers, and administrators asked nothing more than to devote their lives to bettering the condition of Africans, whether the Africans wished them to or not. This spirit of sacrifice marched side by side with the hard-headed pragmatism of British entrepreneurs and the vaunting hubris of empire-building politicians. It would find expression later as "the Law"—something unknown to Kipling's "lesser breeds" bent on colonial expansion for expansion's sake. Simply put, "the Law" embodied the notion that with power went responsibility; from those to whom much was given, much was asked. Blessed by fortune, the British saw themselves as their brothers' keepers. Though derided in more effete times, "the white man's burden" was nonetheless a dominant theme in Victorian middle-class

thought and was to exercise a profound and generally beneficent effect on the undeveloped world.

No one could have embraced this uplifting notion more
enthusiastically than Thomas Bland Strange. Filled from his
earliest days with a family sense of duty to his country and to
the Crown, and imbued with imperialist traditions at Edinburgh Academy, he was a ready convert to his friend Charles
Gordon's ideas of service and sacrifice in the cause of imperial expansion, with its ideals of liberty, law, and Christian
values.

Gordon based his imperial patriotism on that of ancient
Rome, and was fond of quoting Macaulay:

For Romans, in Rome's quarrel,
Spared neither land nor gold;
Nor limb, nor life, nor child nor wife, in the brave days
of old.

Strange became, if anything, an even more ardent patriot;
so much so that he was nicknamed "Jingo" by some anonymous classmate, after the music-hall song of the time:

We don't want to fight, but, by Jingo, if we do,
We've got the ships, we've got the men, we've got the
money, too!

It was a singularly apt nickname, and it stuck; for the rest
of his life, at every level of society, he was to be known simply
as "Jingo." Letters addressed merely to "Lieutenant Jingo," at
the town where his unit was serving, would be delivered
without delay or question. Titled generals and private soldiers alike would know him as such, and he personally would
scarcely ever refer to himself by any other name. It was as
Jingo Strange that he graduated from Woolwich Academy on
December 17, 1851, and was commissioned into the Royal
Artillery, an event which was to be as much a milestone for
the gunnery world as it was for the young lieutenant.

TWO

The Rock

Silhouetted against the growing brightness of the vivid Mediterranean sunrise, the enormous bulk of Gibraltar towered high above the Spanish coastguard vessel—huge, menacing, overwhelming. But the captain of the little vessel had neither eyes for the scene about him nor regard for the niceties of the neutrality he might be violating. Down here in the shadow of the mighty Rock, the sea was a pattern of grey and white in the early pre-dawn light as the ship drove before a westerly gale, her lateen rig, set wing-and-wing, stretched to the utmost. Every eye on board strained for the quarry just ahead. The little smuggler, just beyond the reach of the *garda costa*'s brass six-pounder bow gun, had broken out British colours and was now technically under British protection and beyond the reach of Spanish customs regulations. But the coastguard vessel was in hot pursuit, close and closing, and her captain knew that there was little the British garrison in their batteries far above could do to prevent the capture he meant to make. A warning shot from the nearest cliffside battery boomed out, but the splash of the shot far astern showed that he was now too close under the Rock for its guns to bear on him. From that height they could not be depressed to cover the waters close in to the foot of the sheer cliffs. The captain shrugged off their empty gesture and concentrated all his attention on the chase.

The smuggler suddenly put down her helm, shot into a narrow opening in the offshore rocks, and rounded up into a tiny cove. Down came her sails, and she laid herself neatly alongside a rock shelf sloping up from the water. In an instant her crew had abandoned her and stood huddled on the shore directly beneath the beetling cliffs. The ship, her contraband cargo, and her crew lay there ready for the taking, and the *garda costa* captain, aglow with satisfaction, brought his own ship to anchor in the cove entrance and sent a boat away, filled with armed men, to effect their capture. He himself took charge of the operation, and all was going to his satisfaction when his attention was drawn to a figure lowering itself down a rope from the embrasures of the British battery high above. The figure, when it arrived, somewhat breathless and disarrayed from its strenuous descent, proved to be a British officer in artillery uniform. He immediately announced to the astounded *garda costa* captain that he and his men were under arrest and demanded the surrender of the captain's sword. The captain, recovering from his initial astonishment, laughed in derision and gestured to the armed men about him as he informed the visitor of the true facts of the situation. But the tall newcomer was no whit abashed. Pointing up to the cliff above him, he directed the captain's attention to the swarm of British soldiers filling the embrasures of the battery above them, each with a carbine aimed directly at the captain's heart.

It was, indeed, a standoff. Recognizing the fact, the captain made the best of a bad bargain and agreed to submit the matter to the governor of Gibraltar, in whose jurisdiction they were, and to abide by his decision. With a nod and a handshake young Lieutenant Jingo—for this was indeed he—hauled himself back up the rockface to the security of the battery embrasure. There he received the enthusiastic congratulations of his gunners and the

annoyed remonstrations of his superior officer, routed out
of his bed and irritated yet again by the impetuous zeal of
his young subordinate, "always up to something" and with
no care for officer-like propriety. Lowering himself down
on ropes, for God's sake!

A sleepy governor, routed out of his bed in turn, gave the
garda costa captain permission to return to nearby Algeciras
and allowed the smuggler to enter Gibraltar bay, thereby
emphasizing British prestige as the arbiter of all comings
and goings at the Mediterranean's mouth.

It was this aspect of Gibraltar's role that had impressed
Jingo from the day of his arrival here with a clutch of five
other new-made subalterns in a transport fresh from England. The towering Rock, dominating the narrow straits
and holding the key to Mediterranean supremacy, had captured his imagination, and he had set out, with typical
enthusiasm, to explore every corner and to learn every detail
of the history of the storied promontory where fate and the
pen of an army clerk had deposited him.

For a dedicated gunner, Gibraltar was a fortunate posting. Here, as nowhere else, artillery dominated affairs. Gibraltar's guns enforced the rule of law—British law—over
this international waterway, requiring each passing ship to
display her national colours or risk the reminder of a cannon shot in the sea just ahead. The pirates who had once
preyed on this rich traffic had been swept away, and Gibraltar's guns now presided over the peaceful comings and
goings of the world's merchantmen.

The great fortress, at the time of Jingo's arrival, was in the
throes of an intensive remodelling and updating which
would make its already formidable defences more powerful
still. According to Captain J. Sayer's definitive *A History of
Gibraltar*, "no civilian concerns were allowed to impede the
strengthening works; the Rock was a fortress, first and
foremost, and the civil town a mere appendage, so that any

building obstructing a clear line of fire was pulled down, and gun muzzles peeped from the most unlikely places in orchards or gardens." Sayer, himself a civil magistrate in Gibraltar at the time, notes that the immense defences were not made to any single plan, but were intended simply to dominate every foot of land or sea from which an attack might be made on the Rock. There were three principal components; firstly, the seawall, complete with bastions, which girdled the westernmost parts from Europa Point to the approach causeway; secondly, the three powerful "retired batteries" named Jones's, Gardner's, and Civil Hospital; and thirdly, the galleries which honeycombed the upper levels of the Rock. Into these defences were incorporated no fewer than 700 guns, mostly 32- and 68-pounders, the most concentrated firepower of heavy artillery to be found anywhere in the world, served by a garrison of 5,600 men.

Soldiers and civilians alike shared the little town straggling upwards from the edge of the harbour, which was enclosed by a long mole on the westward side of the Rock. The long High Street was given over to shops and saloons to accommodate both the permanent population and the thousands of visiting soldiers and sailors, for "Gib" was a vital staging point on the route to India and the East. From the higher levels the Alameda Gardens and the surrounding homes and terraces enjoyed pleasant prospects.

Jingo found himself part of the garrison of the most formidable fortress in the world during a period of intense activity which provided plenty of scope for his professional talents. There was also a lively social round among the garrison, stimulated by the comings and goings of the Royal Navy. Not least among the Rock's amenities was a magnificent garrison library containing not only every sort of technical manual, but also a fine general section that included much original material on Gibraltar's past history. This was destined to become Jingo's second home on the Rock.

The ancient castle where he and his fellow subalterns were quartered was a survival from the days of the Moors, whose leader, Gib-al-Tariq, had given the place its name. The ruined hillside tower round which Jingo hunted quail had been named "the Queen of Spain's Chair." The queen after whom it was named had watched her army's siege of the Rock from there and had vowed never to change her chemise until the British flag should be lowered from the Rock's flagstaff. Her chemise yellowed with the passage of time, and the ladies of the Spanish court dyed their own with saffron to match that of their mistress—a custom that became traditional in Spain. Eventually the gallant British governor, moved by the royal lady's distress, lowered his flag long enough for changes to be made without breaking the queen's vow.

Everywhere were reminders of the heroic past, and the library furnished details of each story, from the daring capture of the place by a handful of British Marines to the innumerable assaults and sieges by the fleets and armies of France and Spain.

But the Rock posed other challenges. With some of the hardier and more athletic of his fellow officers, Jingo went on rock-climbing expeditions, risking life and limb on the sheer cliff faces high above the sea and becoming as proficient in clambering about the barren mountain-top as Gibraltar's famous Barbary apes.

Another diversion for young officers was riding with the famous Calpe Hunt, an assortment of hounds and horses assembled by a former governor of Gibraltar, which hunted, through arrangement with indulgent Spanish authorities, in the arid hills of the nearby mainland. It was famous, not for its success in catching the wily Spanish foxes—in all his hunts with it Jingo never saw a fox killed—but for the difficulties and dangers it imposed on the hunters. Stone walls, prickly pear, rocks and holes and thickets of gorse, along with the unevenness of the ground and the uncertain footing, made the hunt a hazardous affair, all the more so because of the zeal and inexperience of the riders. These often included young midshipmen from visiting ships, Spanish officers curious to witness this peculiar British custom, and garrison officers with more enthusiasm than practice. Jingo, blessed with the experience of riding over rough Irish country, survived more or less unscathed, but many of his fellow huntsmen were less fortunate.

Another sport much enjoyed by garrison officers was sailing. The five young artillery subalterns had a small yacht of their own, which eventually came to grief in a wild gale off the Barbary coast, so that its crew found themselves marooned without funds among the nomadic Arab tribes-men near the town of Tetuan. Here they were promptly interned by the local Pasha, who placed a guard on them which, he explained, would protect them from any Bedouin bandits. They were at liberty to wander about the environs until they could arrange passage home; in the meantime, maintenance of their "escort" would be charged against them or their government. As they had no money to buy food, they were forced to subsist upon whatever game they could shoot in the scrubland about the town.

One day, while out shooting, they heard the sound of trumpets and saw a long procession winding through the hills to the music of tom-toms and horns. There were ladies carried in litters, and in order to obtain a closer look the five young subalterns made their way towards the wedding party, as it proved to be. The young Bedouin men escorting the bride, objecting to the rude scrutiny of these *Faringi*, opened fire, and bullets flew all about them. There were several very near misses, and the subalterns took to their heels.

Short of food, shivering at night on the bare tiled floors of their windowless house, the little party was growing desperate, when by chance a small felucca put in at the port. Its owner proved willing to transport them across to Gib for the promise of payment there, and the marooned yachtsmen were able to regain their barracks to face the dressing-down that awaited them.

These light-hearted excursions apart, most of Jingo's off-duty hours were spent in a rigorous program of self-improvement, for he was determined to make the most of every opportunity to better himself, mentally and physically. Long hours of reading in the garrison library included military subjects as well as history and the classics. Already blessed with a strong physique, he kept himself fit by regular workouts, and by bouts of boxing and single-stick with his battery sergeant, Crawford Lindsay. (Lindsay would later retire to Canada and become Chief Constable of the new settlement of British Columbia.) Jingo was careful about what, and how much, he ate, and was considered remarkable in a hard-drinking mess for his temperance; he had seen too many promising military careers blighted by drunkenness.

He learned to speak fluent Spanish, with the occasional aid of what he coyly referred to as some "charming dark-eyed dictionaries," and regularly roamed the mainland hills sketching and painting the Andalusian countryside, for he was becoming a promising young artist, with a flair for landscapes.

Jingo's program of self-improvement was nearly brought to an abrupt end by an accident. As part of their drill, the Rock's artillerymen regularly practised firing with red-hot shot, which was devastating to shipping and had been used with great effect in repulsing earlier naval assaults by French and Spanish fleets. It was a difficult procedure requiring precise timing, for each red-hot cannon ball was separated from the propellant gunpowder in the gun by only a wet wad, which would quickly be consumed if the firing was delayed. One morning, while Jingo's battery was practising this procedure, some such delay occurred and the gun exploded, killing or wounding its entire crew. Jingo himself had the narrowest of escapes. He had turned towards a neighbouring gun at just the precise moment and was shielded from the direct force of the explosion by a large tree in the park-like Alameda battery. Stunned, deafened, and shocked, but otherwise unhurt, Jingo was moved by the fortitude of a fellow subaltern, Lieutenant Le Fer. Although crushed and painfully wounded, Le Fer calmly lit and smoked a cigar after directing the surgeon to first treat his nearby gunners, whom he felt to be in greater need than himself.

Determined to become fluent in Spanish, and as assiduous in this as in all other aspects of his self-education, Jingo decided to spend a leave travelling through rural Spain as a Spanish gentleman, hoping thereby to learn more of the native customs and way of life than he would as a British officer. Accordingly, he packed a portmanteau with his British clothes and sent it off to Cadiz. Then he set off for that city, alone and on horseback, dressed in a smart Spanish jacket, many-buttoned breeches, boots, sash, and sombrero.

THREE

Soldier of the Queen

The realities of rural Spanish travel—the fleas, the garlic, the eternal olive oil, and the rough red wine tasting of tar from its leathern bottle—all these Jingo was happy to accept in return for escape from the stereotype of the English officer abroad. All too often arrogant and insensitive, such travellers were apt to be resented, detested—and overcharged!—by Spanish hostlers and hotel keepers. Jingo was just twenty years old and in the best of health, and the world was at his feet.

With a full month's leave ahead of him, he was in no hurry; accordingly he first headed east, along the coastal road between the seashore and the foothills of the Sierra Nevada. His big stallion, Almanzor, his saddlebags bulging, bore him easily through the tiny fishing villages—Estepona, Marbella, Fuengirola—to the relatively civilized comforts of the thriving seaport of Malaga. There he turned northwards into the mountains and the long climb to Granada. This ancient city, the last capital of Moorish Spain, enchanted the impressionable Jingo. The towers and arcades of the Alhambra Palace, once the summer residence of sultans and princes, were now still the semi-ruinous abode of gypsies and goatherds, despite the protests of Washington Irving and Richard Ford, whose books Jingo carried with him. The beauty of the place, especially by moonlight, cried out to the artist in him, and he spent a week prowling and painting in the overgrown gardens of the Generaliffe and the crumbling ramparts of the citadel. One of these paintings, a little watercolour of the towers and gardens, with the snowy peaks of the Sierra Nevada over all, was to become his favourite, and hung on his bedroom wall for the rest of his life.

Descending from the splendours of Granada through a series of breathtaking passes to the old mountain road that twisted and turned among snowy peaks and through green valleys, he emerged, after several days, at Loja. He continued on, past walled, whitewashed villages and tiny farmhouse *fincas* clinging to mountainside terraces dug out by backbreaking toil over the millennia, through Antequera, the oldest town in Spain with its prehistoric temple-tombs, and then north to Cordoba, the fabled centre of Moorish power in Europe. Here the vast mosque, with its multitude of pillars gleaming in gold, stunned the young traveller with its immensity and kept him busy painting through the daylight hours. South again, then, to Ronda, with its jewel-like bullring and lonely Roman theatre, set on the edge of a precipice.

On all these travels Jingo had been kindly received by the locals, who regarded him with indulgent amusement as *el loco Inglese*, once they had penetrated his disguise. Not until he was on the road from Ronda did he encounter any difficulty. At this point his horse cast a shoe and pulled up lame just as he was passing through a district that was notorious for its bandits and had been the scene of numerous robberies and murders of passing travellers. Nothing daunted, Jingo sought out a blacksmith whose surliness was not improved when he disregarded Jingo's caution about the proper way to hold this particular horse and was kicked by an indignant Almanzor.

With Jingo's help—he wound the stallion's long tail around the raised fetlock—the shoe was fitted. But the scene at the forge had attracted much unwanted attention to the young Englishman travelling alone in such curious circumstances. Jingo ignored the dark looks and mutterings and pushed boldly on to the little rundown posada, where he put up for the night. A highly spiced dinner, washed down with a surprisingly good wine was followed by an even more surprisingly lively entertainment furnished by the dancing of Pepita, all gleaming smiles and flashing eyes, accompanied by guitars, castanets, and clapping hands. Pepita, it seemed, was the daughter of the house, and enjoyed the appreciative admiration of several young suitors in the audience. Aware of their resentful eyes, she made a coquettish play for the *Inglese*, stamping her foot and urging him, with imperious nods of her head, to come out onto the floor and dance with her. Nothing loath, Jingo moved out to her and danced a tempestuous bolero, enthusiasm more than making up for his lack of expertise. The dance ended with a burst of applause and shouting from an appreciative crowd, and lowering looks from several young men.

When the evening's merriment was done, Jingo thought it as well to remove his saddlebags and their contents to his room for the night, in view of the reputation of the place for light-fingered locals. Intercepted in the stable by a group of the same young men he had noticed in the bar, now definitely menacing, he thought it best to demonstrate that he was not going to be an easy mark. Catching up his revolver from its saddle holster, he took aim at a water pot sitting on a stableyard wall and shattered it with a single shot, then ostentatiously flicked the cylinder around to show that there were five more cartridges left. With a cheerful "Buenas noches!" he went up to his tiny room under the cobwebbed roofbeams and slept the untroubled sleep of youth and clear conscience. Next morning he rode away, leaving, besides his payment for board and lodging, the tiny gold dollar from his watch chain for Pepita to add to her ornaments.

Seville provided more painting and sketching, but there were no further adventures before he reached Cadiz and the hotel where his portmanteau had been sent. In his dusty Spanish clothes he was nearly turned away by the haughty desk clerk, who was suitably abashed when Jingo reached out his bag from behind the desk, unlocked it, and revealed his army officer's uniform.

In Cadiz he experienced something of life at the other extremity of Spanish society. At a state ball at the Puerto Santa Maria, attended by the Queen of Spain herself, Jingo gained admittance on the strength of his British officer's uniform and found himself dancing with the most beautiful woman there. In his memoirs, Jingo coyly omits her name, referring to her only as "the Marquesa de—," but he declares her to be of the bluest blood in Spain. As he swept her through the lovely, sensuous waltz, he could not help contrasting the full-figured, olive-skinned noblewoman in his arms with his last dancing partner, the tawny, flashing-eyed Pepita. His aristocratic partner was no mere royal cypher, however. Jingo thought her eyes outshone her diamonds, and her fabled temper and independent mind had given her the sobriquet *la tigre real*—"the royal tiger." Spanish women from any walk of life, Jingo was learning, were not to be taken lightly!

Years later, Jingo was to meet his dancing partner again under very different circumstances. On the Channel packet to Dover, homeward bound on leave, he encountered her with her diminutive husband and her even tinier mother, fleeing to England from a revolution in their native Spain. The fact that she did not recognize him stabbed Jingo to the heart, but he made sure of his recognition of her by checking the name on the collar of the little dog accompanying the party.

At Dover the Spanish party got into difficulties. They spoke not a word of English and the customs officer was inclined to be suspicious of their vast pile of boxes and luggage. As the marquesa and her helpless husband looked on wordlessly, Jingo stepped into the breach. Taking the customs officer to one side, he informed him that the little party was simply an aristocratic Spanish family fleeing for their lives to the sanctuary of England; that he was personally acquainted with them; and that he, a British artillery officer, would vouch for their bona fides. Impressed, the customs officer waived all inspection and Jingo tipped a porter to organize their luggage and put it aboard the London train.

As they made their way to the platform, the relieved marquesa looked her thanks, but in the best traditions of *noblesse oblige* Jingo merely tipped his hat and made off, too proud to bring their former acquaintance to the attention of his dancing partner of long ago.

A visit to the bullring in Cadiz revealed to Jingo yet another facet of the Spanish character. He admired the glitter and colour and ritual of the gorgeously costumed confrontation between the magnificent bull and his elegant opponent in the ring, the grace and artistry of the matador, and above all, the courage of both the killer and the killed. But it was the fate of the gored horses, often disembowelled by a furious charge, that moved him most. The cruelty that sent those old, worn-out animals, their tongues cut out to prevent their screaming in pain, to be used to provide spice to an afternoon's entertainment, linked the Spanish bullring, as Jingo instantly recognized, with the gladiatorial slaughters of Roman amphitheatres. This inhumanity to horses, animals which Jingo especially loved, seemed to him a revealing example of the streak of cruelty which ran like a dark thread through all that he admired of the Spanish character.

Back in Gibraltar, barracks life seemed especially humdrum to a young subaltern after the colour and adventure of his travels in Spain. Jingo enlivened it by slipping out early each morning with his friend Le Fer for a cooling dip in the harbour before the burning summer sun made life uncomfortable. The two fell into the habit of slipping into Moorish *haik*—loose, hooded garments reaching from head to toe—for their morning bathing expeditions. Unfortunately for Jingo, an elderly English lady along his route to the harbour noticed that the seeming Moor passing her window had pink heels, and she reported indignantly to the senior officer of the garrison that British officers were wearing native dress in the town. A choleric letter was duly delivered to Jingo from the Town Major's office demanding "reasons in writing for wearing Moorish costume in the city of Gibraltar."

Believing brevity to be the soul of wit, Jingo turned up one corner of the letter and replied in a single word, "Coolness," and initialled it "T.J." The Town Major was not amused, and Jingo was duly carpeted and severely rebuked for his levity. This cavalier attitude towards authority, together with an unseemly rumpus at an officers' ball in a local theatre, where Jingo and his fellow subalterns had resisted an assault by some young men of the town angered by the attendance of their young women as dancing partners, gave him a poor reputation with some of the senior officers. Still, he was deemed suitable for promotion and on November 21, 1853, he was made full, or first, lieutenant.

The Crimean war had broken out, and every young officer eagerly sought a posting to the war front, where careers and promotions could be hoped for. But because of his new rank, young Jingo's application was turned down; only juniors were needed as reinforcements. While the other four subalterns were sent off to the Crimea, he was forced to accept a posting to the West Indies, far from the scene of action.

Yet, though it ended in disappointment, Jingo's Gibraltar service had been an important part of his professional career. He had not only mastered his trade, but he had extended his intellectual boundaries through intensive reading in the Rock's excellent library. He had learned to speak Spanish like a native; had acquired proficiency as a landscape painter and caricaturist; and had become a skilled rock climber. He had developed a taste for adventurous travel, which he would be able to indulge throughout his life. Above all, he had learned the ways and character of a race of people other than his own, and had developed an affectionate appreciation of them, something which few other professional officers bothered to do, and a trait which would play an important part in his future career.

It was a mature and experienced young lieutenant who caught the packet home to England en route to his new posting—an officer who had made the most of his opportunities on the Rock, whatever his seniors might think!

He also carried with him a curious dictum which he confided to his memoirs without comment as to its source: "Bad sort of woman to marry is a woman who dislikes dogs and the perfume of flowers; she never cares much about men!"

FOUR

The Spanish Main

Back in London Jingo was taught an invaluable lesson in the workings of a bureaucratic power structure such as the British Army administration. Desperate to get to the Crimea front line and all the opportunity for adventure and advancement that he saw there, he went down to Woolwich and haunted the office of the Deputy Adjutant-General of the Royal Artillery, who was officially responsible for gunnery postings. When he was finally admitted to see that worthy, he made such an impression that the D.A.G. promised that, on the first "death vacancy" occurring, Jingo would be sent to fill it, "and have the opportunity of getting [his] head blown off."

Needless to say, Jingo was delighted and spent every morning, as he afterwards confessed with shame, poring over the obituaries and casualty lists in the London newspapers, hoping for a deceased officer of suitable rank and regiment.

But alas for such hopes! On one of his visits to the D.A.G.'s office, Jingo's fiery temper got the better of him. Nettled by the insolence of a bombardier clerk in the office, he rebuked him in no uncertain terms and strode out, leaving behind him a confidential clerk who was now his mortal enemy. The clerk wasted no time in exacting his revenge. A story was leaked to a military newspaper revealing that Lieutenant Strange was to be permitted to go to the Crimea "out of his turn," rather than reporting to his company in the West Indies, "where his presence is much required."

The news story was headlined "Another Woolwich Job," insinuating that Jingo had made an improper deal. An embarrassed D.A.G. immediately cancelled the arrangement. The next day's mail brought orders for Lieutenant Strange to report to a unit in Kingston, Jamaica, and after a brief pause in Ireland awaiting transportation, Jingo sailed for the West Indies.

The military establishment in Kingston, Jamaica, to which Jingo was now reporting was already, like all the other island garrisons in the West Indies, something of an anomaly. In the eighteenth century, when all the great European colonial powers had been contending with naval powers of comparatively equal strength for possession of the rich sugar islands, each colony had changed hands many times, according to the fluctuations of local naval ascendancy. When the British finally emerged with the bulk of the islands in their possession, they strengthened their hold by fortifying the principal harbours of the larger islands. In most islands a citadel of some sort ornamented the commanding height of land, and batteries protected the harbour approaches. But by the middle of the nineteenth century the overwhelming might of Britain's Royal Navy, which had grown steadily in strength after Trafalgar until it exceeded all other European navies combined, had ensured that no military power, however great, could capture, let alone retain, any West Indian island against Britain's will. The Royal Navy's powerful West Atlantic squadron, whose rumbustious song was already being heard in every East Coast port throughout the Americas, had made all military establishments in the islands redundant, except for local policing duties.

But somehow the message seems never to have been transmitted from the Admiralty to the War Office, and in any case
bureaucracies, military as well as civil, tend to be self-
perpetuating. Thus Britain continued to maintain garrisons
throughout the West Indies well into the late nineteenth
century, paying a heavy price in human life to do so. In
mosquito-infested, fever-ridden islands like Jamaica, a regiment arriving fresh from England could count on losing half
its strength to disease, especially yellow fever (or el vomito
negro, in the more graphic Spanish phrase), before returning home in five years' time.

Jingo was left in no doubt as to the role played by disease
in Jamaican military affairs. He owed his own posting to a
vacancy created from the death by yellow fever of a young
lieutenant, and his first official duty on joining his unit was
to preside over the funeral arrangements of the most recent
casualty, a youthful gunner. These arrangements were simple in the extreme. There was no funeral parade of the
regiment, no formal firing party, lest the frequency of these
sombre affairs sap the morale of the troops, who might be
led to speculate as to when their own turn would come.
Jingo turned out, early in the morning, in full regimentals as
befitted the occasion, but he was the only military representative. A native working party, armed with shovels, carried
the plain wooden coffin to a boat and rowed it, with Jingo in
the stern, to a nearby sandspit roughly fenced off as a
military cemetery. Here among the mangroves the grave was
dug in the sand, the pit filling with water below the one-foot
mark, into which the coffin was deposited with a splash.
Jingo read the brief military funeral service, with the work
party standing bareheaded about him, after which the grave
was filled with a few shovelfuls of sand. There were even
further horrors in store for the young lieutenant, already
shocked by the grim realities of island funeral arrangements.
A grinning workman rapped the disintegrating mound of
sand over a nearby grave with his shovel so that an appalled

Jingo might hear the landcrabs scuttling about inside the buried coffin.

For a keen young officer, Jamaica proved a frustrating posting. The guns which were Jingo's special charge were antiques, the brick ramparts in which they were set were crumbling, and the hot, humid atmosphere of the coastal batteries where he was stationed made any sort of energetic activity difficult, and impossible after the sun reached full strength in mid-morning. All drills and military exercises of any sort had to be carried out in the relative cool of the first hours following dawn, while social life was restricted to the evening and night. His fellow officers had resigned themselves to their circumstances, and heavy drinking was the main feature of mess life, while a score of drinking establishments in Kingston catered to the garrison's private soldiers. Indeed, on his first day as duty officer Jingo was forced to put the regimental sergeant-major, the senior non-commissioned officer responsible for discipline, on a charge for being drunk on duty.

Jingo would have none of this apathy, drunkenness, and professional stagnation. Determined to make the most of what Jamaica offered, he took every opportunity to explore his surroundings, especially the lovely interior of the island, and to learn what he could of its history. He went boating, and was fascinated to learn that just below the harbour surface were the remains of old Port Royal, once the base for roistering buccaneers before an earthquake had pushed it beneath the waves. He also risked his neck in a small canoe, accompanied only by his young black batman whom he nicknamed "the Demon," in a hunt for "Port Royal Jack," a ferocious shark which kept watch on the crew of the harbour guardship, H.M.S. *Boscawen*. Notorious both for its age and its size, this voracious creature normally kept station on the ship, feasting on its scraps, but when it began to terrorize nearby bathing beaches Jingo went after it with baited hooks and rope appropriate to its size, as well as a harpoon. "Jack" took the line but nearly upset the canoe. Only after a furious half-hour struggle did Jingo manage to transfer the end of his line ashore, where the great brute was eventually beached and despatched. Cut open, the twelve-foot shark was found to have in its stomach an amazing range of objects, including a Royal Marine's uniform tunic, a huge metal colander, a number of hooks, some steel chain, and several smaller sharks.

The heavy drinking was taking its toll of his brother officers. One morning Jingo found a young lieutenant, a former classmate of his at Woolwich, in the mess bathroom in the grip of delirium tremens, shouting and threatening to cut his throat. Jingo was able to restrain and calm him, and afterwards, as part of the young officer's attempt to restore himself to a normal way of life, he promised to accompany him in a program of total abstention from alcohol. Jingo kept his promise, but his young friend was unable to do so for long and died a few weeks later.

Thinking that perhaps he might be able to avoid the dread yellow fever by cutting out meat as well as alcohol, Jingo became a vegetarian throughout his stay in the tropics. Although he resumed a meat diet later, he remained a temperate drinker for the rest of his life.

For all the problems of heat and disease, Jamaica offered a lively social life, with the resident governor and his lady setting the pace with frequent balls and dinners, which garrison officers were expected to attend. Jingo enjoyed himself tremendously at these functions and became a favourite at Government House, where a room was always kept for him (the barracks in Port Royal being at such a distance that an overnight stay was usually entailed). However, on one evening, having to return to prepare for early-morning duties, he attempted to paddle himself back across the harbour to the fort. In the pitch blackness he lost his way and blundered about for hours in mangrove swamps, where he was bitten terribly by swarms of mosquitoes.

By the time he finally arrived at his destination, his face, neck, wrists, and hands were covered with innumerable swollen bites, and he was so dizzy he could hardly walk. When he entered his room and looked in the mirror he saw that the whites of his eyes had turned yellow, a sure sign of the dreaded Yellow Jack. His horrified adjutant offered to send for the garrison doctor, but instead Jingo asked for Mother Wingrove, his old black washerwoman, who was reputed to be able to cure the disease, something the army doctor was notoriously unable to do. The stout washerwoman immediately took him under her motherly wing, undressing him and bustling him like a small boy into a hot bath, the top of which she covered with blankets to hold in the steam. After a good soak there, the half-boiled Jingo was hustled into bed and covered with blankets. Mother Wingrove assured him, "I make you all right soon, my sweet sonny; don't you take no nasty doctor stuff!" Instead she made him drink a hot decoction of herbs, which she called "fever tea."

After a twenty-hour sleep, Jingo awoke next morning weak as a kitten and with an appalling taste in his mouth, but otherwise back to normal. The garrison doctor calling in on him found him restored to health and had the candour to say, "I'm glad Mother Wingrove got you first; I doubt if I could have pulled you through." He attributed the speedy recovery to Jingo's spartan regimen of diet and drink. All the same, he was packed off to an army convalescent camp at Newcastle in the mountains of the interior, a place of clear, bracing air, verdant valleys and breathtaking views of mountain and sea. For two weeks he was able to read and paint and ramble about this idyllic hilltop retreat.

This brush with death turned Jingo's interest to Christianity, of which he knew little more than any other young man of his time and situation. He was fascinated by the native Jamaicans' "black Christianity," with its curious mixture of African obeah, or voodoo, and its blend of rigid piety and carefree amorality. He became a student of the Bible and of theology in general, not so much in quest of a personal salvation but rather as a scholar in search of knowledge. He began to contemplate life as a philosopher and to reflect on the current of circumstance that had washed him up on this tropical island. On one of his rambles he had come across the cemetery of Fort Augusta, across the bay from his own barracks, and had been deeply moved to find almost the entire complement of the 22nd Dragoons buried there—a whole regiment perpetuated in the stone of their grave markers. What folly had sent a cavalry regiment, complete with horses, to this fever-ridden hole where the parade ground was a swamp and the terrain utterly unfit for mounted operations? Some fatuous bureaucrat in Whitehall had sent the regiment to their deaths with a flourish of his pen. Looking about him at the weed-grown graveyard crammed with the bones of young men, Jingo was made aware of the price of Empire. Theirs had been no glorious death, these victims of Yellow Jack on this isolated island, far from home and friends, yet they had died for their country as surely as any hero of a blood-soaked battlefield—and there were scores of them for every soldier killed in action!

From such gloomy ponderings, Jingo sought respite in the Bible, "that most wonderful and beautiful of all books," as well as in a number of the most scholarly works he could lay his hands on. These included Buckle's *History of Civilisation in England*, Paley's *Evidences*, Butler's *Analogy*, and Locke's *On Human Understanding*. At the end of an intensive course of such reading, he acknowledged himself little the wiser in understanding the human condition.

Jingo was returned from such airy contemplations to the realities of army life by the abrupt resumption of his military

duties in Port Royal, where he found the menace of Yellow
Jack had been lifted, at least until another summer season.
His had been the last case, and he plunged with zest into the
quickening pace of life in the island's capital. The sea breeze
had brought cooler temperatures, the beaches and verdant
valleys had never looked more beautiful, and island social
life had never been brighter or gayer. Not for the first time
Jingo found himself entranced by the beauty and grace of
Creole women, whose exquisite coffee-coloured complex-
ions, delicate features, flashing eyes, and graceful figures
made European women in general, and Jamaica's English-
women in particular, seem dull and frumpy. Their grace and
lightness of foot, compared with the "stumping about" of
European womenfolk, made Creole girls overwhelming favourites among bachelor officers for the frequent balls and
banquets at Government House, regimental messes, and
aboard H.M.S. *Boscawen*. Jingo found their company and
conversation delightful.

But he had little time to enjoy this burgeoning revelry; he
was posted on short notice to the Bahama Islands, to replace
a young lieutenant who was being sent to the Crimea.
Leaving his faithful "Demon" with several of his high-
necked shirts, which the latter had been regularly sneaking
to wear at social functions, he embarked on the inter-island
mail steamer bound for Nassau, with stops en route at Haiti
and Cuba. Jackmel was the mail port for Haiti, and during
their stopover there Jingo accompanied a couple of the
ship's midshipmen on a stroll ashore. There was a fort on
the top of the hill, as in so many islands, and prompted by a
professional interest in fortifications and their artillery,
Jingo and his companions climbed up for a look.

They found a scene of complete decrepitude. Trees grew
from interstices in the crumbling walls, ancient guns rusted
in the embrasures, the gate sagged open. Inside, there was
not a sign of life. The sun beat down on a dusty, weed-grown

square; a sentry slept in a hammock in the shade of some trees; the guard, if they could be called that, slept soundly in their guardroom, their rifles in a rack outside.

It was more than the mischievous young officers could stand. Moving quietly, they removed the sentry's rifle, still with rusty bayonet attached, and the other rifles from the rack, and hid them in some bushes. The midshipmen lowered the Haitian flag from the fort's flagpole and hoisted in its place a yellow bandanna surreptitiously removed from its slumbering owner, the yellow flag being the international symbol for quarantine. It was not until an exuberant middy tumbled a pyramid of rusty cannonballs on the parapet that the sleepers awoke. They rushed about in a terrible state, looking for their missing weapons, and surrounded the three miscreants uttering fearful threats. Only Jingo's warning as to what might happen to them if he were to report the missing rifles to their commandant reduced them to silence.

Everything, however, ended happily. Their joke over, the trio restored the missing rifles, left the mollified guard with a tip to buy drinks all round, and departed for their ship. The yellow bandanna was left flying, however. It was not noticed until the departing mail ship fired a gun and dipped its ensign in salute, forcing an embarrassed fort guard to respond with its yellow rag.

During a period of quarantine at the Danish island of St. Thomas, Jingo met the officer from Nassau he was to replace, who seemed far less enthusiastic about the prospect of the Crimea than Jingo would have been. From St. Thomas a fast-sailing schooner carried him on to Nassau, the principal town and harbour for the island of New Providence in the Bahamas.

Nassau proved to be a delightful change from Jamaica. Not only was there little, if any, yellow fever, but the climate of the island, swept by sea breezes and removed from the humid sultriness of the Caribbean, was far more temperate and invigorating than anything Jingo had experienced in Jamaica. The local people were lively and cheerful, in contrast to the surliness he had often encountered at his previous station. But perhaps best of all from the young lieutenant's viewpoint was the responsibility given him. As the senior artillery officer, he was not only in charge of the island's gun defences, but was also a member of the "Board of Respective Officers," which was responsible for organizing the island's overall defences. The senior officer, a West Indies infantry colonel, presided.

Chief among these defences was Fort Fincastle, crowning the hill overlooking Nassau harbour and shaped, in plan, like a gigantic sidewheel steamer, with the bow towards the waterfront. This had once been the site of the stronghold of the notorious pirate Blackbeard, but like so many others in the islands, the fort had been allowed to crumble in the long years of peace when funds were scarce.

It was Jingo's job to put the fort and its artillery into a proper state to repel any attacks upon it, and he set about his task with zest and vigour. His gunners, all reliable men of long service and much experience, were set to work restoring the aging weapons and repairing their platforms, a long and arduous task. Once it had been accomplished to the best of the garrison's ability and to the extent of the funds allowed them, Jingo set his men to a new sort of work. Recognizing that the only threat to the island could come from the sea, and with a myriad of beaches to protect, all of them ideal for a boat landing by any invading force and all without fixed defences, Jingo organized a mobile defence unit. Field pieces were improvised by mounting and equipping some of the fort's guns so that they could be hauled by hired horses around the road that encircled the coastline, where they were screened by low bushes from observation from the sea. The Bahamian Horse Artillery had been born.

Jingo purchased an old navy cutter at an auction and cruised about the island in it, ascertaining, with the help of a nautical chart, the navigable channels that might be used by bombarding ships. Once he had fixed these, he had small unobtrusive buoys placed as markers at measured distances from his guns, so that the range of each anchorage would be known by his gunners.

By the time he had finished this work and acquainted his men with their responsibilities, Jingo could feel satisfied that the fort, or at least its artillery defences, was as ready as humanly possible to repel an attacker. He then relaxed the long working hours he had enforced on his toiling gunners. Apart from morning gun drills and frequent visits to the rifle range, they occupied their time with cricket and football matches, for their lieutenant preferred fun and vigorous exercise to the dreary routine of the parade ground.

His gunners loved him for it. There was no drunkenness, no lapses of discipline; instead there was an eager application to their work in which their lieutenant played a full part. All unknown to himself, Jingo was displaying that gift of leadership with which he had been born, a natural instinct for getting the most out of men and "leading by example." It was a gift which he was to display time and again, and which was unquestionably his greatest natural asset.

The garrison gunners under their enterprising young lieutenant soon learned that business could be combined with pleasure in Jingo's way of doing things. Those marksmen with the best record on the rifle ranges were invited to go on sailing picnics in the lieutenant's boat, landing at one of the deserted offshore islets in campaign kit, armed with their rifles. The object of these expeditions was to hunt the wild pigs with which these islets were infested, and which were pugnacious and dangerous quarry when cornered, especially in deep brush which made it difficult to get a clear shot

as the animal charged. For the men it was exciting sport,
and from the official point of view it provided the garrison
with much-needed fresh meat with which to supplement the
staple army ration of salt beef. The slain pigs were butchered on the spot and packed into hogsheads for the passage
back to barracks.

But the Bahamas had other distractions to offer. There
was an active social life. At one of the numerous evening
functions at Government House, Jingo, who like most of his
young fellow officers had an eye for the ladies, came under
the spell of the beautiful daughter of the American consul, a
languid Southern belle whose tiny feet danced in and out of
a cloud of ruffles and lace, and whose raven hair and
exquisite features were accompanied by a quick wit and a
lively intelligence. Jingo found her enchanting, and every
moment he could spare from his official duties found him at
her side. They went on picnics together and long horseback
rides through the whispering pines of the interior. At every
ball and reception Jingo danced attendance on her. He
found her at least as well read as he, and they had long and
animated discussions about favourite books and authors
and about the political currents of the day. In these discussions Jingo found himself, as often as not, of differing
opinion from his charming but firmly opinionated partner.

In the end, though, it appeared that the emotion was
mostly on Jingo's side. He found himself increasingly cut
out by a friend of his, a naval officer who earned himself the
leading role in the lady's affections. However, he was somewhat mollified when the young lady eventually discarded
both her suitors in favour of a young English peer, whom
she ultimately married.

Being young and resilient, Jingo soon shrugged off his
loss and plunged into the many sporting and social diversions which the island capital offered. Among these his chief
love was sailing, and he became notorious for his penchant

for crowding on sail in his tiny craft, even in the teeth of a northerly gale. But after losing both mast and sail while out with a crew of his gunners and nearly coming to grief, he was told in no uncertain terms by a superior officer that while he himself might be considered expendable, his crew could not, gunners being in short supply. Thenceforth he behaved himself more prudently while afloat.

He haunted the Nassau library, which was better than Kingston's but not quite up to Gibraltar standards, and he joined the literary institute. More surprisingly, he became an ardent gardener, grubbing away for hours in the big garden of the West Indies Regiment's mess hall.

A violent interruption of this pleasant off-duty round was a fire which broke out in Nassau late one night as Jingo was returning in all his mess dress finery from a Government House ball. Whipped by a strong wind off the sea, the fire spread with terrifying speed through the streets of wooden buildings, and in a matter of minutes it threatened to engulf the entire town. Throwing off his gold-laced jacket, but still wearing his shirt, mess trousers, and half-wellington boots, Jingo dashed off to the barracks firehall, where he found his gunners, all of them returned from the all-night leave he had surreptitiously given them, already manning the regimental pumper. Off they all went, many of them hastily dressed, down to the blazing town.

A hose-line was quickly laid to the harbour and the gunners, pumping lustily, sent a column of water soaring into the heart of the flames. The soldiers, being stronger and more heavily built than the Creole firemen of the town brigade, were able to send more water and to sustain it longer. With Jingo directing them, they were the principal force battling the blaze. But the fire had got too much of a start; there was no stopping it with water alone. Accordingly, Jingo clambered onto the roof of a building in the path of the flames and directed his gunners to pull it down. Ropes were passed to him which he secured to the chimneys, and his axemen chopped the roof timbers apart. The fire then spread to this building. Jingo's foot went through the burning roof and a flaming cinder went down the top of his boot. Despite the agony of his burnt ankle he continued to direct the demolition of the house; only when it had been finally pulled down, chimneys and all, was he able to dislodge the hot cinder from his boot. The firemen and gunners then concentrated their efforts at the gap made by the demolished building and were able to halt the advance of the fire. In an hour it had consumed itself and burnt out, leaving a row of blackened, smoking buildings, but the rest of the town had been saved. Jingo and his gunners had saved Nassau, and they found themselves the toast of the town.

This fire, and the performance under his direction of the men he had inspired and trained, was the highlight of Jingo's Bahama posting. The prompt response of off-duty men to this emergency was a clear demonstration of the *esprit de corps* and cool efficiency he had been able to inculcate with his brand of leadership, founded on mutual trust and respect. It was the final feather in the young officer's cap, for although he was unaware of it at the time, his Bahama stay was drawing to a close.

FIVE

Shipwreck

F ar away in the Crimean peninsula, wounds and sickness were wasting the British and French forces encamped about the fortifications of Sevastopol. The Allied commanders, anxious to bring their increasingly tedious campaign to a close, called for more men, especially gunners to pound away at the stubborn Russian defences.

Their call arrived in the Bahamas just as its gunners were enjoying the islands at their most idyllic. Jingo had taken them on a weekend expedition to one of the Out Islands, and they were setting up tents and cooking their supper of turtle, fish, and pork as a steam warship, H.M.S. *Vulture*, closed Nassau harbour. By the time the man-of-war's boat reached them, they were enjoying a singsong, accompanied by the ever-present banjos.

"You are wanted for Crimea!" was the message delivered to Jingo's men. "The ship sails at daybreak and everyone must be aboard by then, with all kit and gear, ready for inspection." With hardly time to shout "Hurrah!" the artillerymen were on their way, tent and supplies stowed, boat loaded and propelled by sail and oar. Their indefatigable sergeant had all his lists prepared and handed over to a gimlet-eyed garrison adjutant before dawn had broken. Next morning all were aboard *Vulture*, Lieutenant Jingo saluting the quarterdeck as he came over the side.

The grim old Royal Navy captain, commanding officer of *Vulture* and a veteran of the West Indies station, was suitably impressed by Jingo's knowledge of naval etiquette, but he was even more appreciative of having a company of experienced gunners on board for the voyage to Jamaica. He had lost many prime hands to yellow fever and consequently was short of men for the warship's guns. The artillerymen were glad to fill out the vacancies in the ship's watch and quarter bill, and being veterans of many of Jingo's sailing expeditions, they proved able not only to man a gun but to knot and splice like any able seaman.

"Why, your fellows are handier than half the red marines afloat!" the captain exclaimed to Jingo, and promptly invited him to take his meals with him for the length of his stay aboard.

At Jamaica, the remains of an artillery regiment, ravaged by Yellow Jack, joined the Bahamas contingent. The combined force, under the command of a languid English captain, with Jingo as the only other officer, was to embark in an ancient hired transport, the *Emma Eugenia*, of only 400 tons burthen. The night before embarkation, Jingo was painfully wounded by a blow to the head from an oar swung by a gigantic native as he attempted to break up a brawl between the Jamaican and a sailor from the guardship, H.M.S. *Boscawen*. He was still badly dazed and bleeding as he reported aboard the transport on sailing day, but he was happy to be leaving on what was to be the last leg of a voyage to Britain.

The *Emma Eugenia* was old and tired and lubberly, able to sail only before the wind, which fortunately served as she left Kingston Harbour. But if the ship aroused some concern among her passengers, who included the wives and children of soldiers as well as a few civilian families, it was as nothing to the alarm awakened among even the most hardened travellers by her crew. Her captain, though pleasant and unassuming when sober, was seldom to be found in that condition once the ship had cleared the harbour. As he kept the sextant and charts in his cabin and did whatever navigating was done, the position of the ship was a mystery to everyone else on board. A couple of his officers were capable enough, but the captain had reduced their duties to little more than watchkeeping and supervising the setting and taking in of sail. On top of all this, the crew appeared to be made up of the scum of the Caribbean, recruited from the criminal elements of ports on the *Emma*'s itinerary as her original complement died off or jumped ship. They seemed to be in a continual ferment of surly near-mutiny, so that an increasing amount of work aboard was carried out by the passenger gunners, the only reliable and disciplined work force on board. In this happy state the *Emma* surged northwards on the wings of a boisterous following wind, her passengers growing more anxious by the day to reach the welcoming land and be quit of their ill-found argosy.

In the event, they reached it all too soon. One moonlit night Jingo, keeping watch with the second mate, noted that the sea was growing paler, a condition which he knew from his sailing experiences off the Bahamas could only be due to shallow water over a coral reef or shoal. He called this to the attention of the second officer, but had no sooner done so than the ship struck. There was a grinding crunch and the vessel was brought up all standing; then she heeled over until it was difficult to remain on deck without a handhold. Fortunately she had struck while sailing before a gentle breeze and with no sea running, so that her masts did not go by the board, although her standing rigging was badly strained and shaken.

In the turmoil that followed, with the crew running about in alarm and women passengers in night attire clutching their children about them and cluttering the passageways with their baggage, Jingo darted below to inform his senior officer. That worthy, as languid and unflappable as ever despite his bright striped pyjamas, pulled at his moustache and said: "Yas! All wight! Sound the assembly, fall in the men, and tell the sergeant-major to call the roll."

But Jingo had already seen his gunners fallen in on the deck. All that remained was to call the roll, which proved that every man was present.

The calm and competent appearance of the gunners, with their captain, now impeccably attired, receiving the usual military reports and acknowledging the usual salutes, was in such contrast with the confused and frightened performance of the crew that the ship's first officer informed Jingo: "Yours are the only fellows to be relied upon. Can you pick out a good boat's crew?"

Jingo could and did, falling out his old boat's crew from Bahama sailing days. But the first officer was as worried about his captain as he was about his crew. "We must lock up that drunken sweep before we do anything else. If I lock him up, it will be mutiny. Can you explain the situation to your boss and have him take the responsibility?"

The senior officer, however languid in his manner, was a man of quick and decisive action in a tight corner. After Jingo had explained the situation, he took charge of the *Emma*'s captain when he appeared on deck. He shepherded him below to his cabin, making reassuring and comforting noises, locked the door and pocketed the key before returning to the scene of action.

And action there was indeed. As the gunners turned out and lowered their boat, the native crew drew their knives and rushed them. But when their leader was knocked senseless by a marlinespike wielded by a husky gunner, the remainder withdrew sulkily to the fo'c'sle and refused to have anything to do with any attempt to save the ship, by manning either the capstan or the pumps. Nothing daunted, the soldiers dropped a large kedge anchor, bringing its hawser back to the capstan. Led by Jingo, they set the sails aback to help the ship off, manned the pumps to lighten her as much as possible, and heaved away at the capstan bars, directed by the ship's officers. There was no movement in the ship as the strain came on the hawser, which became bar taut. Still the gunners heaved until, with a tremendous twang, the hawser broke, the severed end flying about the deck with a force that could have cut a man in two. A second hawser to a second anchor also parted. The weary gunners continued to pump throughout the long night. As dawn broke, the ship appeared to be in desperate straits, as a rising wind and sea began to grind and slam her on the sharp coral reef.

A supreme effort was called for; yet despite appeals from their officers, the native crew refused to lend any help. Weary and worn, the soldiers, ship's officers, and passengers managed with great effort to lower the ship's best bower anchor, an immensely heavy affair, onto the boat and sent it away shackled to its weighty chain cable. Though now almost exhausted, the little band was able to shift everything of any weight right aft, where the ship was still afloat. Finally, after a last desperate effort with the capstan, the ship slid off into deep water to an exultant cheer from all on deck.

The vessel was now afloat, but only just. Incessant labour at the pumps was still required to keep the rush of water into the hold in check. Noonday observations by the ship's officers showed them to be off the coast of Florida; the drunken captain had failed to allow for the sideways set of the powerful Gulf Stream. With a sail fothered under the ship's bottom, reducing the inflow somewhat, pumping became more a matter of routine than of emergency, and with her crew of ship's officers and artillerymen doing the work on deck and aloft, the *Emma Eugenia* ploughed her way slowly and uncertainly across the broad grey Atlantic, encountering headwinds, cold weather, and, off the Newfoundland Banks, prolonged thick fog. No celestial observations could be made for days, so nobody on board had any idea as to the ship's true position. At last, after days of increasing anxiety, the skies cleared and they were able to establish their position, hundreds of miles off the intended course. Gales, violent and protracted, brought all progress to a standstill; then rationing of both food and water became necessary as supplies ran dangerously low. The voyage was a nightmare of labour and hardship, the pumps always going, the ship half derelict at times.

Then one night, while on watch, Jingo smelt the rich, earthy reek of peat smoke and gorse—the scent of "ould Oireland," for sure! The crew laughed and told him he was imagining things. But next morning, plain as could be, the Old Head of Kinsale stood up proud on the eastern horizon. On then, through the Chops of the Channel, past the Bishop and the Lizard and the Eddystone and the Shorn-cliffe Downs white with the tents of the German Legion (Prince Albert's poor relations, a disrespectful pilot called them). At last they reached the South Foreland, the Thames estuary, and Woolwich Wharf.

"Why, the war's over!" a lounger answered Jingo's shouted query.

The whole odyssey had been in vain. He had lost the race to reach the war, lost his hope of adventure and distinction and promotion. Casting a scornful eye over Jingo's salt-stained uniform, workworn and shrunken, the lounger, a supercilious brother officer, sneered: "Who's your tailor?" Jingo knew he was back again at "the shop," the home of peacetime "bullshit and gaiters."

SIX

The Great Mutiny

The year 1856 sorely tested young Thomas Strange. He arrived back in England just in time to greet the arrival home of the triumphant troops from the Crimea. For Jingo, already envious of the fighting reputations won by these hardened veterans while he was moping about the West Indies, there was further humiliation to come: he and his gunners were relegated to the role of helping the London police hold back the crowds along the parade route as the troops marched through the city to a gala reception at the Palace.

But the ultimate humiliation still lay ahead. Jingo, terribly conscious of his unadorned chest in a city suddenly filled with bemedalled veterans, was attending a ball with a "lively, brown-eyed little brunette," as his partner. During an interval in the dancing the pair found themselves surrounded by young officers, all wearing the newly issued Crimea medals. Turning to Jingo, the young lady asked in all innocence: "But you have no medals! Where did such a large fellow as you are manage to hide himself during the war?"

Cut to the quick, Jingo returned his wondering partner to her mother, left the ball, and never saw her again.

In time, of course, he recovered from his embarrassment at having missed the war and settled into the routine of peacetime soldiering. He was stationed first at Aldershot, where he was vastly impressed by the soldierly bearing of the King's German Legion, an elite unit who sang their marching song "Soldaten Lieder" as they passed in review, and later at Sheerness where he was posted as District Adjutant. He found much of his work boring, but enlivened his off-duty hours with brisk bouts of boxing with a gigantic Norse subaltern named Wolfe, whom his friends nicknamed "the Animal" and who roomed across the hall from him.

Wolfe was something of a celebrity among young artillerymen, being a sort of walking warning of the restrictions under which all gunners laboured. When the army established its first Staff College, open to competition from officers in all branches of the service, fifteen of the first twenty successful candidates were artillerymen or engineers, a reflection of the higher intellectual qualities needed in the technical branches of the service. It was then thought necessary to handicap such officers by allowing no more than four entrants from these branches, thereby allowing officers of lesser ability to qualify from the Guards, the infantry of the line, and the cavalry regiments.

Young Wolfe was one of the gunners so debarred. Although he was not allowed to take the course of instruction, he was permitted to write the final exam, which he passed with high marks. While never subsequently allowed to serve on the Army Staff, he became a notable and much admired figure among his fellow gunners, living proof of their mental superiority to mere horsemen and footsloggers and of the injustice of a bigoted army command.

Wolfe and Jingo were inseparable, and the two tall gunners were soon at the centre of a convivial group of young officers that included Huleatt, "a fighting chaplain," an artillery medical officer named Jerry Orton, and a naval officer known as "Jovial Jock" Baird. With such friends for company, Jingo found that time in his otherwise boring posting passed pleasantly enough.

He spent his long leave in 1857 journeying through France, Spain, Italy, and Switzerland, learning their languages and attending art classes when not roaming the mountains with paintbox and sketchbook. In Switzerland he met another pair of artillery officers, and in their company stopped at a Swiss lake resort, where they encountered a trio of English girls chaperoned by their mother and accompanied by a middle-aged Frenchman, the suitor of one of the girls. The gunners, determined to cut out the fat Frenchman, laid furious siege to the three sisters, Jingo with such effect that he was challenged to a duel by the indignant swain. But before matters could come to such a pass, if indeed they ever would have, a telegram arrived for Jingo ordering his immediate return to England. The great Indian Mutiny had begun.

The British East India Company maintained three armies in India, in one of which, the Bengal army, a savage revolt had broken out. The causes of the rebellion were numerous and complex. One was the introduction into the army of a new cartridge, wrongly believed to be greased with the fat of the pig, an animal held to be unclean by Hindus and therefore offensive, on religious grounds, to the Sepoys in the Company's native regiments. Another was smouldering nationalism fanned by disgruntled native rulers shorn of much of their former despotic power by the British. But essentially the outbreak was due to the insensitivity of British government officials and the arrogance of Company officers too intent on matters of trade to pay attention to the attitudes of the native soldiers on whom much of their power rested. There were 300,000 native soldiers, or Sepoys as they were called, and only 45,000 European soldiers in the Company's service in India, and the revolt of a whole native army, with every possibility of its spreading to the other two, threatened British rule throughout the entire subcontinent.

The situation was not helped by the friction existing at all levels between the officers and men of the British Army and those serving in the regiments of "John Company." Lord Roberts of Kandahar, then serving as a subaltern in the official British forces, notes in his history of the period, *Forty-One Years in India*, that his fellow officers in the line regiments affected to look down upon their counterparts in Company service. The disdain was heartily reciprocated by the Company men, who regarded regular service soldiers as so many clodhoppers, fresh off the boat and quite useless in the unfamiliar surroundings of an India in which they themselves were completely at home.

Roberts, although only a junior officer, did his best to heal this breach, and he deplored the official insensitivity to the unrest, which began with the introduction of the new cartridge at the appropriately named army base of Dum-Dum. The new rifles, a vast improvement on the old smoothbore muskets, were still muzzleloaders, and their ammunition consisted of the ball and its powder propellant made up into a paper cartridge, greased to allow it to fit easily into the grooved rifling of the barrel when rammed home. The grease was made from vegetable oils, not the "unclean" pig, a point which some commanders attempted to drive home by allowing their soldiers to grease their own cartridges. But as Roberts noted at the time, the harm had been done; the rumour, once started, spread everywhere overnight, and native regiments one by one flared into rebellion.

But serious as were the problems posed by the revolt, they were as nothing in their effect on the British public compared with the savagery of the Sepoy assault on British civilians. The bloody butchering of their British officers by native soldiers who, mere moments before, had been loyal and trusted members of disciplined Indian regiments, was shocking enough. But what really stunned the people of

Britain was the cruelty shown to the families of British officers. Hundreds of women and children were killed and their mutilated bodies flung aside by mobs of uniformed soldiers who seemed to have been caught up in transports of sadistic rage.

The response in Britain was not long in coming. What the British people wanted, what they demanded, was not merely the restoration of law and order to a turbulent India but revenge as well. It was not enough simply to restore John Company's rule; public opinion would not be satisfied until the perpetrators of these acts were tried and punished with the full rigour of the law. The British government bustled about with unusual energy collecting troops to be sent out with the utmost despatch. Among the first to go was a contingent of artillerymen which included Jingo's unit, and it was with great satisfaction that Jingo paraded his men before an inspecting officer, Sir Fenwick Williams.

The Gunners had not served in India since the days of Clive, and as British Army uniforms had changed drastically since then, they did not know what sort of dress was appropriate for the Indian climate. In the event, the matter was decided for them by the War Office, which decreed that each man was to be issued with a sort of pillow case, one for each item of headgear; this was to be worn over the regulation artillery busby with the addition of a small crescent of leather attached in front to act as a visor. When the men of Jingo's unit paraded in the new rig for the first time, already feeling ridiculous in their pillow cases, they found that the visors, quickly named "flapdoodles," lacked any support and simply hung down over their eyes and noses. They were admonished by their colonel to carry them in their hand for the nonce, but as he led them through the town on their way back to barracks, Jingo threw his away. Immediately the gunners behind followed his example. A cloud of fluttering

bits of leather marked the route of the disgusted artillerymen, much to Jingo's satisfaction. The colonel, though
annoyed, nonetheless had the good sense to accept that
asking his men to wear pillowcases on their heads was
enough without requiring them to put up with flaps over
their noses. The gunners, in good heart, embarked aboard a
splendid Australian liner; there was to be no dawdling about
in any ancient sailing packet for men bound for India. As
Kipling wrote:

> It's Tommy this, an' Tommy that, an' "Tommy, wait
> outside."
> But it's "Special train for Atkins" when the trooper's
> on the tide.

Their contingent was to be the first to make the passage to
India via "the overland route"—by ship through the Mediterranean to Egypt, then overland to the Red Sea for embarkation in another vessel which would carry them to India itself.
The ship, like all troop transports, was crowded and conditions aboard were pretty basic, but for all that Jingo enjoyed
the passage past Gibraltar, Morocco, and Malta, before the
eventual arrival at Alexandria. Here the party loaded the
baggage on camels and availed themselves of varied means of
transportation ranging from mules to four-wheeled carts,
which the troops dubbed "charabancs." The men were all
dressed in white sea-kit and were supposed to be travelling as
an unarmed party, in order not to infringe upon Egyptian
neutrality. The Suez Canal, of course, had not yet been
begun, and the railway which was supposed to link the
Mediterranean with the Gulf of Suez had only just got under
way. Despite the heat and the flies and the beggars, the men
enjoyed the trip, especially when they arrived in Cairo.

Like millions of visitors before and after them, the troops gazed in awe at the Sphinx and the pyramids. Jingo, typically, climbed to the top of one without any of the proffered assistance from guides and touts. In those days, before the Egyptian government undertook conservation, the public was allowed to wander through ransacked tombs and to view mummies long since robbed of their finery. Jingo was greatly taken by the mummy of an Egyptian woman, still in her teens, with the lovely face of a young girl, still enchanting after four thousand years. So young! So old!

Watching the boisterous behaviour of the noisy troops, picnicking and skylarking in the shadow of the immense pyramids and preyed upon by swarms of Egyptian beggars and touts, Jingo reflected "how much like Goths were these, their descendants. The two races remained unchanged, one barbaric at bottom with a veneer of civilization, the other an ancient civilization overlaid with barbarism."

A few days' march brought the troops to Suez, where they were entertained by a group of women and children who had escaped from India, although many had lost husbands, fathers, and brothers in the Mutiny. Baskets of oranges and bottles of ginger pop and beer were handed out to the hot and dusty soldiers before their officers marched them aboard the waiting transport.

Jingo spent the entire night labouring in the hold, superintending the stowage of precious ammunition and other stores. At dawn, his duty done, he took out his paintbox to try to capture in a quick sketch the flaring glory of the blood-red sunrise. He was reprimanded for this by his indignant colonel, who thought him idling when there was much work to be done. Jingo explained that it was already finished, with everything properly stowed. The colonel, mollified, passed on. All the same, Jingo threw the uncompleted picture overboard, and sought his bunk.

The passage through the Red Sea in a crowded troopship and the stifling heat of a blazing summer sun Jingo characterized as "indescribable," yet he managed to apply himself, utilizing every spare moment, to learning Hindustani. It was "the first language baby Jingo had spoken, and it came back to him as by magic," he wrote in his memoirs.

Calcutta was finally reached on October 11, 1857, and the troops were quickly disembarked and marched to the railroad station, where they entrained for the town of Raniganj.

With Cawnpore menaced and Lucknow under siege there was an air of frenzy among the horde of red-faced staff officers hustling reinforcements up the line. Nevertheless, the gunners were able to shed a good deal of unwanted baggage at Calcutta, including the detested heavy shakos in their white pillowcases. In their place, a smart and comfortable headgear was improvised by Jingo's colonel. A quantity of the light turban material used by natives was purchased in the bazaar, and with this each man improvised a Sikh-style turban, wound about his army forage cap. This provided him with protection both from the hot sun and from sabre strokes, as well as an efficient pillow.

Pleased with their smart new headgear, and relieved to be rid of all the cumbersome impedimenta imposed on them by generals at home unacquainted with the Indian heat, the troops set off in fine fettle, marching, like so many imperial troops before them, up the Grand Trunk Road towards the holy city of Benares.

SEVEN

Blood and Battle

The troops were drawn up in hollow square to witness punishment, the early light of dawn glittering on their burnished accoutrements and on the drawn swords of their officers, rigid in front of their platoons. For all the perfection of their formation there was an air of unease that was almost palpable. Many of the young recruits were already pale beneath their tan and only the muttered imprecations of their sergeants kept wavering heads steady and eyes fixed to the front. At one end a battery of field guns, unlimbered and ready with their crews kneeling about them, stood in line. Facing them, a few paces away, a row of Sepoy prisoners waited, sullen and shabby in tattered uniforms. Jingo stood behind his crouching gunners in the centre of the line of guns, staring fixedly at the wretched handful of prisoners. Like everyone else, he dreaded what was about to happen, but unlike most of the onlookers, he was to be no mere spectator. His guns, his gunners, were about to execute these prisoners, and he was determined to carry out his unpleasant duty without flinching.

Tried at the central compound at Benares, these Sepoys had been found guilty of mutiny and desertion and a long list of other offences: murder, rape, torture, mutilation. Because of the hideousness of their offences, it was decreed that they should be executed by the native Indian method traditionally employed for the most serious offences. Rather than being hanged or shot, the usual British Army forms of capital punishment, these men were to be blown from guns.

It was, in fact, a remarkably humane death. The guns were charged with powder but not loaded with shot; death from the blast was instantaneous and painless, whereas a hanging which failed to break the neck could leave a victim strangling for minutes, and a man shot by firing party might well thrash about, mortally wounded, until despatched by an officer's revolver. But what Sepoys dreaded about death by gun was what happened after the actual execution. For the bloody fragments that were left were collected by native sweepers of the lowest caste, a defilement which would require ages of degraded transmigration for a Hindu's soul before he could hope to be re-embodied in the soldierly caste he would lose by such a death.

But if the actual execution meant a quick death for the victim, it was a gruesome business for everyone else taking part in it, and Jingo longed for it to be over. He looked at the prisoners awaiting their fate with varying degrees of composure. They were fine-looking men, with the handsome features of the Oudh tribe, and it was hard to think of them as murdering mutineers. Their officer, a distinguished-looking veteran with a white beard and carefully upswept moustache, still wearing the medal of the Sikh campaign, stepped from their ranks and saluted the British brigadier.

"Sahib," he cried. "I have often faced death for the Sircar (Government); let me show my Baba logue (children) how to die."

"Yes," said the brigadier. "Pity you did not show them how to live like loyal Poorbeah soldiers."

The old officer made no reply but marched proudly up to the flank gun and saluted it smartly. He touched the muzzle with his right hand and then the caste mark on his forehead, before looking steadily at the gunner crouched at the breech.

"Ready!" he commanded. "Fire!"

An explosion, a cloud of smoke, and a heap of clothes and flesh lay on the ground.

"Now, men," said the brigadier, "follow your officer!"

But if the Sepoys were stoically resigned to their fate, they were in no hurry to embrace it. They had to be led to the six waiting guns and secured by ropes to the wheels before being blown to bits.

Their pitiful remains were left to the waiting sweepers to be gathered up and hastily buried. Wiping a spot of blood from his cheek, a grim-faced Jingo led his battery about the business of moving off his guns, in the wake of the shaken regiments as they marched away to breakfast to the music of their bands. It was just retribution, military fashion, no doubt, but for Strange and his gunners it was the most unpleasant experience of the war and the first blood they had spilled.

It would certainly not be the last, though, as Colonel Maberly, their commanding officer, explained to them. They were to be part of a self-contained field force under General Franks, which was to fight its way through rebel-held territory to join Sir Colin Campbell in an attempt to capture Lucknow. This city, the principal rebel stronghold, was held by a force of more than 60,000 men, all trained native soldiers, and had already defeated two earlier British assaults. Its capture, and the defeat of so large an army, would break the back of the Sepoy resistance and bring the Mutiny to an end.

The newly arrived gunners were to be part of the field force's siege train, and Jingo himself was drafted as Commissary of Ordnance. As such, he was responsible for organizing the transport of a vast amount of ammunition and supplies and for administering the huge number of elephants, camels, and oxen, with their drivers, needed for the job. It was an exercise in logistics entailing hours of dreary desk work, but as a plum Jingo was promised the job of "general's galloper," responsible for carrying messages wherever required. Jingo prepared for it by buying himself a horse, which he named Butcha, a sturdy little grey stallion which seemed capable of carrying his six-foot-two frame with the requisite speed.

Their first outing was not a success. Butcha had never encountered elephants before and on meeting a team of them hauling the heavy artillery, he reared and fell backwards in his alarm. Jingo was hurt and shaken but escaped being crushed, and both horse and rider eventually learned to live with elephants and to love them.

The huge animals possessed a delicacy of touch surprising in beasts capable of immense brute power, and they were crafty enough to know how to make the most of it. Faced with any task requiring more than the usual amount of effort, they would stubbornly refuse it until promised "baksheesh" by their mahout, upon which they would immediately complete their task. They often worked in partnership with their mahouts to steal everything in reach as the artillery train passed through a town, and Jingo would frequently be forced to ransack the baggage and return to its indignant owners the loot which an elephant had passed up to its rider.

The backbone of the field force was made up of three regiments of the line, the veteran Tenth Foot and two raw new regiments, the 97th and 20th, together with a brigade of Gurkhas led by British officers, and a mixed artillery contingent of field batteries and heavy siege guns. Screened by squadrons of irregular Punjabi horse, and followed by a large baggage train, the column moved off to the north, a vast cloud of dust crawling across a parched and treeless plain.

Near the village of Secundra, in a belt of low jungle, the first Sepoy resistance was encountered—a large force of mixed native infantry and artillery. With his usual impetuosity, General Franks led his men in dashing style, using his artillery in close support of his skirmishing line so that Jingo, in this his first battle, was caught up in the thick of the fighting. Finding himself in the tumbled debris of a captured Sepoy battery, he scratched the initials "R.A." into the bronze barrels of its two field guns to show that they had been captured by the Royal Artillery, using the point of his sword for the purpose. With his colonel at his side, he found himself so far in advance of the main British force that they were coming under fire from their own troops. Jingo was forced to wave his handkerchief, tied to the end of his sword, before fire slackened. It was not the way that Jingo had imagined he would use the weapon, but in his first action Jingo's sword had proved to be most useful.

A day later, after a hot and dusty march, a second Sepoy force was encountered at Chandra. After a long afternoon of fierce and confused fighting, the column was forced to encamp in the face of a dangerous and still undefeated enemy. Warning his officers that extreme vigilance must be exercised by sentries and officers alike throughout the night, General Franks emphasized that there must be "no lurking in doolies," a dooly being the curtained litter used for carrying wounded men.

As he went his rounds of the outposts during his night watch, Jingo was accordingly incensed to note a dooly lying near his sleeping artillerymen with a suspicious bulge in its curtains. Suspecting some fellow officer of putting comfort before duty despite the official injunction, Jingo administered a kick to the protruding backside, only to be horrified to hear a stream of oaths bellowed in the unmistakable voice of General Franks himself!

Appalled by what he had done, Jingo fled to the shelter of
the nearest gun and flung himself down to sham sleep, while
his furious commander raged in the darkness behind. In his
first battle, he had kicked his commanding general in the
backside; what hope was there for a military career begun in
so inauspicious a manner?

But Jingo had not reckoned on the forbearance and good
nature of his genial general. The next morning, with the
merest suspicion of a smile on his grizzled features, General
Franks intimated that he had, indeed, recognized his midnight assailant but did not hold it against him, and at the
end of the campaign he mentioned Jingo in his official
despatches for distinguished conduct. It was to be the first
of four such commendations during the Indian campaign,
but of all the distinctions he achieved, it was to be the one
that Jingo, in later life, would treasure most.

Early morning marches were the order of the day, and the
beauty of the Indian countryside through which the column
was passing made a deep impression on the young officer,
who recorded this vivid passage in his journal:

On the 22nd of February, 1858, in the early morning,
the force was ordered to deploy on the march. Once
off the roads among the dew-laden fields there was no
dust. In the distance, catching the rising sun, glittered
the golden minarets and domes of Sultanpoor, while a
pale moon grew faint in a sky whose rose tints melted
into zenith blue. Graceful groups of the rounded
foliage of mango groves broke the level aspect. The
scarlet of the long lines of British Infantry contrasted
with nature's green, and the glint of burnished
accoutrements. The sheen of dancing spears shone
above the brilliant turbans of the Irregular Horse,
followed by the more sombre hue of the Artillery and
the crawling columns of the Gurkhas in the rear, with

white bullocks drawing their guns, while high above all loomed the broad foreheads of the elephants as they trundled the heavy guns like baby carts behind their huge forms, walking with their peculiar slouching gait and noiseless footsteps. All made a picture frame in the memory. Put it face to wall! It is irresistibly recalled by the note of a bugle. A happy inspiration had seized the Bugle-Major (a Celt of course). The mellow bugles of the Light Infantry rang out the lively march of —

> The young May moon is beaming, love,
> And the glow-worm's lamp is gleaming, love,
> How sweet to rove through Morna's grove,
> While the drowsy world is dreaming, love!

And so some marched to death, and all were light-hearted.

The idyllic mood of the morning march was rudely shattered by word passed back from scouts: a large rebel force lay deployed across the line of the route.

Taking Jingo as his galloper, General Franks pushed on ahead to make a personal reconnaissance of the enemy position, which he knew to be close to the walls of the town. The two came under fire at a bend in the road. Before beating a hasty retreat, they just had time to observe that the rebels had established a heavy battery to command the turn in the road, with no fewer than fourteen cannon peeping through the embrasures. Jingo was sent back by his general to bring up the column's horsed artillery, and was nonplussed when the major commanding the batteries began to move off his force at a rapid trot before he had had time to communicate information about the concealed enemy guns on the road just ahead. Riding up alongside the battery major, Jingo could not make himself heard above the noise of the rumbling and banging of the gun carriages. At the last moment, as the leading gun teams neared the fatal bend that would lead them on to annihilation, Jingo stood up in his stirrups, gestured to the left with a swordarm signal, and bellowed, "Left take ground!" Obediently, the column wheeled left into the open fields away from the hidden guns, while its incredulous commander, scarlet with rage, screeched at Jingo: "Damn you, sir; how dare you take command of my battery!" For answer, Jingo pointed silently to his right, where the hidden battery was now just coming into view and sending its opening rounds bouncing across their front. Instantly recognizing the danger so narrowly averted, the major grunted "Quite right!" before leading his gunners on a wide circuit through the fields to a flanking position.

Their fire soon enfiladed and destroyed the enemy battery, which was captured smartly by a charge led by the intrepid General Franks himself, with the irrepressible Jingo at his side. Both survived a hail of case-shot which decimated the group of horsemen all about them, and arrived in the rebel battery at one end as the last of the rebels scrambled away out of the other.

But the fire-eating general was in no mood to linger and savour his victory. Anxious to get to Lucknow, he reformed his column and set up camp for the night, ready to move on at first light. Jingo was left to dispose of the captured Sepoy artillery. The task proved to be both difficult and dangerous. After a great deal of effort and experiment, the smaller guns were destroyed, but three enormous bronze 24-pounders posed an even greater problem. Eventually Jingo had them packed with powder, with a couple of balls jammed on top, and lowered them, muzzle down, into a deep dry well, with a common fuse attached. This was then lit, and the result was a tremendous explosion which sent the three guns soaring high into the air, streaming flame like enormous rockets, before plunging to earth. One of them fell through a tent—fortunately empty—in the nearby encampment. Jingo was visited by a stream of indignant officers, all of whom cursed him roundly as a dangerous maniac and pointed out that the guns had proved to be a greater menace in his hands than they had been in the enemy's. It was a chastened and mortified Jingo who was forced to deal with the fallen guns where they lay. Each was destroyed by more pedestrian methods and laid to rest in its own grave.

Eight days later he made amends. The column had fought its way through desultory opposition in the hostile territory of Oudh and arrived at Selimpore on the evening of March 4. Next day it was scheduled to make the long march necessary to effect a junction with Sir Colin Campbell and attempt the capture of Lucknow. Haste was imperative. Unfortunately for General Franks, a small but strongly defended fort, Moonshee Gunj, lay a mile off the line of march, posing an awkward problem. To besiege it would take time, time that he could not spare, yet on the other hand he could hardly leave it in the hands of a rebel force which could cut his line of communications and destroy the vital supplies already moving up it.

Franks resolved the problem by detaching a small force of mixed artillery, infantry, and cavalry to capture the fort by a sudden direct assault. With Colonel Maberly of the Royal Artillery in command, the assault began, following a personal reconnaissance made by General Franks himself. The general again used Jingo to transmit his orders to the attackers. The Royal Artillery's little field pieces were pushed up to within 400 yards of the outer defences, and in short order rendered them untenable. White-turbaned rebels were soon streaming away down a protective ravine, pursued by British lancers.

But a strongly built inner keep, or tower, proved a tougher nut to crack. Its guns swept the inner courtyard and the attackers found themselves forced to take shelter behind the captured outer wall. The assault had ground to a halt and the general, impatient to resume his march, could spare it no more time. The force was ordered to rejoin as the column marched on, and Jingo was sent to order the engineer officer, McLeod Innes, to blow open the gate of the citadel with a bag of gunpowder.

It was more easily said than done. On arrival at the scene, Jingo found the body of an officer, Lieutenant Percy Smith, lying in the only courtyard gate, and a little knot of attackers, mostly gunners, huddled behind the outer wall. Braving the musketry fire from the tower, Jingo had Smith's body carried clear of the gate, and with the assistance of the gunners he wheeled one of the fort's guns into position to fire into the stout gate of the keep. But the door was far too thick for the gun's small shot to have any effect. Despite the risk, there was nothing for it but to attempt to place a charge directly against the door and blow it in. The only gunpowder available was beside a native gun in the courtyard, which was commanded by musketry fire from the citadel. After extemporizing a bag from a piece of carpet, Jingo and McLeod Innes dashed out and began to fill it with the Sepoy powder. Instantly they came under heavy fire from the loopholes of the keep. Innes, while stooping over the bag, was hit and fell, shot through both thighs. He was carried off by a stretcher party. Undaunted, Jingo kept on, filling his improvised bag to the top before withdrawing to the temporary shelter of the outer wall. Here he recruited an infantry officer, Captain Fred Middleton of the 29th Regiment, to assist him, and the two made a dash for the gate, Jingo carrying the heavy bag of powder, Middleton beside him with a flaming portfire, or torch. Both arrived unhit. Jingo tamped the powder bag firmly against the gate, fuse uppermost, and Middleton applied his torch. Then they bolted for the safety of the sheltering wall. Alas, the native powder was poor stuff. The resulting explosion blew away part of the gate, but the main structure of the door remained as strong as ever.

A peremptory message from the general now arrived, ordering Jingo and his men to rejoin him immediately; the fort keep would have to be left to the enemy. But nothing else of value must be left. Determined to render the fort impotent to do any further harm, Jingo had the three outer guns wheeled away and then, with the aid of a few free spirits, he dashed into the inner courtyard, again under heavy fire, and manhandled the last gun there out of the gate and across the moat bridge to safety.

Although a minor incident in a long campaign, this abortive attack on a small fort was a highlight of Jingo's early career. His dash and gallantry, his courage under fire, and above all his initiative and confident command had all been amply displayed and won both his general's commendation and the respect and admiration of his colleagues. Innes, who had been wounded while working with Jingo on filling the powder bag, was awarded the Victoria Cross, Britain's highest award for valour. Had it been Jingo who was hit rather than Innes, it might have been Lieutenant Strange, V.C.

But of even greater significance, although unrecognized at the time, was the successful cooperation with Captain Middleton. Many years later, and in a far-off land, that association was to be renewed.

By now, young Jingo felt himself a part of this Indian Army, an odd blend of native Indian and European elements with its own distinctive way of doing things. He had learned, for example, that field batteries here were accustomed to operate with far more dash and *élan* than he had been used to in England. Instead of the staid pace, amounting to a trot at most, at which horse batteries moved on Woolwich Common, Indian Army batteries were accustomed to move at a headlong gallop in the face of the enemy, deploying and opening fire with a speed thought impossible in home units. The Irish riders of the gun teams thought nothing of putting their horses at fences and even brick walls that might have daunted a steeplechaser, sometimes with disastrous results if a gun axle gave way. Such impetuosity demanded both judgment and nerve. Jingo recognized that riding the wheel horse over such an obstacle, knowing that several tons of metal and wood were directly behind and would crush one to death in the event of failure, required courage amounting to heroism. His Irish gun teams and their native gunners on limber and mounting were equal to the test, and Jingo exulted in their bravery and skill. In India, his gunners operated with the *élan* of cavalrymen, and Jingo would soon make great use of their daredevil recklessness.

At Lucknow, General Franks's column joined the besieging force commanded by Sir Colin Campbell, irreverently known throughout the army as "Sir Crawlin' Camel," because of his agonizing caution and slowness of movement. This vast force included the armies of Generals Havelock and Outram and had been encamped about the city for weeks, while its cautious commander collected reinforcements and mustered what resolution he could. As his contemporary, Sir William M. James was to write in *The British in India*, "No other general had ever thought it necessary to mass such an amount of force, or deemed it expedient to proceed with such extreme deliberation and caution."

Campbell had already carried prudence to extremes in his earlier campaigns. At Cawnpore, James wrote, he had arrived at the city after a leisurely approach "not an hour too soon" to save the city from disaster. Lucknow would test this timid commander to the limit.

The royal city, seat of the kings of Oudh, lay in a loop of the Goomti River with a canal bed on its open side. It was thus a naturally strong defensive site, and its strength was further enhanced by a series of strongly walled palaces lying outside the perimeter of the town itself. It was these immense buildings that were occupying the attentions of the besiegers when Franks's force joined, and it took the artillery a considerable time to reduce them to the stage where they could be assaulted by the impatient infantry.

For Jingo, the siege rapidly took on a sort of dreamlike quality, enhanced by the nature of the buildings under attack. Vast airy structures of pink or ivory reared themselves above a waving sea of green foliage; golden minarets lanced the perfect blue of the Indian sky among the pearly bubbles of temple domes and frothy arcades of slender pillars and pierced stone. He found himself directing his battery fire against a sort of fairyland, which was yet a place of infinite menace, for the palace compounds had been heavily fortified and were fiercely defended. His sense of dreaming was the result of sleeplessness; in the entire siege he was able to enjoy only one full night's sleep, since he had volunteered for double duty. During the day he acted, as usual, as staff officer to Colonel Maberly, directing the attack from the southward, but all night he served as battery officer in the forward gun emplacements, for the artillery was short of officers. He catnapped when he could in the intervals of action, so that time lost its meaning and life became a mad round of galloping and firing and being fired upon in an unlikely world of beauty and menace, filled with men in exotic uniforms and flowing beards, for there were loyal Sikh regiments in the besieging army.

At long last, Jingo was relieved of his double burden in time to enjoy a night's sleep before the final assault on the perimeter palaces and on the city beyond was to be launched. And it was while he was waiting for the attack to begin that he fell into conversation with a young cavalry officer in the uniform of a regiment with which he was unfamiliar. The cavalryman chaffed Jingo about the

Gunners' famous one-word motto "Ubique" (Everywhere), with its implied derision of regiments which listed each battle honour on their colours. Before he could take offence at this criticism of his beloved unit, Jingo fortunately recognized the officer as Hodson, famous throughout India as the "irregular leader of irregular horse."

Hodson was noted for his headlong dash and courage and was the hero of innumerable encounters. Roberts, his contemporary and no mean judge of martial qualities, considered that "he had done more in the Queen's service than any man alive." But there was a blot on his career. Sent to arrest the King of Delhi, last of the Mogul kings and one of the leaders responsible for the rebellion, Hodson had brought in the old man without incident; but while attempting to bring in his two sons and grandson from their hiding place in Humayan's tomb, he ran into trouble. With only a handful of men as escort, he was surrounded by a mob bent on rescuing the two princes, considered to be the future leaders of the rebels. Faced with the seemingly inevitable massacre of his few troopers and the rescue of their all-important prisoners, Hodson acted with characteristic decision. He drew his revolver and shot the three prisoners dead. Then, with his men behind him, he spurred his horse at the heart of the mob. The soldiers cut their way through a crowd stunned by the sudden turn of events. The ruthlessness of the action shocked British and Indians alike. The rank and file soldiers applauded his audacity, but Hodson's fellow officers thought the shooting of prisoners, particularly by his own hand, unworthy of so gallant an officer. Roberts, in his journal, notes his shock at seeing the bodies of the three young men laid out on a stone platform awaiting burial, and his regret that Hodson, whom he admired, had been guilty of such merciless action.

But this incident apart, Hodson was a legendary figure and much admired by his contemporaries in the cavalry and artillery regiments. Jingo found him a soldier's soldier, and the two chatted together for some twenty minutes as they waited for the attack to begin. At last a bugle sounded the "Advance," and in the rush of eager Highlanders swarming past them Jingo lost sight of his companion.

If the siege had seemed like a dream, the attack, when it came, was pure nightmare. Jingo afterwards recalled it as a series of manic episodes—kilted Highlanders displaying their bare buttocks as they swarmed over the palace ramparts; desperate hand-to-hand fighting with sword and bayonet through the silken luxury of opulent harems and gilded throne rooms. Jingo found himself caught up in the frantic onrush and swept along with a regiment of ferocious Sikhs down a street lined with arcaded shops, each harbouring a knot of desperate and dangerous rebels. It was kill or be killed. Several times Jingo escaped death by inches, saved by his own reflexes or by the prompt reaction of a chance and anonymous comrade. Once he fought barehanded against an assailant who leaped upon him from the shadows of a narrow room, and who was despatched by a shot from a musket of a native trooper. The trooper, as it happened, was bent only on robbing the rebel of his turban and the money kept there, for the Sikhs knew the rebels had just been paid. But if he owed his life on occasion to the support of these new-found comrades, Jingo more than held his own end up. At the end of a long day's fighting he was rewarded by a gift of sweetmeats from a grinning group of Sikh troopers, along with the wish that the sahib might join their regiment. He was the style of officer they appreciated.

Sword in hand, Jingo began to explore the captured palace, now mostly abandoned by its defenders. In one room he found a couple of Irish infantrymen swathing themselves in silk curtains, and admiring themselves in a huge harem mirror; in another he had scented rosewater poured over his head in a palatial bedroom suite. But it was the stuff of nightmare, all the same. Dead bodies lay everywhere, and in the fountain courts the marble channels ran brimming with mingled rosewater and blood.

It was in such a courtyard that word reached Jingo that Hodson had been shot; that he was lying somewhere, unattended but still alive. Fearful of what might happen to him in this vast slaughterhouse, Jingo set out to find him.

His search ended in a nearby bungalow, where the dying Hodson lay, blood gurgling in his chest and staining his lips with every breath. He was not unattended, however. He had been brought here by a party of his own horsemen and a doctor was bending over him, but it was apparent that nothing could save him. He had been shot through the chest as he entered a darkened room in the palace. A rush of Highlanders behind him had avenged his fall. He was surprisingly composed now, in his final moments, and whispered a message for his wife, telling her that he loved her and that his last thoughts were of her. Tears streamed down the cheeks of the bearded troopers about him, and Jingo, saddened beyond words, turned away to leave him to die in the arms of older friends than he.

Back in the palace, the nightmare of shooting and looting went on unabated. Opening yet another door, Jingo found himself in a sort of boathouse occupied by a houseboat formed like a gigantic fish—a fish being the royal symbol of the kings of Oudh. The huge craft was covered with scales made of beaten silver—later looted by jubilant soldiers—and was fitted inside to accommodate ladies of the harem in opulent style. Latticed windows allowed these passengers to view the passing scene. The furnishings inside were most ornate, with silver lamps and gilded mirrors. It seemed somehow the ultimate Arabian Nights touch. Jingo pocketed a little paperweight as a memento; then, with a damascene sword and dagger wrapped in a shawl as his share of the loot, he found his way out of this ravaged dream palace and made his weary way back to his quarters.

An appalled eyewitness to the attack on the palace complex, half luxurious royal residence and half fortress, had been William H. Russell, the celebrated roving representative of the London *Times* and dean of all front-line war correspondents. In his book, *My Diary in India*, he wrote: "It was one of the strangest and most distressing sights that could be seen, but it was also most exciting! Discipline may hold soldiers together till the fight is won, but it assuredly does not exist for a moment after an assault has been delivered, or a storm has taken place."

Leaving the city open on two sides so that its defenders would have ample opportunity to evacuate it, Sir Colin Campbell, prudent as ever, sought to avoid any further bloodshed. However, he allowed a three-day sack of its palaces as reward for his troops and punishment for the perfidy of the kings of Oudh. The loot was sold and the proceeds divided among officers and men. Jingo received something over seven pounds as his share which, in the traditional manner, he turned over to the Home for Soldiers' Widows.

Yet, as always when men accustomed to discipline are turned loose to indulge in indiscriminate plunder and destruction, Campbell's "authorized sack" of the palaces led to all sorts of irregularities. Such prolonged looting was easier to start than to stop, and it got so out of hand that it began to threaten the good order of the army. In an attempt to restore discipline, Campbell authorized severe punishments for anyone caught looting, and set armed guards to patrol the palace compound, but even these measures met with mixed success. As Sergeant Pearman, serving with the Third Light Dragoons at the storming of the palace, noted in his memoirs, troopers found with plunder in their possession after the stipulated three-day period were triced up to triangles and given one hundred lashes, "layed on heavy." As a result, much valuable loot was simply destroyed by soldiers anxious to rid themselves of incriminating evidence. Pearman himself saw jewel-encrusted golden sword hilts, priceless jewellery, and irreplaceable *objets d'art* thrown down a well, never to be recovered.

Not all such valuables were lost to the world, however. Pearman also noted that some artillery gunners, craftier than mere cavalry troopers, buried a great deal of loot in a garden, from which it was surreptitiously retrieved, piece by piece, and sold on the black market to souvenir-hungry soldiers not fortunate enough to have been present at the sack. Nor were the stiff punishments entirely beneficial to army discipline; according to Pearman, many officers went scot-free with valuable and unreported plunder that would have earned a private soldier a painful flogging.

The period of mopping-up operations following the assault and capture of the city covered days of desultory fighting and random shooting in a city infested with snipers and looters. It was, ironically, in this sort of vexing interlude that Jingo very nearly lost his life. Temporarily attached to the staff of a Colonel Napier, he was ordered to clear a native magazine crammed with enormous jars of gunpowder and to pour the powder down a well. The difficulty was that the magazine was in a building that was burning fiercely, with the flames already only a few feet away. Jingo pointed out that the magazine could not be cleared in time, but to no avail.

"When I want your advice, I shall ask for it," was the tart rejoinder, and Jingo was left with no choice but to obey. He took a handful of volunteers—the fewer the better for so suicidal a mission, he felt—and plunged into the burning building. The jars, great stone things reminiscent of those that hid Ali Baba's forty thieves, required two men each to move, and the little party set to rolling them along on edge, out through the intervening rooms to the square. Here they had to be manhandled across a space still swept occasionally by rebel rifle fire, and emptied down the well. It was heavy, backbreaking work, carried out in the noise and heat of the conflagration raging only a few feet away. The men toiled with sweat streaming from them. Each time they plunged back into the doomed building they knew might be the last. Half the jars had been removed and the smoke was now filling the magazine itself, when at last the inevitable happened. There was a tremendous explosion, and Jingo knew no more—

When he came to, he was in hospital. Some angel, well disguised as a bearded orderly, was pouring beer down his throat—cool, heavenly nectar!—and from him Jingo learned what had happened. He had been blown bodily out of an open door. Though his hair, eyebrows, and moustache were singed and his face and hands burnt and blistered, he was otherwise unhurt. Some of his working party had also survived the blast which, in the freakish fashion of such explosions, had killed some and spared others in what seemed an entirely capricious and unaccountable manner.

When he was able to do so, Jingo went to visit his fellow survivors. He was shocked at the state of some of them. They lay still, more dead than alive, with an occasional attendant to brush away the flies that swarmed about them. One of them already lay as if dead. Bending over him, Jingo recognized the bombardier who had been beside him when the explosion had occurred. He had been blinded and dreadfully mangled, and death could not be far away. Jingo knelt beside him and spoke to him. The young gunner recognized his lieutenant's voice, reached out a bandaged hand to him, and whispered: "Tell my mother I died like a soldier." "No, no, not yet; you must live to see her," Jingo responded. But within hours he was, indeed, writing to the dead man's mother to tell her how gallantly her son had died.

The last days of fighting in this ravaged city, stinking of death, darkened by the smoke of burning buildings, were nearly the last days for Jingo. As he was directing the fire of a mortar battery against the high walls of a fortified compound still held by the rebels, he was struck on the head by a bullet and knocked to the ground. He regained his senses with a doctor bending over him, and found himself unhurt save for a walnut-sized lump on the side of his head. The bullet had knocked his cap off and then, spent, had lodged in the turban underneath. The coil of cloth had saved his life. Curious, the doctor unwound the soft white cloth to find it was a muslin nightdress, no doubt once worn by some dark-eyed charmer and snatched up by Jingo in the sack of the palace harem. The doctor, something of a wag, affected to believe that it had been granted to Jingo by a harem beauty in loving token for services rendered, and worn by him as a proud *gage d'amour*, a speculation which brought the embarrassed Jingo much chaff from his laughing messmates and more bother than the bump on his head.

But romance of a more tangible sort also entered his life in Lucknow's last terrible days. In his own account of his innumerable adventures in the ravaged ruins among which his gunners still fought, Jingo is singularly reticent—almost coy—about the details of an encounter with a mysterious native lady. She was apparently the wife of a wealthy merchant, living in isolated splendour in an upper room of an abandoned mansion with only a handful of womenservants about her. Jingo broke into the room quite by chance while searching the house. In a panic, the elderly maids scuttled through the door opposite to where Jingo stood; he turned away.

His journal takes up the story. "But—in the centre of the room stood—She! A dusky beauty, whose brown tints contrasted with the white of her gauzy garments, whose little hands were together in the native attitude of submission, and whose head was bent."

Jingo was mesmerized; he hardly knew what he was doing. With a vague idea of staying this dainty vision, he lifted her gently in his arms, where she lay unresistingly, her head drooping on his shoulder, as he whispered in her ear: "Oh, foolish one! The sahib-logue do not make war upon women." Her arms folded softly and confidingly round his neck as he carried her across the room to a charpoy, where she seated herself cross-legged, her shapely legs shining through her divided skirt of gauzy muslin, her eyes downcast.

"No Ghora logue shall harm you while I am here, but I will go back now lest they should come to look for me," Jingo told her, and at her urging he promised to come back—some day!

Duty and a bout of fever kept Jingo busy in another quarter of the city for several days but, haunted by his promise, he returned—twice—to find her frantic to come with him, to leave the devastated city and share with him the fortunes of the army's campaign. This was impossible, and Jingo told her so.

And then, again in his own words: "At last he tore himself away, and was a little surprised, and perhaps piqued, at the Oriental calmness with which she accepted 'Kismet.' And the Lieutenant who loved, rode away. It had been so before, and since—and will be so again."

Jingo was heartened to learn, as he left with the departing army, that the lady had found another "protector," a garrison officer, who would be staying in the city.

Jingo himself left the city with the Oudh Field Force, a flying column commanded by General Sir Hope Grant, to break up the numerous small rebel armies roaming the countryside. He was attached to its Artillery Division as staff officer and looked forward to his new posting, but as he rode out through the Lucknow gate his thoughts turned again to "She."

It was all undoubtedly in the grand tradition of the romantic cavalryman's admonition to "love, and ride away." Now, sadly, with the mechanization of the army, it has become merely the modern tankman's "Screw, and bolt!"

EIGHT

The Bubble Reputation

The road, little more than a dusty track through the thick jungle scrub, curved round to the right, rutted by the wheels and pocked by the hooves of the Sepoy battery which had passed this way scant moments before. Behind Jingo came the rattle and rumble of his own gun teams—sixteen horses hauling the two long nine-pounders and their limbers at a breakneck pace. They were hot on the trail of the retreating rebels and yearning to come to grips. Jingo scouted anxiously ahead, for the cavalry escort that normally screened his guns had somehow lost themselves in the scrub behind and had yet to catch up. At the moment, his two guns of "Q" Section, Royal Artillery, represented the leading edge of General Grant's flying column.

He came around the bend—and there they were: two guns unlimbered and deployed across the road, the rammers already withdrawn—Jingo had heard the thud as the case-shot was rammed home. The Sepoy gunners were blowing on their slow-match to light the portfires. Jingo had just time to recognize the uniforms of the famous Black Horse Battery, the crack unit of the rebel artillery, before making the decision of his life. No time to turn, to retreat, to unlimber, before the devastating explosion from those guns that would sweep him, his men, and his horses into oblivion. He shouted out, at the top of his voice, the traditional cry of the foxhunter: "Tally ho!"

With drawn sword, he hurled himself towards the waiting enemy. Behind him, without breaking stride, came the galloping gun teams, their guns and limbers thundering after, and their little trumpeter sounding—without orders—the "Charge." A Sepoy soldier, one of the corporal's guard left as an escort for the rebel guns, levelled his musket at Jingo, but before he could fire the point of Jingo's sword caught him in the chest and dropped him lifeless behind the galloping charger. The two batteries collided with a shattering crash, a mad mélange of rearing horses and interlocked wheels, the British gunners slashing at their startled native counterparts with long cavalry sabres.

It was all over in the twinkling of an eye. The rebel gunners abandoned their charges and fled into the thick jungle on either side, leaving a relieved and exhausted Jingo to receive the congratulations of his jubilant gunners.

Moments later a furious brigadier rode up, his horse in a lather and himself in a blazing rage. "Damn you, sir! How dare you disobey orders? Where's your cavalry escort?"

His fury quickly abated when Jingo pointed out the captured guns. Shaking his head in rueful admiration, he exclaimed: "Devilish dashing thing, Jingo. Going out with two guns and coming back with four. Never heard anything like it, by gad!"

Such an exploit, using gun teams as cavalry to capture enemy artillery, had never been carried out before. It proved to be the end of the once-renowned Black Horse Battery, and it marked Jingo for life as a celebrated character. Years later, it would be recalled in his obituary in the *Times*.

Unique though it might be, it was by no means Jingo's first charge. A few days earlier, bringing orders from General Sir Hope Grant to the Queen's Own Hussars for a charge on a rebel post, Jingo had promptly aligned himself with the first rank and had experienced the exhilaration of a full-blooded cavalry charge. He had thus learned at first hand the futility of slashing about in the approved manner with the standard cavalry sword, dulled in constant drill by its contact with its steel scabbard. The point, he was told by an experienced trooper, was the most effective part of a sword wielded by a galloping man, and it was to this lesson that he probably owed his life in his celebrated onfall.

With Grant, Jingo found plenty of action, and innumerable scraps and skirmishes enlivened the incessant marching and bivouacking. He learned all the aspects of his trade under the most demanding conditions, often under fire and in weather that varied from intense heat to drenching downpour. Above all, he learned how to move horses, guns, men, and material across deep and swift-flowing rivers, an experience that was to stand him in good stead in later years on the far-off Saskatchewan.

At the close of the campaign he was promoted to second captain and posted to become second-in-command of a battery in the Punjab. His leavetaking from his old unit was something of an emotional experience for Jingo, who always prided himself on a proper military stoicism. He was especially moved when the men of his battery presented him with a handwritten tribute, duly signed by all of them and quite contrary to military regulations. It was a singularly lonely young officer who journeyed northwards through Cawnpore, of dreadful memory, and Agra with its gleaming Taj Mahal; past Delhi, past Amritsar and its golden temple, to arrive at last in Mooltan, a sunbaked city on the edge of an arid desert where his new battery was stationed.

The fighting in India had made Jingo unquestionably the best-known young artillery officer in the army, mentioned in dispatches four times by four different commanding officers, and familiar, as "Gunner Jingo," to every senior officer in the country. He was known to his superiors for his dash and competence in the field, liked and respected by his peers for his character, and adored by his gunners. He arrived at his new posting with an established reputation, which he immediately began to enhance.

He enjoyed the Punjab and found its Muslim people, with their martial qualities, especially appealing. Given responsibility for the battery's training, he set about new procedures and exercises more in accordance with battlefield conditions than the old parade ground drills. He combined exercises with sport, his battery manoeuvres becoming competitive games, setting unit against unit in friendly competition which emphasized teamwork and pride of achievement, so that his gun teams soon became noted for their speed and accuracy in exercising under battle conditions in the field.

Unfortunately, a singularly obtuse and obstinate commanding officer provoked a near-mutiny in the battery by unfair—and irregular—deductions from the men's pay for additions to their diet they did not want, but for which they were required to pay. The men preferred to have the money rather than the extra food their C.O. thought they should have. For quoting regulations to his commanding officer Jingo was placed under arrest, until higher authority stepped in, relieved the erring colonel of his command, and restored Jingo his sword. Yet although he was proved right and reassured by his brigadier, the incident had been a painful one. Jingo was well aware that such disputes did harm to the reputations of all concerned in the close hierarchy of army command. A recurrence of the ague he had first suffered in Lucknow added to his problems.

For a convalescent, the baking heat of the desert was especially oppressive, and Jingo was granted sick leave. He chose to spend it, not lounging in idleness in a hill station but rather on a long journey of exploration.

It was not merely the weakness brought on by a dangerous and debilitating illness that afflicted Jingo at this time. The truth is that he was exhausted mentally and physically by the demands of a long and arduous campaign—"battle fatigue" it would be called today. In addition there was the strain imposed by being cooped up in an isolated station with an incompatible, and seemingly jealous, commanding officer in an environment that tested the endurance of the healthiest. The relief at getting away from it all shines through the pages of Jingo's diary, where he records, in ecstatic terms, the joy of seeing hills, trees, even rocks, after weeks of staring at arid and featureless plains baking in the equatorial heat.

He had set off, carried like an invalid in a dooly, but with the first whiff of cooler air he began walking. When he reached the foothills he was striding along, bent on penetrating the distant Himalayas, whose snow-capped peaks gleamed on the far horizon. On his walk northwards, he was accompanied at first by a friend, a Captain R. Burnet; but later, when Burnet's shorter leave expired, he went on alone, with only various guides and porters, hired en route, for company.

The journal of Jingo's Himalayan travels reveals a good deal about his changing character. Nowhere else does he show so clearly his wide range of interests, his philosophies, and his prejudices. He records a remarkable series of impressions of a traveller in a land totally unknown to Europeans, and of the impact of an alien way of life on an observer long accustomed to the regimented routine and parochial outlook of the British soldier. The journal is all the more striking in that it was written down, day by day, by a man racked by dysentery (which he attributed to drinking melted snow) and by recurring agonies in his left shoulder and side (cause unknown).

The conditions of travel would have taxed a healthy, well-equipped traveller: Jingo was neither. He could hardly breathe in the high altitudes above 17,000 feet; he was constantly cold, often frost-bitten, frequently soaked to the skin. He wore slippery English boots and knickerbockers over long flannel drawers, topped with the inevitable Norfolk jacket of the travelling Englishman.

Excerpts from his journal reflect his progress through the Himalayas:

June 20th: Mist and rain as usual, mountains clothed with scraggy evergreen oak, a little like the cork tree of Spain, though not so pretty and umbrageous. Coming down, the valley to Gibee was more than usually lovely—camping by the music of falling waters, shut in from the mist of the mountains above by tall pines— the heat will be unpleasant, and the flies— horrible!

June 26th: We are going to make a detour by an unfrequented path, crossing the objectionable river (over which the bridges are broken) by a rope of grass; sounds insecure, but no acrobatic performance is intended.

June 27th: There is a filthy grime, a dirty old man of the mountain, who tries to take a rise out of me by saying that never so big a man crossed the rope, and that it may break. He also descants upon the impractability of the path, which he terms "a very falling down road." On the way we met a flock of sheep and goats carrying loads. They come over the passes from Tibet. Saw the snow nearer and clearer than before, not like a vision of cloudland, as it appears from Simla. It does one's baked-up heart good to see the snow look real. One can see the rope bridge far below, spanning the Beas like a thread. The river is about 150 yards across, and seems to have cut its violent course, by force of its own wild will, through adamantine walls that rise nearly perpendicular to a height of seven or eight hundred feet. No pen or pencil could convey the wildness and grandeur of this dark chasm...

June 28th: Steep ascent next morning to a green summit, where the breeze blew, oh, so fresh! What would they give in Mooltan for such a life-giving air! From this ridge we can see last night's camping ground, and today's halting place below us, although they say they are ten miles apart. As we descend, the Kooloo valley opens before us in a more tranquil style of beauty than anything we leave behind us. The river meanders and makes islands as it goes along, as if it loved to linger there before it goes dashing and foaming with ceaseless roar through those glorious gorges to the sea.—I wonder how they manage marriage settlements here, for every lady has many husbands. How very unkind of fate! When some of the dear girls at home have not got even one...

July 4th: From Boorwah a gradual ascent of the Rhotung Pass (13,000 feet) begins, and after some distance the path becomes something between a young cascade and an insane staircase of unlimited length. Scenery extremely fantastic, an infinite variety of beautiful waterfalls—one in particular I should select if I were to become Undine; it seems to come from cloudland to lose itself in spray. We crossed a small glacier—the eternal snow about here is extremely dirty—the scenery becomes very wild, no trees. The ground is a watershed between two large rivers. We are at the sources of the Beas, which we have followed for miles, until here it rises from a hundred little rivulets of melted snow that run from the glaciers. The Chenab rushes down the other side of the Pass. We

crossed here at the foot of the pass by a bridge of
most peculiar construction—three ropes of twisted
brushwood, each about an inch and a half in
diameter, support the footway, which consists of small
hurdles about a foot wide laid upon three ropes, a
parapet about two and a half feet high is also formed
of brushwood ropes, and the whole swings about
somewhat unpleasantly.—We are now in the valley of
Lahoul; Koksur, a collection of a few mud huts,
contains Mongol-looking men, with extensive
cheekbones, quite different in character from the
Caucasian people on the other side.

Jingo was one of the first Europeans to visit Tibet, crossing
the high tablelands and sketching the sheer-fronted monas-
tery buildings frowning down from their heights. He penetrated areas where white men had never been seen before,
and visitor and native stared at one another in curious
silence, for Jingo's Indian dialects were unknown here.
Jingo, for one, was not impressed; the mendicant monks,
lined up at the roadside to demand baksheesh from the
passing traveller, or lounging about at ease while local
women toiled about field and home, and prayerwheels spun
in wind or stream, seemed neither contemplative nor de-
vout. They were, however, exceedingly dirty, like everyone
else; Jingo was revolted by the filth and squalor of the tiny
villages, and eaten alive by the ravenous fleas when he
paused overnight. It was a relief to escape into the mountains again, and to bathe in the glacial streams.

A complicating factor was the obsession with *shikari*, or
hunting, or what Jingo himself wryly called the "typical
Englishman's compulsion to kill something." Among officers in India, to go exploring for exploring's sake was, at the
very least, eccentric, but to go hunting was perfectly normal, and justified any expense or hardship. Accordingly

Jingo pursued anything that moved, and since the huge Himalayan brown bear was the only creature to be found in any numbers in that place and at that time, he was determined to bring back a bearskin or two as proof and justification of hardships endured.

But the bears were both wary and ferocious, and Jingo's rifle proved to have insufficient stopping power for so large a beast. His first quarry shrugged off his first hit, and since it was unthinkable for a true *shikari* to abandon a wounded animal, Jingo was committed to a daylong hunt, through a snowstorm, on steep and treacherous mountainside. It ended only when a second shot sent the wounded bear over a 400-foot precipice, down which Jingo scrambled in order to skin the beast and lug its dripping pelt back up the mountainside. Darkness had fallen by the time he arrived back at the bleak campsite where his few porters huddled about a flickering cowdung fire. This being the Himalayan summer, the bearskin was not even in good condition.

Hunting mountain bear was not only unpleasant, uncomfortable, and unrewarding, it was also downright dangerous. Another bear, a large male, absorbed six bullets before it fell dead in mid-charge at Jingo's feet. After the kill came the messy business of skinning, the exhausting trip back to camp, the head-to-toe bath in an ice-cold stream to wash away blood and grease, and then the trouble and expense of finding a native porter to carry the heavy pelt several hundred miles over difficult country. Even so, Jingo seems never to have questioned the joys of a mountain *shikari*.

From the journal:

> July 8—Marched to Kulung, fine clear day, and cool breeze blowing from the snow. Saw a live Lama. He wore a red robe (the sacred colour) and was, without

doubt, the dirtiest emanation of the Deity I ever set
eyes on—

July 10—Reached Pul-um-oo, a place, if such can be
called a place, which boasts no human habitation, yet
has a name. It is a camp of nomadic Tartars who live
in small black tents made of goats' hair blankets. They
gave me some delicious milk. Crossed to their camp
over a most extraordinary chasm with the wildest of
torrents beneath, spanned by a rainbow of foam. The
overhanging rocks nearly met above and were joined
by two pieces of timber—such fantastic freaks of
nature I have never seen before. Went on about four
miles beyond this camp and was brought up short by
another torrent, utterly bridgeless and wild...

July 13—The descent from the Rumjuk valley was
gradual, but unpleasant, owing to the loose sharp
fragments of rock, etc. Had to cross numerous icy-
cold streams. The summit of the pass, snow, nothing
but snow and cloud, and needle-like masses of black
rock projecting here and there. A snowstorm came on
while we were at the summit, and we could not see
twenty yards before us—At the foot of the pass, as we
came down, we found ourselves in the Ladak country.
On that patch of brilliant green is a flock of queer
little mares feeding (this is entirely pastoral country),
and a fine Ladaki keeps a vague lookout after the wild
little beasts. He wears a picturesque cap, hanging over
one side, similar to the Catalan peasantry, only the
colour is not red. He caught a mare for me to cross the
stream upon, and showed all his white teeth as I
caught the rope he had twisted round her jaw and
vaulted on to her back. He is altogether the finest
fellow I have seen for a long time—We came upon
another Ladaki camp, consisting of the same black
blanket sort of tent, with a hole in the top for a

chimney. Window ventilators I don't imagine they desire, for the cold in winter must be intense, judging from what it is now in July. Some men, as we approached, ran up the mountain like wild animals, evidently afraid of us, but the ladies of the camp came out to meet us, and were remarkably civil and hospitable, spreading a sheepskin for me to sit on, and offered fresh milk, curds and a sort of paste, looking like a mixture of flour and curds. The milk was delicious—yak milk, I suppose, for the herds about consisted only of yak mares and sheep. The whole picture was most novel—

July 18—The Tesseldar sent a sepoy to attend me—A picturesque, tall fellow, all hair and teeth, and tulwar, and knives ad lib. He carries a shield on his back—probably the part most exposed to the enemy—

The bright blue sky contrasts with two giant mountains in the background, 23,400 feet in altitude, one white with snow, named Kunnoo, or clothed in white, the black brother named Nunnoo (naked). The blue tints of the glacier were more vivid than usual as it was so close, and the hot sun set off several young avalanches all born in thunder. As I sat looking at the wondrously beautiful creation before me, a great pinnacle of snow, a perfect castle glittering against the sky, came down with a thundercrash and melted into snow vapour in the gulf below.

July 28 — Marched 20 miles, 18 of them over glacier. Crossed the Pass Bo-bung at the foot of the Pir Lamoula mountain, a perpendicular mass of snow, with the head in cloudland, giving birth to an enormous glacier. A red cliff was pointed out in a whisper as the abode of the spirit of snow and storm; meet dwelling place for the evil demon who issues from his home of eternal snow to overwhelm the

belated traveller.—We had to cross about 8 miles of
frozen snow, with some very ugly crevasses in it—not
pleasant to walk over a snow bridge, say, a foot wide,
with a cold blue eternity of crevasse fathoms deep on
either hand. Was the only one of the party who wore a
pair of slippery English shoes. Took them off to cross
the first bridge, but it did not improve matters much,
for the sun shone out and the thawing snow made my
stockings as slippery as shoes. The second bridge a
trifle worse, about 30 feet longer, could not see the
bottom but could hear the gurgling snow river rolling
below.

July 29th—Dumohi—The valley opened in most
lovely green and brushwood, undulating meadow
filled with wild flowers in a thousand varieties, acres
of tall purple loosestrife, meadowsweet, silver wort,
and heaps of new and beautiful flowers, until the soft
air is laden with perfume. Sun not so dry and
scorching as in Ladak. The feathery foliage of the
aspen and silver bark of the birch show through the
greenery, while tall dark pine adds sombre shadows to
the fairy picture.

For Jingo, the Vale of Kashmir was like paradise after the
hardships of his mountain odyssey. Yet, perversely, he
seemed to prefer roaming the wooded uplands in the company of a Sikh soldier and hunter, Zubber Khan, looking for
game, to lounging in comfort at a lakeside resort, which he
abandoned after the briefest of stays.

He admired the fabled Kashmir nautch girls, but thought
their dancing dreary and their music hideous. He much
preferred to sketch the ordinary native women, going about
their domestic chores with natural grace, to watching the
professional posturing and writhing of the dancers. But
Kashmir itself he thought enchanting, and he marvelled at

the folly of the British in abandoning such a heavenly place while determinedly holding on to the baking deserts of the Sind.

Days of deer-stalking in the wooded hills and nights of campfire discussion with Zubber Khan restored Jingo to health. The agonizing and inexplicable pain which had so tortured him in the Himalayas had nearly left him, and he regained the weight he had lost in those weeks of bad food and endless toil. He enjoyed the long discussions—more often, debates—with his wise old companion. Jingo thought Zubber's Muslim notion of paradise as an endless romp with complaisant houris throughout all eternity smacked more of hell than heaven—"Have your relations with women on this earth been so satisfactory that you would be content to have no other joy in Paradise?"— but the old *shikari* had no use for the shadowy Christian notions of a heaven where no specific delights were promised.

> October 20th—My 'liver wing' troubles me again. A Mussuk bath of ice-cold water poured over me daily may not be exactly wise—could not sleep with pain last night. Can't do hillwork today, a difficulty in breathing.

On November 14 Jingo parted with the old *shikari* who had been his constant companion for so long, and with whom he had enjoyed so many philosophical discussions beside a campfire:

> Zubber Khan comforted himself with repeating that I am as good a Moslem as he is, and we disputed the point no more. Though poor, he would accept no money from me. He accepted my hospitality as far as food and ammunition went, and I gave him the rifle he liked best when we parted. Black or white, I had no

truer friend, nor more unselfish, cheerful, plucky companion, as true a gentleman as ever wore a sword. November 15th—Rode into Mooltan cantonments.

The lovely country, the relaxed rambles, and the peaceful pipesmoking evenings all had their effect, and it was a Jingo restored in body and mind who rejoined his battery at its new quarters in Ferozepore, a more northerly and healthier station.

When he reported for duty on his return, Jingo found his battery in a sad state, decimated by cholera, and badly shaken in morale. He set about restoring spirits by a program of athletic sports and by an elaborate steeplechase fixture in which gunners raced the horses of their gun teams over the hurdles. But he was himself brought low when his little trumpeter, a cocky sparrow of a boy from the slums of London who had sounded the "Charge" at the action with the Black Horse battery, was taken ill. Jingo sat up with him all night at the hospital, holding the little body in his arms to soothe the wracking convulsions. Death came gently with the first light of dawn, leaving a battery bereft of its mascot and its captain filled with a sadness greater than he had ever known.

Jingo had been deeply moved by the death of his little bugler, and he recorded it with rare sensitivity and a depth of emotion accorded to none of the other innumerable tragedies encountered in his long soldier's life. His description bears repeating:

> As his soft, dark eyes at last closed peacefully, and the livid blueness passed from the little thin face, leaving it like wax, a pink ray of dawn shot through the hospital window and lit up the dead boy's face with glory. He had been a bright, honest, plucky, little scamp. He

had chucked the defaulters' book into a well to wipe out the records against the veteran drunks of the Battery. Alas, for good intentions! It was fished up. Let us hope that this one was not put into a certain pavement, but counted to him for righteousness. He would not lie, and took his punishment like a man. His mother wrote to the Captain about "her sainted boy," and he was not denied the title. He had as good a right to the glory that came through the hospital window as most of the wry-necked saints in church windows have to their halos.

This last, tiny sacrifice was the final one exacted by the cholera epidemic. The healthier station and Jingo's active regime re-invigorated the battery and its bad patch was soon forgotten. These were, for Jingo, truly the piping times of peace, and he enjoyed them to the full. He revelled in the short pre-dawn marches through the dewy countryside, the noonday halts when the sun made further progress unpleasant, the afternoons of easy routine, and the evenings of pleasant camaraderie. His gunners became experienced and proficient, morale was high, and the station pleasant.

There now occurred the most momentous event in Jingo's life, and it is typical of the man that he should record it in his autobiography with the words: "Captain Jingo's turn had come. He went up to the hills single, and returned double."

Although his marriage would last for more than half a century, providing a deep and abiding happiness, a selfless and supportive companion, and a family of five children, he does not even mention his bride's name!

What happened was that, on leave in fashionable Simla, the popular hill station where officers and their families spent vacations away from the searing heat of the Indian plains, Jingo had met the charming widow of a young fellow officer. Her husband had died suddenly only a year before. Her name was Maria Elinor Taylor, and Jingo having fallen in love with her, laid siege to her with all his characteristic impetuosity. They were married in Simla on November 4, 1862, and they returned together to Ferozepore when his leave was up, to the astonishment of his gunners, who regarded the thirty-one-year-old Captain Strange as a confirmed bachelor.

We are told little about the appearance of the bride, but we can surmise a good many of her personal qualities. Certainly she had great charm and was able to dazzle everyone she met, of high or low degree. The gunners of her husband's battery, no mean judges of character, seem to have adored her. She seems not to have been of strong constitution, but she was to survive Indian heat and humidity, as well as the deep snows and ferocious cold of the North American winter, with equal composure.

She was, to begin with, an archetypal member of that unique class of women, the Indian memsahib. Often pictured nowadays as languid creatures, attended by swarms of native servants, indulging in endless flirtations in an ambience of tinkling teacups and twirling parasols, maintaining the middle-class snobberies of Cheltenham or Kensington in the midst of an alien culture, the reality was something quite different. Such a picture might reflect life among the viceregal garden parties of Delhi, but for the wives of the officers and administrators who made up the greatest element of the British presence, life in India was not easy. For one thing, the proliferation of servants was often more a burden than a blessing. The caste system prevented the man who opened the gate from sweeping its sill; the syce who held the reins of the mistress's horse could not be expected to clean its stable; the maid who attended her boudoir could not be asked to make the bed. The horde of servants mandatory for every

Anglo-Indian household made personal privacy quite impossible; husband and wife could never be entirely alone, even in the bedroom. Standards of dress and deportment prevailing in temperate England had to be maintained in sweltering India, the niceties of civilized behaviour observed among all the appalling stinks and unbearable sights of teeming Indian slums. Death was always at one's elbow; the coiled snake in the bathroom drain, smallpox, cholera, and septicaemia were everyday hazards. Children were a particular problem. Childbirth, often with only a village midwife or an alcoholic regimental surgeon in attendance, was an extremely hazardous business. And the need to send one's child, at the age when maternal ties are strongest, off to a distant homeland for the mandatory British schooling was a heart-wrenching business that had to be borne by every young mother.

The wife of an army officer in India had, in short, to be tough and resilient and able to greet adversity with a smile. Even so, there were limits. When Jingo and his bride were met by Jingo's uproarious gunners, dragging a nine-pounder field gun garlanded with flowers, as a hymeneal carriage, Maria declined, with thanks, the offer to ride sidesaddle on the bronze barrel across the bumpy plain. She elected instead to mount her husband's charger and make her entry into camp astride its bony back, wearing an officer's fatigue cap and bedecked with flowers. She was made welcome by the colonel and, what was more important, by the colonel's wife, with a heartiness that speaks volumes for her charm. It was a triumphant moment, and she never looked back.

The couple had arrived just in time to make a long march across India to Lucknow, a march of more than 400 miles, to take part in military manoeuvres and exercises at a huge camp in what was to become a regular event in the army calendar. The battery excelled itself in the mimic battles against units from the whole Indian Army, winning the prize for the best shooting and the congratulations of its senior officer, Sir Hugh Rose, notable more for his biting criticisms than for his praise.

Back in the barracks after an exhausting return march, life resumed its accustomed routine, but the arrival of a major fresh from England changed Jingo's status. Outranked and superseded in command of the battery, Jingo lost both face and the extra pay allowed for the post, and accordingly was not unhappy to receive a new posting. He was to accompany a draft of time-expired soldiers home to Britain by way of the Cape and to receive a new posting on arrival. He had hoped to be allowed to join his old friend Gordon, now "Chinese Gordon," in charge of the artillery of his "ever-victorious army," but his new married status put that posting beyond him.

On the long voyage home aboard the troop transport, a sailing vessel, Jingo and his soldiers cheerfully worked with the ship's crew, and by the time the trooper arrived in the Chops of the Channel they took great pride in their ability to lay aloft, with the nimbleness of experienced sailors, to help set and take in sail.

Woolwich now became the centre of Jingo's life. A year's staff training, under General Eardly Wilmot, to fit him for higher command, led to an appointment to the instructional staff at Woolwich gunnery academy, a plum open only to gunners who had displayed exceptional ability. Jingo hugely enjoyed the experience. All new young gunnery officers came through his hands, and he delighted in passing on to them his notions on how artillery should be used in the field, notions which had stood the test of hard experience. Artillery could no longer be relegated to a static role in the rear, he was convinced. Field guns, protected by a shield and given high rates of fire by breech loading, could operate with cavalry in the field, and he had seen their effectiveness when so deployed.

A born teacher, Jingo revelled in the enthusiasm and ability of his young officer students—Prince Arthur, son of Queen Victoria, was one of them—and he made a notable impact on them. His success did not pass unnoticed; in 1865 he was appointed commandant of H.M. Repository, Woolwich, Britain's chief arsenal and the heart of the artillery establishment.

Woolwich barracks today is little changed from the establishment that Jingo knew. The incredibly long front, some quarter of a mile, still faces its vast parade ground. The impressive central façade, with its figure of Fame dispensing laurel wreaths—playing at quoits, as Jingo saw it—still stands, together with the immense sea of brick on either side, offset by contrasting architraves and gateway arches. Across the road the garrison church that Jingo attended is a roofless ruin, bombed out in World War II, and is now a tiny park, with trim flowerbeds, paths, and garden benches.

Inside the barracks the great officers' messroom, with its marble figure of Armed Science, is still famed as the finest in the British Army. Its collection of mess silver is a national treasure, celebrated as much for its artistry and history as for its intrinsic value. Its sheer size is staggering. The silver collected over the years by each battery mess is stored here when the battery is stood down, to be re-issued when the unit is re-activated in some future emergency, and the collection is the richest display of the silversmith's art to be found anywhere in the world.

Mess dinners in such surroundings are impressive affairs, but never more so than on ceremonial occasions. At such events the magnificent room, with its long table, lit by candles and chandeliers, and ablaze with silver and crystal, achieves a rare synthesis of military tradition and sheer spectacle, with each uniformed guest attended by a soldier servant in gorgeous 18th-century livery, complete with knee breeches and powdered wig. The formal mess routine is climaxed by a procedure unique to artillery messes. After dessert dishes are cleared and the port decanters and crystal are placed, attendants at each end roll taut the linen runner that covers the long expanse of table. At a given signal, the cloth is snapped off at one end, leaving the decanters and glasses still standing, by some magic, on gleaming wood-work where they had stood, a fraction of a second before, on snowy linen. It is a feat that never fails to impress mess guests, a trick made possible by much practice and, presumably, some cost in broken crystal in rehearsal!

Jingo's time at Woolwich was enlivened by his appointment to command and train the militia gunners of the Volunteer Artillery for the annual Easter manoeuvres at Aldershot, an elaborate affair involving units both of professional and of part-time soldiers. In the mock battle that followed, Jingo's amateurs distinguished themselves by theoretically wiping out the Household Cavalry (or the "tinbellies," as they were disrespectfully referred to). Unfortunately, this triumph was dimmed somewhat when his criticism of some of the tactics, expressed to a friend who was also a newspaper correspondent, appeared in the *Times*, and he received a severe dressing-down at the War Office. He had learned a valuable lesson, however; never talk privately to a journalist.

His reputation seems to have suffered little. In 1869 he was one of two British officers sent to observe French war games on the plains of Chalons. Not the least of the lessons he learned here was the manner in which large formations of men could be concealed on a seemingly featureless and unwooded flat plain. It was a lesson which was to prove of great value in operations on the vast Canadian prairie.

Jingo was prevented by Prime Minister Gladstone himself from following the French army as an official observer during the brief Franco-Prussian War, lest he compromise "British neutrality." Nevertheless he went with a friend, at his own expense, to survey the battlefield at Metz in order to understand the various moves made by the two armies, narrowly avoiding arrest as a spy by the German occupying force still encamped there.

In July 1871, Jingo was promoted to major. The promotion proved to be a turning point in his life. He was now forty years old, happily married, and the father of two sons, Henry, nearly seven years old, and Alexander, five. Active, energetic, and in the prime of life, he could see that there was little room for further advancement in a British peacetime army that was undergoing an inevitable period of retrenchment as contingents returned at the end of overseas commitments. England, he felt, was becoming a little country needing only a little army, run, he considered, by little men. Increasingly, his thoughts turned to the New World, and to possible opportunities there.

In August the new self-governing Dominion of Canada applied for an experienced British officer to organize a Canadian regular army to replace the withdrawing British imperial garrison. The position was offered to Jingo. He accepted it without a moment's hesitation and before the year was out he had embarked, with wife and family, for a new life in the New World.

NINE

Monsieur le Commandant

The Major Strange who sailed up the St. Lawrence River in the dark December days of 1871 was a far cry from the flamboyant subaltern who had established such a reputation for himself in India and, to some extent, in England. Gunner Jingo was left behind when the ship sailed for Canada. It was an experienced and responsible artillery officer the Canadian government had requested and was expecting, and in Major Thomas B. Strange they had secured exactly the officer they had hoped for.

If ever a man was born for a job, Strange was born to be the founder of a new army. Enthusiastic and innovative, he was steeped in army life and appreciated the role of discipline and tradition in a successful military force. He was first and foremost a motivator, a proven creator of *esprit de corps*, who believed in morale above all else. Best of all for a country without an established military tradition, he was a leader who inspired by example. In soldiers' terms, he "led from the front."

Not the least of his assets was a commanding presence. He stood six feet two and always held himself erect, and his hawk nose and piercing eyes were set off by a bushy black beard, worn long, in the Victorian military tradition which set much store on whiskers. Lean and tough,

he was physically hard as nails, and he enjoyed an intimi-
dating reputation for being "handy with his dukes," and a
dangerous man in a scrap. All in all, a daunting figure,
and one to command respect in any setting, even in one so
unmilitary as the raw new nation of Canada.

But if the man was made for the job, the job was equally
ideal for the man. Major Strange had inherited from Gunner
Jingo an enthusiasm for improvisation, for devising new
methods and new tactics to suit new conditions. Jingo had
enjoyed working with individuals in small groups, rather
than with masses in the abstract, and thus Major Strange
looked forward to teaching, inspiring, and working with a
small force. Above all, he relished the opportunity for independent command, far from the interference of bumbling
senior officers. Canada was to be the supreme challenge of
his life, and as the ship steamed on towards Quebec and the
new career that awaited him there, he recognized the challenge and looked forward to it.

The task before him was complex, as well as challenging.
At the time of Confederation four years before, the country
had experienced a series of raids by bands of Irish American
vagabonds calling themselves members of a "Fenian Society,"
dedicated to the overthrow of all British influence in North
America. These lunatic forays were easily brushed off by the
small garrisons of British regular troops, aided by local militia units. But the withdrawal of imperial troops that accompanied the granting of self-government meant that the new
nation would have to depend for its defence on its own
resources, which amounted to a few scattered companies of
militia, mostly infantry units. A professional national army
was obviously required; and since the country's principal
defences were the fortified bases at Halifax, Quebec, and
Kingston, artillery forts built by the British and now taken
over by Canadians, the most urgent need was for gunners to
man the heavy artillery at these key points, backed up by the

infantry regiments of the existing militia. These new gunners would have to be trained—hence the need for Strange—at special artillery schools, which would later be expanded to include training for all branches of the service.

The Canada in which the Stranges were arriving was a nation in name only, representing merely the latest effort to form a political union of a number of disparate elements. Chief among these were the French- and English-speaking enclaves, originally established in 1791 as Lower Canada (the southern part of what is now Quebec) and Upper Canada (central Ontario), respectively. Following the rebellions of 1837, Lord Durham in 1841 had recommended their union into the single province of Canada. He believed the French enclave would be absorbed into a larger English-speaking society, but a high birthrate and a determined and all-powerful Church had kept a resilient French-speaking culture alive.

Nevertheless, by 1850 Montreal, the commercial centre of French Canada, was entirely dominated by English-speaking entrepreneurs and a largely English-speaking population, and Quebec only marginally less so. These cities apart, French Canada was an entirely rural region of subsistence farmers, spreading far northwards from its original territory in the St. Lawrence valley and ruled by a Roman Catholic Church with absolute sway in all matters, secular as well as clerical, and dedicated to maintaining a distinct French language and culture throughout its parishes. Confederation in 1867, engineered largely by the political genius of John A. MacDonald, re-established French Canada as a distinct entity, now the Province of Quebec, but the arrangement, linking Quebec as it did in equal partnership with the English-speaking provinces, was regarded with suspicion and many reservations by the Church.

The French-English divide was to prove a major obstacle to Strange in his attempt to form a representative Canadian national army, but it was by no means the only one. A recent and continuing influx of Irish immigrants, fleeing the famine and economic hardships of their native land, had created problems in the ports of Montreal and Quebec, where they had been landed, destitute and often diseased. Though they shared a common religious faith with their host communities, they found themselves unwelcome and resented in a provincial Church whose attitudes, language, and procedures differed from what they had known. Ostracized at the same time in the secular community, they gathered together in ghettos within the cities, a resentful and unstable element at the heart of the new nation.

Overriding all other difficulties faced by the new army's commander was the total unpreparedness of everyone in power, elected or appointed, to meet the needs of the new force. There were no uniforms, no bedding, no victualling arrangements; above all, there seemed to be no money. Lack of funds for almost any kind of military provision was to bedevil Strange throughout his Canadian career, a distinctive national tradition which survives to this day.

Geography was a major factor in any consideration of the new nation's defence. In 1871 the Confederation consisted of Nova Scotia and New Brunswick as the Maritime provinces—Prince Edward Island would join two years later—together with Quebec, Ontario, Manitoba, and, on the far Pacific shore, British Columbia. This last, a British colony since 1853, entered Confederation in 1871, the year of Strange's arrival, on the strength of a promise that a national railroad would be built to link it to the East. The enormous expanse of prairie between the British Columbia coast and Manitoba, an area known only as "the Northwest," was thinly populated by nomadic Indians, herds of buffalo, and a scattering of people of mixed French and Indian descent, known as Métis. Still owned, though scarcely administered, by the Hudson's Bay Company

(HBC), and filled with agricultural and mineral potential, it was being eyed with increasing interest by a United States already busy exploiting its own prairie territory to the south. It was this powerful neighbour, still restless and aggressive after its own Civil War, that brought about the hasty union of the prosperous and established Maritimes, a reluctant Quebec, an ambitious Ontario, a raw new Manitoba, and an apprehensive British Columbia, into a single Canadian entity. And it was this neighbour, overtly friendly but given to sudden bursts of belligerence, that would be the principal preoccupation of Major Strange and his new little army.

The Canadian government founded this army in 1871 when it authorized the establishment of two batteries of artillery at Kingston, Ontario, and Quebec City, which would incorporate schools for the training of artillery gunners. Kingston, heavily fortified since the days of Frontenac and an established naval base, was the strategic "choke point" controlling entry to the Great Lakes system. Quebec City, dominating the enormous expanse of the St. Lawrence and its tributaries from its eminence high above the river, was the key to Canada.

According to the original plan of 1871, "A" Battery at Kingston was to consist of 4 officers and 132 other ranks, including a small detachment at Stanley Barracks in Toronto, and was to be commanded by Major George A. French, an Anglo-Irish officer. An able and efficient soldier but something of a martinet, this Royal Artillery officer had been formerly a member of the Royal Irish Constabulary.

"B" Battery, with a larger establishment of 6 officers and 153 other ranks, was to be based in Quebec City's citadel with responsibility for satellite forts at Lévis across the river and St. Helen's Island nearby. Major Strange, in command, was to be the army's senior officer and was given the local rank of lieutenant-colonel. He was also made commander of the garrison of Quebec which, after the departure of the 60th King's Own Rifles and the Royal Artillery, consisted of his own Canadian gunners. He was given the additional resounding titles of "Inspector of Artillery and Warlike Stores for the Dominion of Canada" and "Commandant of the Citadel of Quebec." Whatever he may have lacked in more tangible assets, he could not complain about a shortage of honorifics!

The 60th was a famous regiment which, as the Royal American Rangers, had been the first unit of Wolfe's victorious army to enter Quebec City. As it marched from the citadel for the last time, its flag was lowered and handed to Strange, to be re-hoisted by him as representative of the new Canadian army. He now had to find and form a new guard for flag, citadel, and country.

Quebec City in 1871 was unique, and not just in North America. There was no city quite like it anywhere else in the world, and Strange fell in love with the place and its people from the moment of his landing. In its topography, it was the most impressive city in the New World. Its great rock, topped by the citadel, towered high above the wide St. Lawrence, with the busy town of Lévis on the opposite bank framed in the dark woods of the Canadian wilderness. Penned between the river and the beetling cliff behind, the Lower Town was a sort of time capsule, preserving in its narrow streets and crowded houses the atmosphere and heritage of the past. "There is but one Quebec in the wide world," Strange noted in his journal.

The Upper Town, with its wide boulevards, busy shops, and elegant townhouses, was still enclosed within its eighteenth-century walls. Beyond stretched the grassy levels of the Plains of Abraham, where the disciplined rolling volleys of Wolfe's red-coated infantry had blown away a French empire and altered the balance of world power in less than ten minutes.

But if Strange was impressed by the city, he was even more captivated by its people. A fluent speaker of French, he found himself immediately at home in a society which still preserved many of the aspects and standards of eighteenth-century France. A wealthy, educated, and highly sophisticated community of merchants and professional people enjoyed a gay and active social life in the Upper Town, especially during the winter, a season of balls and elaborate parties. In the Lower Town, a larger community of artisans and labourers brightened a toilsome round with the innumerable feast days and recreations of a traditional European peasantry, presided over by the Church.

As commandant of the citadel and commanding officer of a brand-new army unit that included many of its most eligible young men, Strange found himself at the centre of the community's considerable social life. Much as he enjoyed this frivolous round, it did not distract him from his overriding concern, the forming and fitting-out of an efficient battery. The unit's task would be not only to man the new nation's artillery, but also to act as its only full-time military force, providing effective mounted and infantry capabilities as well as training schools for the Canadian militia. It was a tall order, but Strange set about it with his customary energy and enthusiasm.

The drivers of his gun teams would be used, when required, as a mounted unit to back up the gunners when these were acting as "infantry." All were to be trained to man, maintain, and fire the fixed artillery of the fortress and its satellite forts, as well as to operate as a battery of field artillery. All this required an unprecedented flexibility, as well as intensive training of both officers and men. To add to their burden, the gunners were expected also to act as instructors to large classes of part-time militia soldiers.

From the first, Strange was optimistic, putting his faith in the quality of the officers and men he was able to recruit. "Canadians as a people have military aptitudes of the first order," he wrote in his journal, "and a Canadian gentleman generally has the makings of a good officer." He was especially pleased with the selection of officers with which the government had initially provided him. Captain C.E. Montizambert and Lieutenant Maurice Duchesnay were both of old French-Canadian stock, and had ancestors who had served in the British Army; Lieutenant Charles Short, an English-Canadian, was a descendant of General Sir Isaac Brock, the hero of Queenston Heights.

Strange, well aware of the inherent tension between French and English, was careful to maintain a balance between the two races in the formation of his battery. Being perfectly bilingual, he was equally at home with both. As a nucleus for his non-commissioned officers and men, he was fortunate in being able to recruit some Canadians who had served in the British Rifle Brigade, together with an ex-sergeant of Artillery, named Lynder, and a young Englishman who had failed a British Army exam. The latter became Sergeant-Major Larie of "B" Battery.

Officers and men were soon imbued with the enthusiasm of their dynamic leader. Convinced that they were indeed a select group, they quickly responded with the sort of *esprit de corps* to be expected of the chosen few.

This spirit was soon severely tested. From the beginning, the little force was plagued by official parsimony; in this least military of countries, both government and civil service displayed a reluctance to spend anything more than the barest minimum. Make do or do without was the order of the day. To operate its field artillery and to move its scores of heavy guns, "B" Battery was given only eight horses, a ludicrously inadequate establishment. Tents for field exercises had to be borrowed from a helpful lumber magnate.

Added to this official policy of austerity was the problem posed by the haste of the British pull-out. With only days, often only hours, between the arrival of a Canadian unit and the departure of the British, there was never time for a proper listing and handover of stores and arms. Before Strange's arrival, everything possible left by the British had been sold by Canadian officials. The very beds for the gunners had been sold to an American contractor, and Strange arrived in the nick of time to prevent their being carried out of the citadel's gate just as his weary gunners were arriving to bed down for the night. Even the sentry boxes had been shipped out. The battery's first days were spent in improvising living accommodation in camp-like conditions in the middle of a Canadian winter.

Once stoves had been lit in the glacial casemates and his men installed in chilly, uncomfortable, but bearable quarters, Strange turned his attention to the citadel's defences. The citadel's *raison d'être* was its heavy artillery, now to become the principal charge of his new battery. To his shocked surprise, he found it non-existent; the huge guns had been dismounted and were now merely so many bumps in the deep snow covering the stone ramparts. Enquiries established that they had been removed to enable the Royal Engineers of the previous British garrison to repair the artillery platforms so that they could bear the weight of the enormous guns, which were much heavier than those for which the ancient citadel had been designed.

To re-establish these monsters on their rampart mountings was accordingly the new gunners' first priority, and they set about it with an energy and ingenuity that surprised even their veteran commander. Lacking an experienced assistant, Strange himself directed the digging out of each heavy gun, and he found that his new gunners included many former timber cutters and lumbermen, accustomed to rolling and lifting heavy and cumbersome logs. This experience stood them in good stead as the big guns were rolled and trundled and parbuckled onto their mountings. In driving snowstorms and biting cold that reached thirty degrees below zero, the gunners laboured on, high above the frozen river, undaunted by the seemingly endless toil or the rigours of the Quebec winter.

"No man was ever served more loyally than I was," Strange confided to his journal. "My Canadians made up for their lack of artillery training by the resourcefulness which comes of life in the forest lumber camps; they were never beaten." The measure of their accomplishment can hardly be appreciated by mere numbers, but the list of guns mounted gives some indication of the magnitude of their task.

The battery was responsible for mounting and maintaining no fewer than 181 pieces of ordnance, ranging from the enormous eight-inch-bore rifled guns of the citadel and the equally huge carronades firing 64-pound shells, to eight-inch mortars and 5.5-inch howitzers. In addition, there was the regular battery of nine-pounders on wheeled field mountings. It was a tremendous task, but by spring Strange and his gunners had put the citadel into defensible condition, and Canada could boast a considerable and serviceable artillery establishment.

Hand-in-hand with the work on the guns went the outfitting and training of the men. Strange found that the government had provided no uniforms or small arms for its new regular army, and furthermore a tight-fisted civil service could not be induced to supply funds to purchase any. Strange made good the deficiency in characteristic fashion by appropriating the uniforms already supplied to the Quebec Volunteer Artillery, a militia unit of which his right-hand man, Captain Montizambert, happened to be adjutant. Suitably dressed in artillery blue, and with rifles and ammunition from the same source, "B" Battery presented a proper soldierly appearance, and under their experienced commander and his excellent officers their drill and deportment soon reached a high standard.

But from the very beginning it was morale rather than anything else which was Strange's main concern. As an old soldier, he knew that pride was the key to good discipline. It was pride, not pay or patriotism, that could conquer fear and inspire an army unit to feats of courage and endurance far beyond the capacity of individual soldiers, so that its cohesive spirit made it greater than the sum of its parts. In this new battery, Strange was conscious of laying the foundations of a national army, and with characteristic vigour he set about inspiring it with pride in itself as an elite unit.

A battery band was quickly formed, its martial music lifting sagging spirits on parades and route marches. It even accompanied the battery on winter exercises and provided music for the sleighing parties and dances. These were part of an organized social life instituted by Strange to lighten the burden of discipline that was the other side of regimental life in a professional army.

Sometimes the social side was indistinguishable from a military exercise. The long and severe Canadian winter was a dominant element in any military operation at Quebec City; it had been a major factor in defeating previous enemy sieges. Strange was determined to make winter conditions help rather than hamper the new Canadian force, and from the beginning he led his troops in a series of exercises designed to make them mobile in all winter conditions and capable of retaining their effectiveness in the worst of weather. By introducing competition between the units of his command, he made these exercises a kind of sport in which everyone became a team competitor.

Taking advantage of the smooth, snow-free ice of an early freeze-up, Strange led his men on skates on a gruelling foray into the teeth of a strong gale as far as Cap Rouge. Then the little army turned about and, with coats spread as sails, whistled home on the wings of the wind, their colonel narrowly avoiding a gaping hole en route.

Strange made full use, too, of the knowledge and techniques of the Indians, who were the most accomplished woodsmen of all. Huron guides were assigned to both sides in the war games and exercises, and the gunners became adept at using such native tricks as crossing rivers on a felled tree—a *pont sauvage*.

It was from these guides that Strange became familiar with the native manner of making war. Mostly it involved small raiding parties rather than large bodies of men, and the favourite method of fighting such a party was to lay an ambuscade. Careful scouting on both sides was necessary to lay, or to avoid, such ambushes. This knowledge of the native style of warfare was to stand Strange in good stead later in his career on the distant plains of the Northwest Territories.

Sometimes a battery would set out on snowshoes, its field guns mounted on sleds in place of the customary wheels and drawn by the shaggy horses of their gun teams, for a long route march in the winter woods. Strange made full use of the experience of his French-Canadian gunners, for his habitants were thoroughly at home out of doors. Overnight bivouacs in the deep woods became a common experience, and the battery, band and all, became accustomed to sustaining itself for days at a time in the wilderness. The hard marches and nightly sing-songs around roaring campfires engendered a strong sense of regimental fraternity.

Curiously, Strange, who had never before experienced really cold weather and who had spent most of his career in the tropics, revelled in the arctic conditions. He became celebrated among his gunners for his habit of taking his morning bath by simply rolling naked in the snow before briskly towelling himself dry, a practice which nobody else emulated. He was also proud of being able to move about comfortably with uncovered ears in winter temperatures that forced native Canadians to wear earflaps down. But as his blood thinned with time, he sometimes suffered frostbite; then his gunners would rub snow on his affected ears and nose, hugely enjoying his discomfiture.

A weekend expedition to Montmorency Falls, part exercise and part sleighing picnic, nearly ended in disaster, for here Colonel Strange became once again the dashing Jingo of his youthful days. In wintertime, the falls, higher than Niagara and a famous site for visitors, became encased in ice formed by frozen spray, which made an enormous dome or mountain 200 feet high. Young daredevils would climb this ice mountain by steps cut in one side, dragging their sleds behind them, and then plummet down the more precipitous side, steering their sleds with their feet and roaring down the long stretches of frozen river. Captain Montizambert—"Monty" to everyone—was an old hand at this dangerous sport, and duly piloted his commanding officer down the perilous run, frightening him half to death in the process. "There, Colonel," he remarked; "guess you couldn't do that on your own hook, even though Englishmen don't need earflaps!"

It was a challenge which Jingo simply couldn't refuse. He dragged the sled to the top, and even though he was appalled at the near-vertical steepness of the slope before him, with the icy torrent of the waterfall thundering behind, he was determined not to back out. Pushing off, he shot away at great speed. Halfway down, the sled veered slightly from its course. Jingo, in his attempts to correct, put his heel down too firmly, and the sled slewed violently sideways, flew into the air, and flung Jingo violently upside down into an icy hummock, knocking him unconscious. He was revived by a solicitous Monty and found to have suffered a badly cut head and various contusions. But his daredevil reputation was intact and his men were made aware once more that behind the portentous figure of Colonel Commandant Strange lurked the irrepressible Gunner Jingo.

As a less dangerous winter pastime designed to foster friendly relations between his new army and the civilian population, Strange organized the Tandem Club, a mixed group of soldiers and civilians that sponsored a program of two-horse sleigh rides. Their jingling night-time cavalcades through lamplit streets and starlit countryside, and their midnight suppers at wayside inns, where the gunners' band would be waiting to play for dancing, became a popular part of Quebec's social life, as did the plays and skits staged by the battery's theatre group, with casts drawn from both military and civil talent.

The end of the long Canadian winter brought a new diversion. Anxious to provide his French-Canadian officers with the quick "eye for country" of their British counterparts, Strange introduced cross-country fox hunting. A pack of hounds was imported from England, and the Stadacona Hunt Club was formed. Since there were no foxes, a scent drag was used. Strange, as master of fox hounds, led the way as the hunt, made up of cadets, battery officers, naval officers from visiting warships, and large numbers of enthusiastic civilians, streamed across the countryside, learning which fences could be jumped, which gates should be opened rather than hurdled, and all the other expertise involved in galloping horses over broken country.

In the first year of service in Quebec City, Strange and his gunners established a rapport with the mixed Anglo-French populace beyond the most sanguine expectations of his political masters. He had been determined to build the new Canadian army on a foundation of mutual trust between soldier and civilian, and he was succeeding in giving the nation's fledgling force the deep popular roots it was to need in the years ahead.

The emergence of Canada's new artillery unit as a *corps d'élite* was a remarkable demonstration of Strange's genius for working with a relatively small body of men, and imbuing them with his own brand of enthusiasm. The competitive drills and exercises, the introduction of "fun and games" into the grim business of soldiering and the tedium of garrison life, the lively regimental social round—all these showed Strange at his innovative best. But by their very nature these innovations clashed with the necessarily hidebound routines of the Ottawa establishment. Politicians might approve the emergence of a smart and efficient Canadian military force in so short a time and from such an unpromising beginning, but civil servants bound by form and precedent looked askance at the highly irregular methods employed to produce and operate it. Those smart blue uniforms—surely they had been pinched from an established military unit? Where were the forms authorizing such an unheard-of procedure? How was ammunition to be granted to a unit which had not officially been issued with rifles? Why were guns being fired when the country—so far as official Ottawa understood—was not at war? Who had authorized the local purchase of blankets, horse feed, harness, sleds, and all the rest? "It was the reign of King Cash Balance," Jingo noted dourly in his diary.

The new army was being created by the drive and ingenuity of an individual commander whose qualities of leadership amounted almost to genius, but it was necessarily at the expense of formal routine. "Proper channels" and "regulation procedure" and "departmental authorization," all with the necessary forms, filled out in triplicate, sometimes threatened to swamp him in a sea of paper, but it was never to inhibit his urge to get the job done. From the beginning to the end of his career, Jingo was to be regarded by officialdom as a maverick.

TEN

Father Figure

The roar of the angry mob rose to a new pitch as the frail figure of the mayor appeared in the door of the looted warehouse, propelled forward by the firm grip of a black-bearded Colonel Strange. Jammed into the narrow confines of St. Paul's Street, the crowd reacted to this appearance of officialdom like a tiger sighting its prey; it surged furiously forward, showering the building and the little huddle of men in its doorway with rocks and bottles. From the heights above, some madmen were rolling boulders down onto the street, threatening the lives of everyone below, fellow rioters as well as the soldiers drawn up in silence in front of the building.

Moments before, the soldiers had driven the rioters from the warehouse. The mob had already threatened the legislative buildings and had almost succeeded in releasing the prisoners from the city jail. Now it was determined to loot the warehouse and plunder the shops, and prepared to take the life of anyone who stood in its way.

It was the summer of 1872, insurrection was in the air, and the spirit of the Paris mob had spread throughout the French-speaking world.

Struck by a stone, the little mayor attempted to dodge back into the shelter of the doorway but was prevented from doing so by a pair of husky soldiers obeying their colonel's silent signal. "Read the Riot Act!" he was instructed; and when he confessed to not having brought one, Strange produced a copy from his sabretache and handed it to him. The mayor hastily mumbled out the official command ordering the crowd to disperse or suffer the consequences, and though his words went unheard above the roar of the mob, Strange now had the authority he needed to act. While the mayor scuttled back into shelter, Strange ordered Captain Short to clear the street. The little cavalry unit of mounted gunners rode towards the mob, which immediately began to recoil upon itself, and pressed their advantage by walking their horses up against the leading edge of the crowd. Individual rioters were already slipping away down sidestreets, and the soldiers had begun to assert control when a gunner's horse slipped on a tram track, tumbling him at the feet of the mob. At the same time, Captain Short found himself separated from his men by a tramcar. Instantly the mob surged forward again, beating both isolated soldiers with clubs and fists. It took a charge by Strange's dismounted gunners, acting as infantry with bayonets fixed, to rescue their fallen comrades and restore order.

Within months of its formation, "B" Battery was called upon time and again to support the civil arm and to restore law and order by a government and populace helpless to defend themselves by normal police methods. The new nation was already in danger of dissolving into civil disorder and anarchy, and its new-born regular army had first to be employed against Canadian citizens, rather than against the alien enemy whose assaults had brought it into being.

In Quebec City and Montreal, most of the rioting was between Irish Catholics and French Canadians, a shared religious faith proving no bar to bitter racial enmity. The tiny municipal police forces proved powerless to control the fighting; only the Canadian Army could effectively intervene and separate the warring factions. Strange found that the Irish, massed under their green flag with its gold harp, were the more truculent, and he usually dispersed them with his mounted "cavalry" section, while his infantry, advancing with their rifles at the trail rather than at the charge, were enough to break up the French-Canadian element and send them back, brandishing their tricolour, to their stronghold in the St. Roch quarter of the city.

Strange and his gunners quickly became expert in crowd control. Bayonets would be fixed before the men left barracks, for not only was the sight of bared steel a very real deterrent, but the weight of the bayonets tended to make the rifles muzzle-heavy, thus reinforcing Strange's orders, which were to fire only when absolutely necessary, and then to fire low at feet and legs rather than hearts and heads. In all the fierce rioting during "B" Battery's nearly ten-year stay at Quebec, only one man, an agitator brought in from the Paris Commune, was killed by military gunfire, and although many gunners were wounded, none died. Strange was equally proud of both records.

The insurrections that threatened the life of the new Dominion were not confined to Quebec. There was trouble also in Ontario and Nova Scotia, and in the West. In September 1872 Strange sent Lieutenant Taschereau, with forty men and two rifled seven-pounder field guns along with a similar detachment from "A" Battery, all the way to Manitoba, to keep the peace among the Indians and Métis there. Canada's new army was proving its worth, helping to keep the country's dissident factions from tearing it apart.

It proved itself helpful in other non-military ways, too, being called out on occasion to supplement the efforts of the local fire brigade in putting out serious fires. On one occasion it was instrumental in saving a large part of the city from total destruction, when the old wooden houses of the St. Roch quarter went up in flames. Strange, perceiving that the efforts of the firemen could not possibly extinguish the holocaust, put his men to work creating a gap or firebreak by blowing up a number of houses in the path of the flames. The effort was successful, the fire was brought to a halt, contained, and extinguished, but not without cost. Lieutenant Short and Sergeant Wallick were both killed while destroying a house, the first deaths sustained by the battery. The city itself, as Strange observed, would be their monument.

The annual clash between Orangemen and Catholic Irish on the "Glorious Twelfth" of July, a traditional feature of early Canadian life, provided the battery with a pleasant marine excursion. The gunners embarked in the steamer *Corinthian* for the trip upriver to Montreal, where they helped maintain the peace and were commended for their "good discipline, conduct, soldier-like patience and forbearance under trying circumstances."

For Strange himself, the years in Quebec were the happiest, as well as the most challenging, of his life. On a personal level, his wife and family of five—three daughters had been added to the two older sons—enjoyed an active social life and were welcomed into the homes of the city's oldest and most distinguished residents. Especial friends were Joly de Lotbinière and his family. Because of its long military tradition, dating from the earliest days of New France, the family now sent its sons into the British Army.

The viceregal drawing room was always open to the Stranges. Both Lord Dufferin and his successor as Governor General, the Marquis of Lorne, became personal friends, and extended their hospitality both at their Ottawa home and at their summer residence at the Citadel. It was to the Dufferin's young daughter that Strange first explained that tricks that could be played with static electricity in the dry Canadian winter air. Shuffling his feet on the viceregal carpet, Strange showed her how a spark—and

Thomas Bland Strange, "Gunner Jingo," in all the formidable finery of a Victorian major-general.

A drawing by Jingo made in India in 1858. Artillery officers were taught to sketch the terrain in which they were campaigning and many developed into accomplished artists. Jingo enjoyed sketching and made a habit of recording the people and places around him wherever he went.

The ice dome at Montmorency Falls; Jingo sledded down the steep slope and was knocked unconscious when his sled flew out from under him.

A crew of gunners drawn from both "A" and "B" Batteries, posing with their nine-pounder field gun at Fort Garry barracks in Winnipeg in 1874. This is believed to be the earliest photograph of a Canadian regular army gun team.

Canada's new artillerymen exercising gun teams in the field.

Jingo's "B" Battery mounting guns on the ramparts of the Citadel at Quebec City, c. 1873.

Strangmuir, the pioneer ranch house and barn built in the 1880s by Jingo on the prairie south of Calgary.

Cowboys of the Strangmuir ranch pose outside their bunkhouse. This may be the building that survives on the site today.

National Archives PA 124101

Crowfoot, chief of the Blackfoot Indians and Jingo's neighbour at Strangmuir.

Glenbow Museum NA 1315-16

The inside of Fort Edmonton at the time of the Northwest Rebellion.

Sam Steele, Jingo's intrepid cavalry leader.

Steele's scouts, a drawing by Jingo.

Jingo's sketches of the "hayclad" and "flourclad" barges that the Alberta Field Force used to get up the North Saskatchewan River.

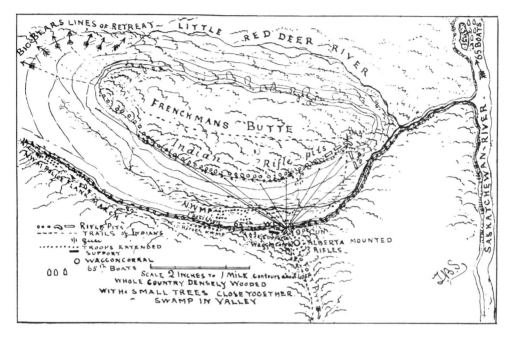

Jingo's sketch of the battle lines at Frenchman's Butte.

Big Bear, chief of the Plains Crees, after his capture.

The hard-pressed 65th voltigeurs pull a nine-pounder gun out of the muskeg on the way to Beaver River, one of the most difficult marches in the 1885 campaign. The painting is by W.S. Blatchly from *The Canadian Pictorial and Illustrated War News*, July 18, 1885.

a shock—could be transmitted by touching someone. The feat so fascinated both the girl and her mother that Lady Dufferin used to light the gas with it as a parlour trick.

The creation of the "Schools of Gunnery" (which developed into nothing less than academies for training in all branches of military service) was the supreme achievement of Strange's career, and became the foundation of both the Canadian Army and what was to become the Royal Canadian Mounted Police.

In order to train the hundreds of militia officers and men sent to these schools each summer, Strange had to rely on the NCOs and men of his unit to act as instructors. This was not normally a responsibility for men in the ranks, and it laid a heavy burden on their military ability and knowledge. Accordingly, Strange set out to make them paragons of behaviour and bearing, worthy of being role models for the impressionable young part-time soldiers whom they were to instruct. Uniform regulations were strictly enforced; in town, white gloves were to be worn at all times, and any drunkenness, smoking, or unsoldierly behaviour brought swift punishment. But in setting the highest standards for the unit, the carrot was used as well as the stick. A recreation room, equipped for various games and relaxation, was set up, an unusual addition to a Victorian barracks. Competitive sports of every kind were organized, with handsome prizes keenly competed for, and there were prizes and badges for the best shots in both artillery and small arms. There were evening classes in a variety of subjects, and a library and reading room also offered coffee for a quiet afternoon.

But sports and physical activities were the most popular. Gym classes were held three times a week, and cricket, football, swimming, and sailing were battery favourites, as was the annual unit picnic with its traditional competitions. Canada's national sport, ice hockey, whose origins are variously ascribed to British regiments stationed at Kingston or Montreal or to students at Queen's or McGill universities, may well have had its real origin in the gunners' off-hours scrimmages with field hockey sticks on their frozen barrack-square, later transferred to frozen lake and river rinks. Certainly, contests between teams of gunners and students were among the first scheduled ice hockey games.

Strange was confident that his gunners, brought to a high pitch of disciplined enthusiasm by this regimen, would be able to inculcate it in others. His confidence was not misplaced. His men took to their role as instructors with surprising ease and composure and were able to establish firm fraternal bonds with the amateur gunners who passed through their hands. Strange was determined that there should be no feelings of "them and us," no distinctions made between the professionals and the amateurs. He made it clear that any disrespect or contempt displayed towards these summer soldiers would be punished, but in the event there was little occasion for such severity.

In all this, Strange was conscious that he was laying the foundations for a new army, with a new sort of leadership. He was aware that the class distinctions inherent in the British social system, and the resulting gulf between leaders and led in the British Army, did not prevail in the New World. He had always had an aversion to the upper-class officer who depended entirely upon his NCOs for the day-to-day management of his men, the lisping exquisite whose only function was to lead soldiers into battle without displaying fear. His own style was to lead by example, never asking his men to do anything he could not, and did not, do himself. At the same time, he sought to avoid the rough style of the United States Army, where command was enforced by kicks and curses.

He aimed at a Canadian style of leadership, a style midway between the two other national examples, one that emphasized mutual respect and restraint between the leader and the led. It was a style well suited to the Canadian militia system, where officers and men alike were drawn largely from the same middle class of society. It had always been fashionable for young men of good family to serve in the ranks of the militia regiments, which traditionally performed a social as well as military function in their depots scattered across the land.

The quality of the officers was, for Strange, the key to the quality of an army, and he was at pains to ensure that the young gunner cadets passing through his hands were exposed to the hallowed traditions and mystique of the Royal Artillery. The RA mess at Woolwich was traditionally the most magnificent in the British Army, and its standards of deportment and etiquette were emphasized at cadet dinners in its Canadian counterpart.

It quickly became clear to Strange that the narrow curriculum laid down for an artillery school, teaching only artillery subjects, was far too confining for the job that had to be done. A great deal more would have to be taught, ranging from simple infantry drill and formations—required to move large bodies of men about—to the duties and proper behaviour of officers, both commissioned and non-commissioned. From the beginning Strange and his staff assumed these responsibilities. He petitioned Ottawa to enlarge the school's function, and thus to authorize what was already being practised, and over the years this was officially done. The school began to provide instruction in everything from equitation to musketry marksmanship.

Another point Strange stressed to the government was the need for an officer training school, a Canadian version of the Royal Military College at Sandhurst, to develop young officers for both the Canadian regular army and the militia and to provide character-building training for young men in all walks of life. Again and again he drew the urgency of this need to the attention of his Ottawa superiors, and was accordingly much gratified at the founding, in 1876, of Canada's Royal Military College at Kingston, Ontario.

Situated on the site of the former naval dockyard on Navy Bay and overlooked by the Martello Tower of Fort Frederick, the new college was close to the artillery establishment at Tête de Pont barracks. From its beginnings, Strange took a close personal interest in the school. Its curriculum, with its emphasis on character building and physical fitness, reflected his own philosophy, and it established a tradition of mental and physical toughness which would survive for a century.

Gunners the world over enjoyed a fraternal bond unique to their calling, a link to their Middle Ages beginnings as civilian practitioners of a dark art, looked at askance by the armoured foot-soldiers and mounted knights of medieval armies. It was a bond which Strange was anxious to develop in his New World gunners, and in 1876 he formed the Dominion Artillery Association, with himself as its first president, to maintain the standards and further the interests of the "profession" in Canada. It was the first such Canadian military association, and it set the pattern for later organizations in other branches of the service. In particular, its establishment of an annual competition in artillery shooting and drill for the country's gunners was to prove most effective in making Canadian artillerymen second to none. In 1881 Canada sent its first team to take part in the artillery competition at Shoeburyness in England, and returned with the prized Governor General's award for all-round excellence.

The thousands of young men who passed through the two schools in their first ten years became the new Dominion's principal pool of trained and disciplined manpower and a national resource of immeasurable importance. It was therefore natural that it was to them, and to the regular army officers and NCOs who had trained them, that the Canadian government turned when the need arose for the creation of a national gendarmerie to police the great expanses of the western plains, soon to be opened up by the railroad. According to the government, if the land was to be settled and the prairies converted to farmland, the nomadic tribes of plains Indians would have to be stabilized and their wanderings in pursuit of the fast-diminishing buffalo herds confined to the newly created reservations set aside for them. Moreover, the swarms of American brigands and bootleggers would have to be shunted back across the border. In view of the vast distances to be patrolled, it was evident that a mounted force would be necessary, and accordingly a troop of light horse was authorized to be raised in 1873. The new force was originally to be called the North West Mounted Rifles, but when it was realized that the initial body might have to be sent out via the United States, because of the unfinished state of the Canadian railway, this was changed by a simple stroke of the prime minister's pen to become the North West Mounted Police (NWMP). By existing treaty, police from one country could cross the borders of the other, but troops could not.

To head this new force, the obvious choice was Colonel G. A. French, who commanded "A" Battery at Kingston. French not only possessed the necessary executive qualities required for the post, but he had already had experience in the Royal Irish Constabulary, just such a force as the government envisioned for the Canadian West. He accordingly became the first Commissioner of the NWMP. For its other officers and constables the government looked no further than to the men who had earned such a reputation for its young regular army and to the militia officers and NCOs they had trained. French's adjutant was Captain W. H. Cotton of the Ottawa Garrison Artillery, and most of the new force's senior personnel, including its succeeding commissioners and superintendents, were drawn from the two gunnery units and their schools.

The most notable such acquisition was Samuel Steele, an enthusiastic young militiaman and gunnery school graduate who was destined to become famous as "the ultimate Mountie" and who would soon be linked with Strange in an outstandingly successful partnership. "Smoothbore Steele," as he was named because of his early artillery associations, was already a prodigy among his fellow gunners, noted alike for his great physical strength and for his energy, courage, and marksmanship. He was named a Sergeant-Major or Special Constable on joining the force. At the same time a fellow gunner, A. H. Griesbach, was made Regimental Chief Constable, so beginning a career which would take him also to the top as Commissioner.

Altogether, more than thirty percent of the North West Mounted Police's original establishment and its initial reinforcement, together with virtually all its senior officers, were drawn from the graduates and staff of the battery schools, and the standards of the new force reflected in large degree those of its parent body.

The planned opening-up of the Canadian West now presented the government with the problem of its defence, and Strange, as Inspector General, was accordingly sent across the continent to the West Coast in 1878 on a Pacific defence mission undertaken jointly with the British. The detachment of gunners that had been sent out to maintain order in Manitoba had been incorporated into a permanent garrison, alternating between Fort Garry and Fort Qu'Appelle. With the Mounted Police now establishing forts across the prairie, the government's principal concern was the defence of the Pacific ports and the western terminus of the railroad under construction.

Travelling by rail across the United States, Strange enjoyed the comfort of the new Pullman cars and the spectacular scenery. In Salt Lake City, he marvelled at the domestic arrangements of the wealthy Mormons, whose big houses had a separate entrance for each wife, up to a maximum of half a dozen.

A bathe in the Great Salt Lake, shared with a stout Mormon and his half-dozen wives, all red-headed, produced an embarrassing contretemps. Jingo writes:

Having had quite enough aquatics, the extreme brine being very painful to the eyes, I made for my bathing-box with the least possible delay, but encountered a procession of Mormon ladies with pink parasols. As my hired garments were scanty in the extreme, the situation was highly unpleasant, especially when aggravated by the giggles under the sunshades, which were only lowered at the moment of my passing. Inserting my hand over the top of the door of my bathing-box, I maladroitly knocked the key off the nail on which it had hung. My companion had already reached the shelter of his box, and I shouted to him to climb over the partition between the two and open my door from the inside.

"Alright, old fellow," was followed by a crash of wood and the exit of the yelling Mormon ladies from their own compartment, in extreme *déshabillé*. My friend had scaled the wrong partition, which had broken and precipitated him into the red-headed seraglio.

Once arrived at the Pacific, Strange was all business, and together with the British representative, Colonel W. J. Lovell of the Royal Engineers, made a thorough inspection of the British Columbia coast. Its defence had been severely compromised already by British indifference in abandoning the San Juan Islands and the lower Alaska coastline to the Americans in earlier arbitration.

Strange's recommendations, he noted bitterly, were merely noted and filed away by the Ottawa bureaucracy, but they were subsequently implemented in part during the Russian scare of 1878-79. They included making Esquimalt into a defended naval base, the Pacific equivalent of Halifax, the fortification of Victoria and Vancouver harbours with heavy guns, and the formation of a four-battery brigade of militia gunners to man them.

Strange was never much impressed by "the Russian menace," recognizing that so long as the all-powerful British Royal Navy continued to rule the waves, little danger could come to Canada from overseas. But time after time there had been invasions and rumours of invasions from the United States. Canadians had been apprehensive, ever since the end of the American Civil War, that the victorious armies of the North might march across the border in yet another attempt to fulfil the Yankees' dream of annexing their northern neighbour. It was Strange's mission, as Inspector General of Ordnance, to see that Canada's border defences had the gunpower to repel any attack upon them, and he was not sanguine about the capacity of the available collection of antique smoothbore cannon to do what was required of them. Since there was no possibility that the Canadian government would replace them with expensive new rifled guns, Strange turned to the notion of modernizing them by a method developed by an Irish inventor, Sir William Palliser. This entailed the fitting of a rifled tube of wrought iron into the bore of an existing smoothbore gun. Long-nosed conical shells, with brass studs which fitted into the spiral grooves of the guns, thus had a rotation imparted to them which doubled both their range and hitting power, and gave them an accuracy far beyond anything possible with smoothbore firings. With such guns, Strange was convinced that Canadian forts would have artillery capable of coping with anything that could be brought against them overland. But the re-tubed guns, imported from England, would cost £111 apiece, and the government balked at spending even this amount. Accordingly, Strange set about the task of modernizing the guns with Canadian resources.

Captain Edward Palliser, a brother of the inventor, was brought over to supervise the experimental conversion of a number of old 32-pounder guns into 64-pounder rifled cannon. A Montreal firm, Gilbert and Son, undertook the work, which was successfully completed on two guns. The cost of £700 was donated by Sir William Palliser. With a change of government, the work was discontinued; finally, a further ten modernized guns were imported from England and their expense accepted.

Strange now set himself to organizing a domestic supply of ammunition, the existing practice of importing this from overseas being both expensive and uncertain under wartime conditions. He pressed the matter to his Ottawa superiors, and eventually was successful in persuading the government to establish the Government Cartridge Factory in the old Artillery Park at Quebec City. This later became known as the Dominion Arsenal and was to serve the country well through two world wars.

Equipped finally with both modernized guns and a supply of ammunition, Strange set about distributing them to best advantage. Three forts, connected by a road and an earthwork rampart, were constructed at Lévis to strengthen Quebec's southern defences, and were armed with three seven-inch rifled guns and sixteen old carronades. This formidable work was to be the last Canadian fortification of what was soon to become "the world's longest undefended frontier." Ten other rifled guns were installed on the Quebec ramparts; five at Saint John, New Brunswick's vital port; two more at the citadel in Halifax; and six at the port defences around Victoria, B.C. With these guns mounted and in place and with trained crews to man them,

Canadian coasts and ports were better defended than they had ever been before, a circumstance of which Strange was justifiably proud.

To the commandant of the citadel at Quebec City, the defences of that place were a particular and personal concern, and Strange set about testing and improving them as part of a continuing program. As much as possible, wartime conditions were simulated; the garrison was turned out to repel mock attacks at midnight or in a blinding snowstorm, the circumstances likeliest to suit the purposes of an attacker.

These realistic exercises proved useful in exposing weaknesses in defence; it was found, for example, that the original breech-loading mountings would seize up in freezing weather. But it was the people of Quebec City who proved the greatest impediment to the warlike drills, for there was a storm of protest from angry citizens awakened by midnight firings of the citadel guns. Even daylight practice had its hazards. On one occasion when the garrison was firing at a target on the river ice far below, a premature round sprayed the Lower Town marketplace with iron fragments. Strange prudently cancelled further practice shooting from the citadel ramparts.

But citizens and soldiers alike were to join in one memorable midnight cannonade, even though the guns were not shotted. On December 31, 1875, the one hundredth anniversary of the defeat of American General Arnold Montgomery in his unsuccessful attack on the Quebec City walls was celebrated by Strange and his garrison. The citadel was packed for the occasion with ladies and gentlemen dressed in costumes of the eighteenth century attending a pageant and grand ball, for Strange was seeking to emphasize the importance of the battle in establishing a Canada separate and distinct from the American republic, and the role of the citadel gunners in repelling Montgomery's onslaught. Sharp at midnight, the revellers trooped out onto the windswept parapet to watch their Canadian gunners fire a *feu de joie*, the guns thundering out as one. The explosion of smoke and flame shook the city and knocked over a lamp in Strange's quarters, resulting in a highly embarrassing fire and a good deal of grousing by Quebec citizenry.

A visit in 1872 from Goldwin Smith, a celebrated intellectual of the time, had been partly responsible for Strange's decision to emphasize the American defeat, and its decisive effect in establishing a parliamentary society in Canada separate from the United States. As a guest at the Strange home, Smith had jeered at his host's efforts to establish a Canadian army and strengthen the country's defences, claiming that Canada must inevitably become part of the United States within very few years. Strange was disturbed that so learned a man could be so manifestly wrong, and so unaware of the pride in their new country of all Canadians, of both French and English origin.

In 1880, as part of a reorganization instituted by a new militia commandant, Major-General R. G. Luard, "A" and "B" batteries exchanged stations. Strange and his unit moved to Kingston, Ontario. For officers and men alike the move was painful, entailing the severing of long-established friendships as well as the breaking-up of domestic establishments and the founding of new ones.

Like Quebec City, Kingston had always been a garrison town, from its earliest beginnings as a French fort, and it, too, was an old university town dominated by a fortress. A large proportion of Kingston residents were of Scottish origin, and among them Strange was surprised to find a family of his cousins who had emigrated from Scotland more than a hundred years before.

"B" Battery soon accustomed itself to its new role as the Kingston garrison, occupying Fort Henry as well as Tête de Pont barracks. Colonel Strange quickly became one of the little town's notable citizens, and a singularly imposing one at that. His eyesight, in his fiftieth year, had begun to fail somewhat, but for a field officer in a fighting service to appear in spectacles was simply out of the question. Officers in the British Army, however, might improve their vision by wearing a single eyeglass, and accordingly Strange had taken to wearing a monocle. The effect of this eyeglass, screwed into his left eye, which peered fiercely out over a tangle of black beard, could be daunting in the extreme. It was especially so for the young cadets of the Royal Military College, now housed in the Stone Frigate, once the old naval hospital, where the colonel was a frequent visitor.

Part of the battery's new responsibilities was the defence of the city of Toronto, formerly the town of York. During the war of 1812, it had been captured and burned by an American force, an act regarded as barbarism by the British, who promptly responded by capturing and burning the town of Washington, the much larger capital of the United States. The fixed fortifications of Toronto's early days as York had long been abandoned. Two ancient cannons were all that remained of the battery on Gibraltar Point, the elbow-shaped sandbar that protected the harbour. A crumbling earthwork and a few dilapidated buildings marked the site of Fort York; a decaying shed, sunk into the hillside of the Don Valley, had once served as the magazine for the local garrison.

Toronto was now a bustling, modern city, far too big to be defended by any mud fort. Its waterfront stretched from the Don to the Humber Rivers, and its northern limits had long ago engulfed the old Potter's Field at Bloor Street and were moving even further up Yonge Street, originally a military road. The British had built Stanley Barracks, a typical imperial army establishment, on its western shore near the city's exhibition grounds and had established a small regular army presence there as a training cadre for the local militia.

Toronto already had the largest, best-trained, best-equipped militia establishment in the country, and Strange continued the policy of relying for the defence of the city on this volunteer army, which included all branches of the service, together with a detachment of his gunners in a training role.

By 1881, after ten years of service in Canada, Strange was at the height of his military career, confirmed in rank, and enjoying the confidence of the Canadian government and the regard of the country's military establishment. His name was now familiar throughout Canada, and indeed, the British Empire, where his Woolwich contemporaries had also achieved high rank. He was on familiar terms with a wide spectrum of Canadian, British, and American society, ranging from visiting princes, peers of the realm, and politicians of every stripe, to soldiers and civilians in all walks of life. As an intellectual soldier, an unusual (some thought, contradictory) qualification, he was at home in any company and respected in all.

With his reputation and striking appearance, he had become a father figure to Canada's soldiers, and indeed was described by the new commandant of the Canadian militia, Major-General Luard, as "the father of Artillery of Canada." His accomplishments were too numerous to list, but chief among them had been the creation, single-handed, of a professional military force. This alone was a marvel of improvisation, and it was made possible only by his dynamic energy and the enthusiasm he was able to impart to all about him. He had organized and put into a high state of efficiency the artillery defences of the new nation, had equipped it with effective guns, trained its crews, and supplied its own arsenal. He had written the Canadian artillery's first manual, had organized its first service association, and had helped found its officer training college. But above all, he had trained men; no fewer than 2,700 gunners had passed through his hands in "B" Battery, and countless thousands of young cadets had learned their business in his training school. At fifty years of age, he had every right to look back with pride at his accomplishments, and ahead with confidence at the tasks yet to be done.

It all came to an end with shocking suddenness. A terse note from England informed him that he must resign his Canadian post or forfeit the British Army pension he would soon qualify for, and which he had earned by his previous service. Canada offered no pension, he had no private means, and he had a large family to support. He had no choice but to resign; fifty, fit, and furious, he was forced out of his profession at the height of his powers and at the peak of his career.

All remonstrances, all appeals, were in vain. Whitehall insisted he must leave his Canadian post. Ottawa would offer no pension if he stayed. As a small sop, the British higher command promoted him to major-general, once it was clear he did not intend to stay on in the army, so that it was as Major-General Thomas Bland Strange, a veteran of thirty years' service in the Army, that he officially retired in December 1882. The break was complete; Strange threw away his uniforms and set out as a civilian to make his way in a civilian world, determined to put the past behind him and to carve out a new career that would support both himself and his family. General Strange was history; it was the irrepressible Jingo, still as dynamic as ever, who set out from his snug Ontario home, bound for the untamed prairies of the Canadian West.

Curiously, neither the Canadian government, which tendered him a vote of thanks in lieu of anything more expensive, nor Strange himself seems to have had any conception of what he had accomplished during his decade of service.

Quite apart from his achievements in establishing the country's regular army and a valid system of defence, his units had supplied a third of the new North West Mounted Police force, including virtually all its senior officers, and the corps of officers and NCOs who would provide the foundation on which the new national army would be built. But it was the men he had trained, whose character he had moulded and whom he had inspired by his enthusiastic leadership, who were his chief legacy to the nation he had served so well. Over the next two decades these men went on to become provincial lieutenant-governors, chief justices of the Supreme Court, presidents of banks and railroads, lawyers, politicians, professional men of every sort, serving in senior capacities in every national institution. These institutions would shape the face of the emerging country, so that in helping to mould the new generation of leaders, Strange had imparted much of his unique spirit to the country he had grown to love.

ELEVEN

Cowboy Tom

The solitary horseman, saddlebags bulging with supplies, rode steadily away along the riverbank, the only
moving thing in all the vast sweep of the prairie. Jingo
watched him go, growing smaller with increasing distance,
until he disappeared altogether around a bend in the river.
There was no one now save himself. He turned and looked
behind him at the fresh-cut logs, neatly stacked in three
piles, that were the only signs of human activity in this
wilderness of grass, wood, and water.

Those logs, cut with such infinite labour and floated
across from the scrub-covered island in the river, represented
two weeks of back-breaking labour by two awkward axemen, for neither he nor his partner had ever worked in the
woods before. The unaccustomed toil and, Jingo suspected,
even more the prospect of spending a Canadian winter on
the bald prairie, had proved too much for his partner. The
young Englishman, fresh from a sheep farm in sunny Australia, and lacking Jingo's grim resolve, had backed out of
the deal the two had made only a few weeks before in the
warm comfort of a Montana bar. Jingo had been forced to
buy him out, paying for his share of the four horses, covered
wagon, and supplies the two had bought at Fort Benton. It
was a disheartening end to an adventure on which the two

had embarked with such high hopes, and which had left him here in the wilderness, leaning on his axe, with only a paltry pile of logs to show for their whole enterprise.

From the beginning, it had been Jingo's dream, his drive, his enthusiasm, that had kept the project going; his young and feckless partner had merely acquiesced for lack of any fixed purpose of his own. Forced so abruptly from the Army only weeks before, Jingo had never considered abject retirement to pensioned penury. England held out little appeal; Canada was his country now, and he was attracted, as always, by the prospect of adventure, the heady mixture of freedom and danger that existed on the frontiers of civilization. Urban life in eastern Canada was already too confining for his restless nature; he had seen something of the great plains on his previous trip across the United States, and it was now to the Canadian West that his ambitions turned. It was also a place where, with hard work and good luck, a man might reasonably expect to make a fortune, and Jingo, a middle-aged man with a large family, was determined to make one in the shortest possible time. And so he had gathered together what ready money he had, packed a single suitcase, and in the summer of 1881, a year before his official retirement, he had set out on his new adventure. Once he had established a home in the West, he would bring out his wife and family, he assured them; in the meantime, they were comfortably ensconced in Kingston with relatives and friends nearby.

Jingo travelled west through the United States, going by rail to Bismarck, North Dakota, and then by sternwheel steamer up the Missouri River to Fort Benton, Montana. Here he encountered the young Englishman who had had some experience raising sheep in Australia, and who was interested in the prospects of similar large-scale sheep-raising in America.

Jingo explained his project to his new acquaintance. He was convinced that the current government policy of settling immigrants on small holdings, to be cleared and operated as subsistence farms in traditional eastern Canadian fashion, was unsuited to the enormous stretches of prairie grassland. Only large-scale methods could be successful here, he believed, where everything assumed big proportions—land, sky, weather, opportunities, problems. His plan was to acquire a huge area—70,000 acres—on the north bank of the Bow River, southeast of the NWMP's Fort Calgary, and to raise large herds of horses and cattle in what he was convinced was ideal rangeland with ample water, grass, and space. The cattle could be marketed in the east, the horses sold for remounts to the British Army.

It had been a beguiling dream, but now Jingo was utterly alone in this western wilderness, with winter coming on and no roof over his head. It was no longer a matter of building a homestead merely to establish his claim to this land; it was also a matter of sheer survival. For a retired general with few woodsman's skills and aching muscles, it was a daunting prospect, but Jingo responded to it with characteristic resource. Somewhere to the east, he knew, was an encampment of Blackfoot Indians, the only possible source of assistance. Without hesitation he set off to ride there.

On arrival, he rode boldly in among the teepees, and was fortunate in encountering the Indian agent, a Mr. Pocklington and his interpreter, Mr. Lheureux. He was introduced by them to the Chief, old Crowfoot, and was able, after the presentation of suitable gifts, to hire a couple of his men to help in building a cabin. With these two assistants, Old Brass and Cutface, the latter so named because he had once cut off the nose of an unfaithful wife, Jingo arrived back at the campsite, together with horses, teepees, and the natives' wives. As the Indians were setting up camp, another visitor arrived, and was engaged to assist. He proved to be the adventurous son of Alexander Morris, a distinguished lieutenant-governor of Manitoba, and he was to became a tower of strength for a grateful Jingo.

The little party set to with a will, the men cutting and trimming and placing logs, the two women collecting the light poles and grass for the roof and chinking the spaces between logs with mud. From the beginning, things went with a swing, and at night the workers relaxed about their campfire, a surprisingly amicable group. The flickering firelight emphasized their differences—the stoicism of the men, the seamed faces of their wives, the grizzled beard of the old soldier, and the fresh-faced youth of young Morris— but for all their differences of age and background, they got along very well together. As Jingo was later to recall in his journal: "We were a curious crowd, but got on famously. I had the good luck to shoot an antelope, and we had bacon, flour, tea and tobacco. What more does a fellow want, with good company?"

The log house was quickly built, and Jingo moved in on his birthday, September 15, 1881. The work of getting in supplies for the coming winter was no sooner begun, how- ever, than unsettling news arrived from the east. The appli- cation made for the property, under the title Jingo had chosen, the Military Colonisation Ranch Company, listed the name of the young Australian who had subsequently backed out. A new application would have to be submitted, and it was not enough for Jingo merely to send it in by mail or through his Montreal lawyer. He would have to take it in person, a requirement which reflected eastern bureaucrats' utter incomprehension of conditions in the West, which existed at all levels of government. For Jingo, it was to entail a trip across trackless prairie of some 300 miles simply to reach the railhead and begin the long train trip east. It was a journey that nearly cost his life.

Winter was setting in, and Jingo was glad to accept the company of two friends, NWMP officers Perry and Provost, who were driving a buckboard east en route to new postings. Leaving young Morris in charge of the homestead, the trio set out on their long journey and soon encountered a fierce blizzard, with freezing temperatures and blinding snow.

With no one able to see more than a few feet ahead, the horses blundered into an unseen hole, the wagon broke down, and the travellers were suddenly stranded on the windswept prairie, miles from any settlement. All three would have assuredly died of exposure within hours but for a sort of miracle. A survey party with several two-wheeled carts, also travelling east, blundered across the little group by purest chance, and the trio and their horses were rescued from what seemed certain death.

Not that their troubles were over. The rest of the trip was a nightmare of starving and exhausted horses, their hooves rotted by alkaline mud; of bad weather and flooded rivers; of bogs, blizzards, and endless labour. It was an exhausted and famished party that walked into the little shacktown that marked the eastern railhead, leading a couple of lamed and starving horses, but for Jingo mere survival was a sufficient blessing.

The return journey in the spring was less perilous, but even more arduous—the longest, most testing ordeal Jingo had ever experienced. He had completed the organization of the Military Colonial Ranch, with himself as principal investor, and with additional capital supplied by fellow officers scattered about the world, who hoped for a return on their investment and a place to which to retire on completion of their army service. Jingo was paying the initial expenses and bearing the greatest part of the financial risk, as well as the physical burden; he stood to lose both his life and his fortune in the event of disaster. Once his claim to the

property had been registered in Ottawa, he set out on the
return journey from Kingston. He was accompanied by his
younger son, sixteen-year-old Alec, together with a friend
of Alec's, the young son of an army officer interested in the
venture, and George Hatton, a militia officer who had
ranched in Colorado and who had been hired as foreman.

Jingo's journal gives a vivid picture of the return march:

We plodded on day by day through alkaline swamps
that the melting snows had left almost impassable.

We marched for near a month, and I do not
remember a day when we did not stick in a swamp,
necessitating generally the unloading of our wagon,
and the carriage of the contents on our backs to terra
firma. As the foreman had sprained his arm by an
upset, and the two lads, only sixteen years of age,
were not game to shoulder sacks of oats and flour, this
duty devolved on ex-General Jingo, who was
supposed to be too old for military service, according
to the wise warrants of the War Office, introduced by
the gentlemen who ride hobbies and high stools.

This march also had an end. There was no blazing
camp fire, no wood on the treeless plains. The
monotonous tinned meats and greasy bacon, and
chips of ship biscuits soaked in the fat of the latter,
were gulped down with pannikins of hot milkless tea.
When old Jingo rolled under the wagon, sharing the
limited space with his son, the foreman and the other
boy, it was not often for deep sleep. His thoughts went
back to those happier days when even the sultry
marches of a hot-weather campaign in India could be
lightened by genial comrades. But those were times
when hope and Jingo were young. Now—hope was
dead—

There was a grim consolation that though Royal warrants considered him unfit to command men, he could at least manage wild horses.

As soon as the two boys were installed in the log hut, built the previous fall, and a field of potatoes fenced, ploughed and sown, the "Boss" and his foreman drove south into the United States, purchased a band of a hundred brood mares and three stallions, hired a few cowboys, and drove the horses back for 160 miles to Canada.

The rains had begun, and the buzz of the merry mosquito was heard in the land. We had no tents, and nothing but blankets and canvas sheets under and over for sleeping in. Not that there was much sleeping done. For many nights the mares had to be circled by mounted men to keep them from breaking back to the country whence they had been driven, where horse thieves abound, who would consider it smart to stampede on their back tracks a band of horses just bought by a "blarsted Britisher." And even after the mares were on the ranch they had to be closely guarded from the same gentry, who did succeed in driving off a couple, by hiring themselves on the ranch as cowboys, and then disappearing with their mounts and one extra. It did not pay the "Boss" to leave the "ninety-and-nine in the wilderness" and go after that which was "lost," and to send anyone else was as equally futile as to apply to the police.

The next two years, 1882-83, were a time of intense activity for Jingo and his increasing number of ranch hands. A further 300 mares were added to the original stock, and 2,350 head of cattle were purchased in Idaho. The work of delivering them was in itself a major undertaking. To secure enough timber to construct the corrals and stables and outbuildings required by such numbers, a working party had to be sent to the mountains to cut and trim logs and raft them down the river to the ranch site; another major undertaking. To feed the large numbers of men needed for all this construction and herding, a considerable vegetable farm had to be laid out and maintained. Through searing summer and arctic winter the work went on, as both stock and work force grew steadily.

The Military Colonial Ranch was a success, and this success drew a steady stream of men hoping for work. Many stayed a week or two only before drifting on to easier berths, for there was little room for idlers in Jingo's bunkhouse; but the best stayed on, and the ranch soon built up a staff of expert and energetic cowboys.

None, however, was more expert or energetic than their boss. True to his instinct to "lead from the front," Jingo had set himself from the beginning to master the skills and craft of the western cowboy. Already an experienced horseman, he quickly adapted to the western saddle and to the shaggy cowponies, so much shorter but quicker than the animals he had been accustomed to. He learned the arts of herding and working with large numbers of horses or cattle and the techniques of cutting out individual animals. He became proficient with the lariat and branding iron, and his annual roundups, to mark or castrate newborn stock, were organized and operated like military field campaigns.

A lover of animals, particularly horses, Jingo was appalled by the cruelties of the roundups, with their branding, bellowing, and brutality, and especially by the near-sadistic techniques of "bronco-busting," where a horse was deliberately subjected to savage ordeals designed to break its spirit.

Brutal work it is [he wrote in his journal]. But time cannot be devoted to gentler methods, which would produce a more tractable animal, and Western men are wedded to their ways. The poor brute, having first been caught around the neck, nearly chokes himself in his efforts to break loose, while he plunges ineffectually. A second lariat takes the fore legs from under him, and down he comes. A cowboy sits on his head, while another brings all four feet together with the lariat, secures them, and a stout halter is slipped over his head, when the rough process miscalled "gentling" begins. The bronco is not naturally vicious, but terror makes him use teeth and hoofs in a dangerous fashion to those who are not accustomed to his little ways. The best hands use a species of magnetic influence, making passes and fixing the eye with their own, until the hand is allowed to play about the nostril and head and gradually over the neck. As long as you hold the bronco's eye and don't lose your self-confidence, you are all right. But all men have not this mesmeric power, and those who have not had better keep clear. The poor animal is kept tied in the corral, he will not touch hay, nor will he drink out of a vessel. Twenty-four hours tame him somewhat, but he has to be thrown again before he can be saddled and bridled. The bronco-buster jumps on his back, and he is let go.

But he does not want to go, and commences the buck furious and prolonged, with all its variations of rearing and sometimes lying down to try and roll over his rider, who is off and on again and again. It is a case of which will tire first. Generally the horse gives in and breaks into a gallop across the prairie. Whip and spur are plied and the poor animal comes back tired out, which passes for tamed. With some, the process has to be oft repeated—

The half-broken ponies that the cowboys rode quickly learned the tricks required of them, in bracing to take the shock of a roped steer, for example; but for all that Jingo felt they fell far short of what a properly trained animal was capable of if more pains were taken with it. To prove his point, he undertook to train a fine-looking horse, given up as incorrigible by the foreman. Jingo worked gently and patiently on the beautiful chestnut, which he christened "Sunbeam," and at the end of a week he had produced a splendid mount which became his own favourite charger in the years to come.

These were intensely busy times for Jingo, as rewarding and fulfilling as any he had ever known. He thrived on the hard but healthy outdoor life, living with his cowboys in their mud-floored bunkhouse, sharing their work and pleasures as well as their simple food. He dressed like them, too, in spurred boots, wide leather chaps, fringed buckskin jacket, and broadbrimmed felt hat, but there was no mistaking him for just another anonymous ranch hand. With his bushy black beard and cavalryman's bearing, so at odds with the casual crouch of the mounted westerner, he was always a distinctive figure, and never more so than when he rode into the muddy shacktown sprouting up around Fort Calgary. To the merchants and street loungers there he was soon a familiar figure, affectionately known as "Cowboy Tom," and as notable for his great physical strength as for his precise English accent, so distinctive among the flat midwestern tones of most Calgarians.

But it was what he said, as well as how he said it, that put him in a class by himself. Years of campaigning with hard-bitten soldiery in foreign parts and coping with the perversities of refractory gun teams, stubborn mules, and obdurate elephants, had left him with a fund of colourful language that was the admiration of all. His cowhands could only shake their heads in rueful wonder at their boss's command of classic cursing, whenever he had recourse to it in some particularly vexing contretemps. Long, sonorous, more often humorous than profane, reflecting both a vivid imagination and long experience of human suffering, these verbal explosions both eased Jingo's burden of irritation and provided interest and entertainment to everyone within earshot. On at least one occasion they helped extricate him from a difficult situation.

The story is best told by Jingo himself, as recorded in his journal.

In crossing the Milk River from the United States for the first time, I was driving a wagon and four-horse team. We had passed no water during the day, and my leaders stopped dead to drink, the wheelers, equally eager, got their forefeet over the swingletrees of the leaders. I was in a fix. A man on the opposite side shouted: "Howld on, kurnel, and oi'll be wid yez." He threw off his buckskin shirt and schapps [sic] and waded into the river, which was waist deep and running swiftly with chunks of ice in it. He quieted the leaders, unhooked and rehooked the traces, and shouted "Let 'em go, and welt the divil out of 'em, Kurnel. Oi'll jump up behind."

With a rush and a scramble they were through the river and up the opposite bank. I thanked my timely friend, and said; "You seem to know me, but I can't remember where I have met you."

"Know yez, is it, bedad? Sure, Oi knew yer voice from the other side of the river! Ye was shoutin' and swearin' at them horses, just loike ye'd do at us on parade, and ye ought to remember me, for, by the same token, ye gave me more solitary confinement on bread and water than Oil ever want again; but Oi don't begrudge yez, 'twas the best thing for me. Tip us your fist, Kurnel, for old toimes, and god be wid the days Oi spint in 'B' Battery."

Jingo goes on to say how he heartily responded, but cannot resist working in a little homily on discipline.

> I was only too glad to grip the honest hand of an old soldier, whose only fault was drink. Soldiers never resent just punishment from an officer they know. Bad discipline nowadays exists where officers don't live among their men, and are not known to them.

Even as the first buildings of the new ranch were completed, plans were under way for the greater ranch house which would replace them. From the beginning, Jingo had envisioned a comfortable home for his family, larger and more permanent than any of the log structures which were beginning to appear on the Alberta plains, as other newcomers arrived to try their luck at ranching. During his first winter on the banks of the Bow River, he devoted the long nights to drawing up plans for the new ranch house, and in the spring he sent the measurements and specifications for the lumber required, together with those for all the doors and windows, to a newly established lumber mill in Winnipeg.

All this material, already cut to size, arrived during the second winter, drawn by teams of oxen across the frozen prairie. At the same time, Harry Strange, Jingo's elder son, arrived from the east with four other young men, sons of the officers who had bought shares in the ranch company, and this eager if inexperienced work force began the business of assembling the ranch house components under the direction of Jingo. All summer they worked hard, for the building season was short. As it was, they were still working on the uncompleted roof when the first winter frosts arrived. Then Jingo found himself sitting on the rafters "hammering shingle nails, in cold so intense that mercury froze in the thermometer and four reflected suns shone in the hazy sky."

But when it was completed, the new house more than merited the work and hardship expended on it; nothing like it had been seen on the western ranges before. There were proper stone foundations enclosing an excavated cellar, and a supporting sill of squared logs. Two-inch planks stood upright in grooves cut into the sills, covered with tarred paper and clapboard outside, and with an airspace sealed with paper and enclosed by tongue-and-groove panelling inside. There were two storeys and an attic, with ten rooms and a covered annex. When completed, the whole house was painted a pale terra-cotta. As soon as the spring temperature rose above the freezing level, Mrs. Strange and her three daughters arrived from Ontario and moved into their new home.

But the difficulties in building the house were as nothing to those involved in sinking a well. It proved to be a deep one, and dangerous too. A landslip nearly filled in the first shaft; fortunately no one was in it at the time. Jingo and his son Harry eventually had to dig out the debris and complete the equally dangerous work of lining the walls of the well with stone, brought to the site from the riverbanks. Jingo considered the well a greater accomplishment than the house.

A henhouse was dug into a bank behind the main building, and root houses, sunk six feet into the ground to escape winter frosts, were completed for the storage of potatoes and other vegetables. These, it was hoped, would be grown in the new-fenced kitchen garden, ploughed and planted in the hard prairie soil with the assistance of four half-broken broncos hitched, for the first time, to a plough.

When it was complete, the new establishment was given a name. Jingo chose "Strangmuir," but Mrs. Strange and her daughters always called it "Nomoka."

In addition to the family the house accommodated a governess for the girls and an Irish cook. There were frequent guests, for Jingo kept open house in the hospitable western manner; among them, none more familiar than Crowfoot, chief of the Blackfoot nation.

The Blackfoot braves are tall and handsome [Jingo noted]. Their flowing blanket costume added to their apparent height. They have not the muscular development of a white man, as they have never worked, and their buffalo hunting was done on horseback. Their aquiline beardless faces show intelligence, and their bearing is dignified and gentlemanly. The hair is left long and tangled, and only feathered upon the warpath. Crowfoot, their chief, was like a dark Duke of Wellington in feature, and he had something of the level-headedness and shrewdness of the Iron Warrior. He had the wisdom from the first to see that the true interests of his people lay in friendliness to the white man...

When my family came up to reside in the terra-cotta coloured mansion, "Strangmuir," we were often surprised by uninvited guests. The moccasined feet would be across the threshold before a sound was heard, and the Indian would quietly seat himself beside the piano, where the girls were practising, ask for tobacco, light his pipe, and go on smoking placidly, and listening while the governess repeated the "One! Two! Three!" with equal stolidity, though the old warrior beside her had an ominous disc of parchment attached to his costume, from which still hung the now scanty tuft of a pale scalp-lock.

Crowfoot and Old Sun [the second chief] were our most frequent visitors. They would sit in the long room, which was schoolroom and dininghall, until dinner came up… Crowfoot's table manners were those of the gentleman he was. He would gulp down gallons of hot tea, and then cool himself off with the fan provided by one of the ladies of the house… Indians whose rank did not entitle them to enter, uninvited, the house of the "White Chief with One Eye Open" (the eyeglass!) would have to content themselves peering in at the windows of the lower storey…

Much as he enjoyed their company, Jingo had mixed feelings about his neighbours. He held the chiefs, especially old Crowfoot, in the highest regard. Ever a keen linguist, he had mastered the patois common to the plains tribes and was able to converse with them on easy terms, and to appreciate the old chief's shrewd understanding of his tribe's changing circumstances. Crowfoot had come to accept the passing of the nomadic era, when his tribe lived by hunting the herds of bison, but his influence, particularly over his more restless young warriors, was limited. The tribal organization among the plains wanderers had always been of the loosest sort, with authority, such as it was, being exercised by a chief simply by the force of his own personality, and by his prowess in the hunt or in war. With the disappearance of the buffalo, brought about by the introduction of the repeating rifle, and the suppression of tribal warfare by the new Mounted Police, the chief's control over his fractious young men became very tenuous indeed, and Jingo was soon made aware of the consequences.

Government policy at the time was to establish each of the tribes on a reservation, as close as possible to its traditional hunting grounds, and to persuade them to become self-sustaining subsistence farmers. In the meantime they were fed and provided with all other supplies by government agents assigned to each tribe. In Ottawa, it seemed a practical solution to the problem of freeing the prairies of the large bands of armed warriors, accustomed to roam at will over vast tracts of land, and make the West safe for settlement by unarmed farmers.

But in Indian country the short-sightedness of official policy was clearly evident. It was absurd to believe that the native people, born to hunt and fight as a way of life, could become farmers overnight; their long-held traditions were not to be changed by mere government edict. Confined to their reservations, the tribes set their women to do whatever crop-raising was required of them, while the young warriors looked about for other diversions. For the Blackfoot band, an obvious choice was the great number of horses and cattle grazing over the unfenced rangeland of the Military Colonial Ranch just across the river from their reservation, the nearest thing to the buffalo herds they had been accustomed to slaughter.

Jingo both admired and sympathized with the warriors whose primal instincts were stirred. But he was not prepared to sacrifice ranch stock to gratify age-old tribal hunting instincts, and he was forced to act when his horses were stolen and his cattle butchered on what soon became a regular basis. His cowboys patrolled the ranges every day but Sunday, and the Indians, quickly learning of this Sabbath break, made use of it to raid the ranch herds and escape unscathed. Protests to Crowfoot proved unavailing. The old chief regretted the raids, but could do nothing to stop them; his young warriors paid no heed to his cautions.

Jingo and his sons did what they could to fill the Sunday void, and on several occasions were able to head off Indian bands found roaming on the wrong side of the river, but the raids continued. In the dry season they took on a particularly sinister aspect, when the Indians resorted to an old stratagem once used to stampede buffalo herds. They would set fire to the prairie grass when the wind was in the right direction, so that the dense smoke was blown down towards the ranch and masked them as they ran off selected groups of horses and cattle.

These grass fires, covering a wide front and moving with terrifying speed, were the most dangerous and devastating threat that Jingo and his men had to face from their Indian neighbours. Every living person, man, woman, or child, had to help fight the flames, which not only posed a threat to stock and ranch buildings in their path, but left behind them a blackened wasteland unfit to graze animals for months afterwards.

Surveying the smoking ruin of his rangeland after yet another of these outbreaks had been finally quelled, Jingo realized that something drastic would have to be done if the ranch was to survive. South of the border, vigilantes and lynch law would have been invoked to put an end to cattle rustling; here in Canada, he must put his faith in the Mounties and the rule of law.

An old acquaintance from artillery school days, Superintendent Sam Steele, was both encouraging and helpful. Already the most promising of the young officers in the new police force, Steele believed in prompt, firm action to establish the new rules prevailing in the Canadian West, something hitherto unknown among the itinerant tribes. Anxious to establish the security of the pioneer ranches now being established in the territory, he responded to his old friend's request with characteristic vigour. Writing, years later, in his memoirs *Forty Years in Canada*, he recalled:

> I would go with a strong party, remain at the [Strange]
> ranch until sundown, and then surround Old Sun's
> camp and capture the thieves before they could take to
> the woods. On one occasion we sent for the chief and
> the headman, and the General [Strange] and I
> addressed them, urging them to keep their people

honest. No doubt the lectures had good effect, but a nocturnal visit from the redcoats did much more.

When Steele himself was not available, he would send as his deputy a Sergeant Fury to sort things out. Fury, a tall, quiet-mannered man, was a typical exponent of the Mounted Police's methods which had tamed the West; be firm, cool, decisive. The scarlet tunic, with all the storied might of the British Empire behind it, could be counted on to overawe mere numbers in any confrontation; go in, get the job done, and get out with the minimum of fuss. It was the traditional Mountie way, and Jingo was an awed spectator of just how well it worked.

Riding into the Blackfoot camp on a buckboard, Strange identified his missing horses, which the sergeant secured to the rear of the wagon, and the man who had taken them was pointed out in the group of Indians now crowding about. When this unfortunate, one Dried String Meat, pulled a knife and resisted arrest, Sergeant Fury spun him to the ground, snapped handcuffs on him behind his back, and marched him to a seat on the buckboard. He then took the reins, knocked aside a tall warrior who attempted to seize the horses' heads and another who slashed at him with a knife, and drove calmly away. Having stowed his prisoner safely in custody, he then returned to the encampment and came back with the astounded pair of warriors who had interfered with his previous arrests. All three were duly charged and paraded before a magistrate in the Calgary courthouse.

It was a superb display of how the tiny police presence, with a mixture of bravery and bluff, was able to enforce the law across the enormous expanses of the western prairie, and Jingo was vastly impressed. He was less so when he appeared to give evidence, to find that an indulgent magistrate had declared the prisoners: "Not guilty, but don't do it again!" and then ordered the horsethief to give Jingo "the kiss of peace," which the "smirking rascal" was happy to do before a furious Jingo could defend himself.

The conflicting approaches to the enforcement of law between police and magistrates was typical of the vacillations of government policy towards native Indians, which alternated between rigid repression and fawning indulgence. Like every other rancher in the West, Jingo believed justice must be simple and firmly enforced, if it was to be understood and respected by Indians accustomed to revere strength and despise weakness. The Christian virtue of mercy was regarded as mere weakness by these warriors, and scorned accordingly; indulgent courts only earned their contempt.

What did earn the respect of the most restless and free-spirited among them was the appearance and character of the redoubtable trio who sought to establish the rule of law in southern Alberta territory: the giant, barrel-chested Steele; the tall, black-bearded Strange, glaring through his monocle; and the dynamic, fearless Fury. Steele, Strange, and Fury—as historian Robert Stewart would later ask, could any trio have been more aptly named?

Beyond the increasing native indifference to the law, there was a more deep-seated problem concerning government policy toward the Indians in the West. Jingo was convinced that Ottawa's attempt to make farmers out of wandering tribes accustomed for thousands of years to hunting as a way of life had no hope of success. The tradition of countless generations could not be ignored; it was folly to assume, as Ottawa seemed to do, that warriors with scalplocks still dangling from their belts could settle down to the drudgery of crop-raising farmers.

To Jingo, the obvious solution was to convert these nations of horsemen into ranchers; the cowboy life appealed to the prairie nomads and offered them a stake in the development of ideal rangeland. He urged the government to grant them the grassland and breeding stock needed to begin tribal ranches, but his urging fell on deaf ears. In faraway Ottawa, bureaucrats dozed on, while on the plains, young warriors, starved for interest and excitement, grew increasingly restless, and tensions between white settlers and Indian tribesmen steadily worsened.

TWELVE

Massacre!

Talking together in low voices as they trudged along the rutted snow of the road, a straggling group of some fifty men approached the little store on the outskirts of the village. Their leaders, a pale-faced man with a heavy moustache and a tall, burly figure, dark-faced above a grizzled beard, pushed open the shop door labelled "Walters and Baker" and went in, followed by about a dozen or so of the others, which was all the store could accommodate. The remainder milled about outside.

In the shop, Walters himself, startled and indignant at the sudden invasion, confronted the crowd from behind his counter. An assistant, brushing crumbs from his mouth, emerged from a back room and stood beside him, gaping in surprise and apprehension.

"Well, gentlemen, it has commenced!" said the pale-faced leader, moving briskly to the counter.

"What has commenced?" asked the shopkeeper.

"Oh, this movement for the rights of the country," was the response. "We want all the guns and ammunition in your shop for our people."

Walters made a grab for a rifle hanging unloaded on the wall behind him, but was instantly seized and made prisoner, along with his clerk, while the intruders began the systematic looting of all the arms and clothing in the shop and the storeroom behind.

It was Wednesday, March 18, 1885, in the village of Batoche, Northwest Territories, and Louis Riel, with Gabriel Dumont at his side, had begun an uprising of the Métis which was to shake Canada to its foundations.

It came as no surprise. For months the Métis of the Canadian Northwest, the offspring of generations of intermarriage between French-Canadian voyageurs and native women, had been petitioning Ottawa regarding the status of their homesteads, clustered, habitant fashion, in narrow strips along the banks of western rivers. Surveyors for the railroad and for the new large holdings of a wave of European immigrants were paying scant regard to the boundaries of old Métis settlements, arousing fear among the Métis that they were to be summarily dispossessed. Similar fears had led to an earlier uprising in Manitoba in 1869-70, when for a few brief months the Métis had established their own nation around Fort Garry under Louis Riel. After the murder of a dissenting settler, Thomas Scott, the rebellion had been quashed and Riel took sanctuary in the United States, but the outbreak had helped Manitoba's Métis secure recognition of their lands and other rights. Now Métis in the remaining Northwest Territories wanted similar security, and when the Canadian government failed to grant it they turned, once again, to Riel.

Now in his early forties, Riel had been born in Saint Boniface, son of a Scandinavian father and a mother of mixed Irish and native ancestry. Educated, eloquent, and intelligent, he was a forceful advocate of native Indian and Métis rights, but was emotionally unstable and mentally unbalanced; some of his time in the United States had been spent in mental institutions. Smuggled back across the border by his Canadian sympathizers, he soon organized the dissident Métis into a coherent group which in the fall of

1884 sent a petition to the Canadian government setting out their concerns and asking for clarification of their status. Titled "A Bill of Rights," the tone throughout was modest and restrained, but it met with contempt in Ottawa. No action of any sort was taken to allay the Métis' concerns, and armed rebellion, as in Manitoba, seemed the only way to attract the government's attention.

A curious aspect of Riel's subsequent behaviour was the conflict between two sides of his nature. To the native people he was an idealist, advocating the extermination of all whites in order to establish a Métis state governed by the Bishop of Montreal as a Canadian Pope. Yet he dealt with the government on monetary terms, threatening to sell the Territories to the United States and offering to quit the rebellion in return for a cash payment or pension for himself.

Whatever the true nature of his interest, he had enough sense to recognize ability when he saw it, and to make Gabriel Dumont, a Métis buffalo hunter and a born organizer and military tactician, his lieutenant and leader in the field. He declared himself leader of a new provisional government of the Northwest Territories, with Dumont as his adjutant-general.

The move came as no surprise to the Mounted Police. On the very day that the Métis government was announced, Commissioner Irvine set out from Regina for Prince Albert with ninety men. Despite severe winter conditions that brought snow blindness and frostbite to some of the group, Irvine's column covered the 300 miles in six days, a remarkable accomplishment even for a body of men accustomed to moving at speed across difficult country.

In the north, however, Superintendent Crozier could not afford to await the arrival of these reinforcements. When a small police party, sent to parley with the rebels, was rebuffed, he instantly recognized that the situation could only be resolved by force. A courageous, thrusting leader who had outfaced threatening groups of native people several times before, he collected every available man in Prince Albert—fifty-two police and forty-three civilian volunteers—and set off for Duck Lake near Batoche. It was his intention to seize the arms and supplies from the store there and deny them to the rebels; but after being caught in open country and beguiled by a false rebel parley, he was ambushed by a large Métis force and forced to retire. Twelve men were killed—nine of them volunteers on an exposed right flank—and seven wounded. Nevertheless, the police managed to wound Gabriel Dumont and to kill his brother, Isidore, and four other rebels. The civilian volunteers killed included young men from every province in Canada, a circumstance calculated to arouse a country-wide response.

Bloody defeat though it was, Duck Lake had at least been a skirmish fought along conventional European lines; the dead were not mutilated, and were allowed to be borne off for proper burial. What settlers in the West were dreading was not a battle with the Métis, but an Indian uprising with all its horrors, and a week later it came.

At Frog Lake, in the Moose Hills north of Battleford, Big Bear's band of Plains Crees pillaged and burned the small settlement, massacred nine unarmed civilians with all the traditional accompanying horrors of scalping and mutilation, and carried off women and children as captives. Everywhere settlers on isolated farms or in the tiny shacktown settlements looked apprehensively at the large bands of Indians encamped nearby.

No one looked more closely than Jingo. As proprietor of the largest ranch in the area and the principal employer in the Calgary region, he felt himself responsible for the safety of dozens of men, women, and children, in addition to his own family. With thousands of head of stock on its unfenced rangeland, he knew that the ranch would be a prime target for any native warband, and its big ranch house ripe for pillage. He jotted down on a piece of paper his estimates of native strength in the district, in order to form some idea of what he and his cowboys might be up against, should the nightmare of tribal warfare spread southwards.

There were, he figured, something over 9,000 Indians in the area, exclusive of Métis, and of this total some 2,500 were young warriors mounted on good horses and armed with rifles, including the deadly Winchester repeater which had proved so devastating a weapon among the buffalo herds. About 2,150 were the warlike Blackfeet, traditional rulers of the valley, but Jingo felt he could count on the friendship and good sense of their chief, Crowfoot, to keep the tribe on its reservation. Poundmaker, however, a chief of the northern Crees and the most powerful and influential of all the Indians in the territory, was a nephew and close friend of the older Crowfoot. If he went on the warpath, as seemed likely, would he take Crowfoot and his fierce warriors with him? There were more than 400 Sarcees, thought by some to have been the most violent and troublesome of the plains people, and between 2,000 and 3,000 Bloods, the best horsemen of all the tribes. The nearly 900 Piegans had more, and better, horses than any other band and were allied to tribes already reported to be on the warpath further north. More than 2,000 Crees, in three widely scattered bands, were reported to be peacefully settled on their land, along with a small group of Chippewa and Assiniboines.

Unlike the Métis, the western Indians had no particular grievances to settle with the Canadian government, and claimed no major injustices. Some were unhappy with their new reservations. All had just suffered through a particularly severe winter; game had been scarce and when government supplies had been delayed by bad weather some tribes had been reduced to near-starvation, but few blamed Ottawa. The most upsetting factor, especially among the Crees accustomed for years to dealing with Hudson's Bay Company traders whose word had been their bond, was the new breed of white men who had come amongst them. Indian agents, all political patronage appointees and including a large number of Irishmen accustomed to cheerful blarney, had upset the native people's traditional reliance on the white man's word. Too many promises, lightly given, had not been fulfilled. Yet on the whole there were few quarrels between local Indians and government authorities, apart from the frustrations inherent in the abandonment of the old nomadic ways for life on the reservations. What was to be feared was the universal restlessness of the young men; in every tribe the warriors longed for action, for the wild excitement of the raiding war parties which could bring new horses to be ridden, cattle to be eaten, scalps to decorate their belts. Jingo knew at first hand how tenuous was the control exercised over them even by so great and wise a chief as Crowfoot. He knew that any further Indian success in the north must bring real trouble in the Bow valley, and just to the south the border area was alive with renegades, white and native, ready to exploit any breakdown of law and order.

To oppose the formidable numbers of potential enemies, Jingo could count on his own cowboys, all expert horsemen and marksmen, a few scattered families of settlers, and an inspector and four Mounted Police constables in Calgary, all that had been left after Irvine had marched north with every policeman who could be spared. Yet much could still be done to avert trouble, and Jingo was in the process of making plans when a telegram arrived, brought by mounted messenger from Gleichen, thirteen miles away, the nearest station of the Canadian Pacific Railway.

It was from the Hon. Adolphe Caron, an old friend and now Minister of Militia for Canada, and it read: "March 29, 1885. Can you get up corps? Would like to see you to the front again. Trust you as ever. Arms and ammunition will be sent upon a telegram from you." To an old warhorse like Jingo, the appeal was simply irresistible, the high, clear, clarion call of duty. Could he get up a corps? Could a duck swim?

In a matter of minutes, Jingo had his four fastest horses hitched to the buckboard and, with son Harry beside him, was preparing to leave for the drive to Gleichen to telegraph a reply to Ottawa when he was stopped by Jim Christie, his new foreman. Christie, an old soldier who had served in "B" Battery with Strange years before, handed him a list which, he said, bore the names of men wishing to volunteer and serve under him in any defence force he organized. The list included both of Jingo's sons and every man on the ranch. Even in his impatience to be off, Jingo recognized it for what it was: a remarkable testament of personal loyalty and trust in his ability to lead them.

"It's all right, governor; the boys will stick to you. Every man on the ranch is down," Christie told him, and let go the horses' heads.

Jingo, deeply moved, folded the list and put it into his pocket before taking up the reins. As the buckboard moved away, he raised his hat to Christie, standing in the stable-yard, and to the ranch hands crowded by the bunkhouse door, and shouted: "All right, boys! Sergeant Christie, take charge!" Having thus restored his foreman to his former army status, he drove away to the telegraph office.

From Flaherty, the Gleichen stationmaster, he received the latest news from the north, all of it bad. Crozier had abandoned and burned Fort Carlton, which was little more than a trading post and quite indefensible, and was retiring

to Prince Albert, now heavily garrisoned by Irvine's force.
But of greater concern to Jingo was Flaherty's news from
Calgary, where reports that the Blackfeet were about to
attack the town were causing widespread panic. It was
obvious that Jingo's first move in organizing the defence of
the area must be to establish calm and confidence among
the Calgary citizenry, and so he arranged to wait for the
morning train to the west, while sending Harry back to the
ranch with the buckboard.

Sitting in the little waiting room, Jingo began to make his
plans. His first priority would be to stabilize the situation in
the immediate area, to ensure the safety of the settlers and
the livestock of the ranchers. Horses and cattle were scarce
among the northern rebels, and great care would have to be
taken to prevent these animals in the south from being stolen
by Indians from nearby reservations and sent to the aid of
rebellious tribes to the north. His first efforts therefore must
be devoted to raising a force for local defence; once that was
established, a second force could be organized for operations in the field against the rebels.

While he was pondering these plans, a telegram arrived
for him from Caron in Ottawa, directing him to proceed
with the mounted corps he had told Caron he would raise,
to Fort Qu'Appelle, east of Regina on the CPR. There he
was to report to General Middleton, the officer commanding the Canadian Militia. This was, of course, none other
than the officer with whom Jingo had served in India, and
who had assisted him in the attempt to blow in the gate of
the fort at Moonshee Gunj. Now grown portly and pom-
pous, as befitted his rank and station, he had been rooted
out of his comfortable Ottawa office and sent back into the
field in command of operations against the rebels. A careful, not to say cautious, commander, he was an experienced
and competent professional soldier directing an army of
willing but untrained amateurs, and he was not especially

happy about it. But he was an able strategist and had prepared an excellent plan of campaign. Whether he was also an able and resourceful commander in the field, capable of coping with so shadowy and elusive a force as the Métis woodsmen under the wily Gabriel Dumont, remained to be seen.

Before leaving on the early morning train for Calgary, Jingo telegraphed Caron, explaining his situation: no corps had yet been raised, and there were as yet neither arms nor ammunition available, but plans were under way to provide a defence force to protect and stabilize the area and a field force to campaign against the northern rebels. He also dashed off a letter to Middleton, already at Fort Qu'Appelle with a considerable force, which he hoped soon to increase to more than 2,000 horse and foot, supported by guns. His weaponry was to include a Gatling gun, the wonder weapon of the age. This was a multibarrelled affair turned by a crank, giving a high, sustained rate of fire, and thus the first primitive machine gun.

The telegrams and letters sent and received from the little Gleichen railway station were to become a flood in the next few days, as Ottawa sent directions to its commanders in the field and they in turn communicated with one another and made their needs and progress known to their remote government superiors.

Middleton had acted with admirable promptness and decision. He was no mere military mountebank, as some Opposition critics were to maintain, although he had already posed for his official photograph in the uniform he had devised for the campaign. It consisted of a simple tunic, breeches, and forage cap, setting off his walrus moustache and comfortable paunch, for he was striving to play down the tendency of militia officers to overdress in "too much fuss and feathers."

Middleton's plan of campaign, which he quickly communicated to Jingo, was simple and direct. Troops were to be moved from the east to the Lakehead by rail. The hundred-mile gap from there to Winnipeg would be covered on foot or by sleigh as weather and circumstance allowed. The troops would include both batteries of regular artillery from Quebec City and Kingston, along with the regulars from the military training schools, but the bulk of both infantry and cavalry would consist of militia regiments. These varied widely in efficiency and equipment. Some Toronto regiments were wealthy enough to purchase the weaponry and accoutrements denied them by a niggardly government policy. For political purposes, it was considered important that French-Canadian units be included, although the government had grave doubts about how well French-speaking soldiers would fight against French-speaking rebels.

Once arrived in the West—and already 350 of them were with him, Middleton told Jingo—these raw soldiers, with a slim stiffening of professionals, would be divided into two columns. The first, under Middleton himself, would head northwest to Batoche, the seat of the Métis rebellion, from Fort Qu'Appelle. A second column, under the command of Lieutenant-Colonel William Otter, a competent and energetic officer whose regiment, the Toronto-based Queen's Own Rifles of Canada, was one of the most effective militia units, would head straight north for Battleford from its rail base at Swift Current. A third force, commanded by Major-General Thomas Bland Strange—for Cowboy Tom had now been restored to full military status—was to establish a base at Calgary and relieve the panic at Edmonton. After that, it would campaign in the northern wilderness in pursuit of Big Bear, both to bring him to book for the massacre at Frog Lake and to liberate the prisoners he had carried off with him. All the soldiers, with their arms, ammunition, and supplies, were to be sent to the first two columns, the ones despatched from the east. The third column would have to be raised, trained, and outfitted on the spot, and strengthened by anything that could be spared from the other two.

Few soldiers in their right mind would have taken on such a thankless task. Jingo would have to give up his British Army pension for the period of his employment by the Canadian government—in the event, he lost it for a period of three years—and organize, recruit, arm, equip, and train a sort of private army, with the minimum of outside assistance and with only the meagre resources of a frontier area to draw on. He would then have to transport this force into unmapped wilderness, defeat and capture the rebellion's fiercest warband, and liberate its prisoners, which included women and children. It was a task to daunt the stoutest heart, an impossible request to make of a retired, middle-aged soldier, and Jingo accepted it with relish. He could hardly wait to begin, and he sat up all night in the station and on the train to Calgary, setting his plans in order.

As events were to prove, he was the ideal man for the job; there can have been few officers in the country better suited by character and experience for so unusual and demanding a task. Since his first days in Canada, as commander of a non-existent force, he had been accustomed to scraping together necessary equipment, and recruiting needed people, from the unlikeliest quarters, always dependent on his own resources and with the minimum of assistance from indifferent officialdom. He had already shown a positive genius for working with relatively small numbers of men, organizing and imbuing them with his own aggressive outlook. But here on the remote prairie, far from any city or town, there were even fewer possible sources of supply and suitable men were both few and very far between. This was to be a job that would test even Jingo to his very limits.

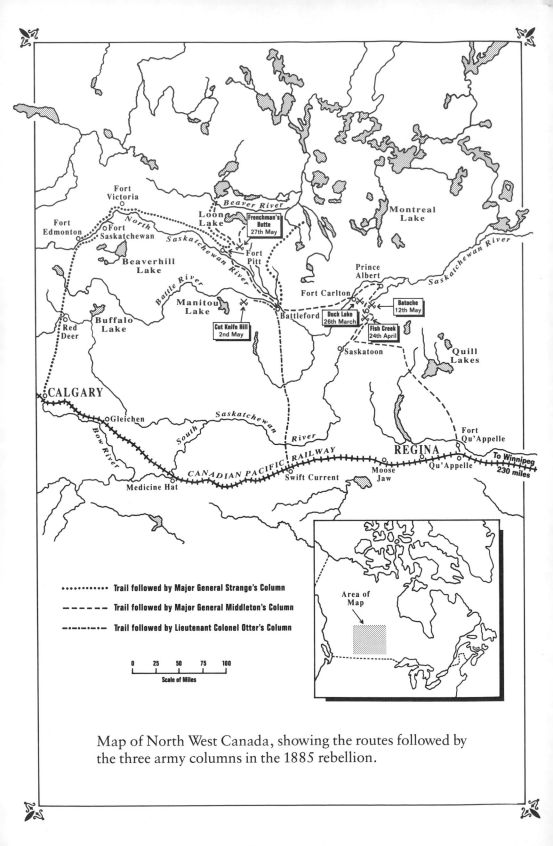

Map of North West Canada, showing the routes followed by the three army columns in the 1885 rebellion.

THIRTEEN

The Buckskin Brigadier

T he party was, in its rustic way, reminiscent of the Duchess of Richmond's famous Brussels ball on the eve of Waterloo. Just as the festivity was at its height and everyone was enjoying the music and dancing, the sound of distant gunfire interrupted the merriment. Not the cannon at Quatre Bras this time, but a fusillade of rifle shots, far off but clearly heard. Like the duchess before her, Mrs. Strange professed not to hear them. She had half expected some such occurrence, ever since Jim Christie, hat in hand, had invited her and her daughters to an impromptu dance gotten up, he explained, for the ladies and gentlemen of the district by the ranch hands eager to repay past hospitality.

Shortly after Jingo's departure for Gleichen, Christie had noticed a band of Indians, without women or baggage, encamped in nearby scrubland. Fearing a raid on cattle or ranch house, he wished to put the place in a state of defence without alarming the womenfolk. The dance in the big bunkhouse had been his idea. Mrs. Strange suspected what was afoot but cheerfully fell in with it. Once she and her daughters were clear of the building, Christie had half a dozen loopholes knocked through the cellar foundations, and sent patrols to ride herd on the stock throughout the night. He had been correct in his suspicions. The Indians attempted to drive off some horses, but were interrupted by a couple of cowboys and driven off after an exchange of gunfire. In a later raid thirteen horses were driven into a slough and smothered to death but, overall, Christie's prompt response was successful in deterring Indian raids on ranch stock. Only about forty head were lost to such incursions throughout the period of the rebellion.

In Calgary, meanwhile, Jingo was having a very rough time of it. The town's mayor, alarmed by the departure of the usual Mounted Police contingent and fearful lest the young men of the place should be lured off to fight rebels away to the north, leaving the inhabitants defenceless, had actively campaigned against any government recruitment attempts. Jingo encountered a hostile atmosphere, made even worse by a letter from the Lieutenant-Governor of the Northwest Territories assuring Calgarians that they would be left to defend their homes. His Honour, Edgar Dewdney, was a kindly, well-intentioned man caught up in a whirlwind of events that were quite beyond him. A political appointee, like every western official, he was entirely a creature of the federal government, and seems never to have understood his role as the Queen's representative and Commissioner of the Northwest Territories, and thus the embodiment of state power in the land.

Attempting to recruit men for his force, Jingo found himself actively opposed and frustrated at every turn. His characteristic response was to call a town meeting, attended by virtually the entire adult population, which he addressed himself.

Never, by any stretch of the imagination, an orator, Jingo dominated the proceedings by sheer force of character, his eyes blazing above his black beard. Adding emphasis to his broken sentences by suitable gestures, he stressed again and again that the defence of Calgary and its surrounding ranchland was to be the first priority of the force he was raising.

Only when the safety of the region was assured and troops were on their way from the east to garrison the town, would men be sent north to strengthen Edmonton and bring Big Bear to book.

For all his lack of eloquence, he was a success. He left his audience in no doubt as to what his priorities were, and they left convinced that enrolment in the new force would not jeopardize the safety of the region. Recruitment henceforth was brisk, opposed only by the mayor and a few diehard councillors. Recruits included young men—virtually all the men in these new territories were young—of every sort, from Englishmen of good family to feckless drifters, from patriotic idealists to paupers looking for army wages, board, and bed. Most were cowboys out of a job, who had sold horses and saddles to raise money. Perhaps the most unexpected were a number of American citizens, mostly unemployed Montana cowhands looking for adventure, who cheerfully took the oath of allegiance to the British Crown and promised to serve Queen Victoria well and faithfully.

Day by day, enrolment in the Alberta Mounted Rifles, as the unit was called, grew swiftly, as word of its purpose was spread abroad. Some of the men applying were expert horsemen and marksmen; these were mostly assigned to what Jingo had called his scouts, for already he envisaged a cavalry arm of light horse to scout ahead of his mounted column. The bulk of the applicants, whatever their calling, had had some acquaintance with horses, the standard mode of transport in the region, but few in the orderly Canadian West were familiar with guns—unlike their American counterparts.

In a remarkably short time Jingo had the men he wanted. Now his concern was to supply them with horses, saddles, and weapons, for the Alberta Mounted Rifles had neither mounts nor rifles.

In the days that followed Jingo fought to arm and equip his tiny force, wrestling not only with local authority—or lack of it—but with bureaucrats in Ottawa 2,000 miles away. To enrol the services of an ex-policeman, for example, required clearance from no fewer than four separate Ottawa departments. Telegrams from Ottawa or from Middleton discussing strategic moves were sometimes sent in plain language and quickly became common knowledge throughout the area, while others of no consequence were sent in code, which could not always be deciphered.

Arms were promised, then refused; again promised, they did not arrive. Middleton urged haste, delayed reinforcements. Caron promised, then procrastinated. Dewdney wrung his hands, helpless and hopeless and fomented trouble among white settlers, some of whom proposed to join the rebellion. Station master Flaherty threatened to abandon Gleichen if the station was not garrisoned. Citizens of Edmonton telegraphed for immediate assistance. Everywhere, it seemed, help was urgently wanted, but nowhere was help available. All news seemed bad, as Jingo noted in his journal:

> I had authentic information that the Indians had destroyed farms, plundered the Hudson's Bay stores, Indian Department officials and missionaries at Bear Hills, Battle River, Peace Hills, and Beaver Lake, and I received messages from all these quarters imploring assistance.

Even more frustrating than the attitudes of government ministers in faraway Ottawa was the obstruction and ineptitude, as Jingo saw it, of pettifogging officialdom closer at hand. Perhaps a single telegram to Ottawa about such an instance may serve as typical of the many.

To the Hon. Minister of Customs, Ottawa.
May 19, 1885.
Sir,
I have the honour to bring to your notice the conduct
of some of your officials in Winnipeg in delaying the
transmission of a supply of saddles urgently required
by the Cavalry under my command, by declining to
forward them to Calgary on the grounds that I was not
authorized to order supplies for the Government.

In the first place, I submit they might have been sent
to Calgary in bond.

In the second place, military equipment for the
Government should not have been charged duty.

The action of your subordinate has seriously
crippled my advance, which has been delayed waiting
for saddles, not anticipating such monstrous conduct
on the part of an official employed by the
Government, at a crisis like the present.

Such an individual is evidently unfit to occupy the
position he holds.

I have to request the saddles be forwarded
forthwith, if it has not already been done.

I have the honour to be, sir, yr obedient servant,
                T. B. Strange, Major General
                Commanding Alberta Field Force

Strange's characteristic of not mincing words made him
popular with his soldiers, less so with officialdom!

And yet, somehow, order began to emerge from chaos,
usually on the strength of unilateral decisions by Jingo
himself. When local ranchers refused to supply mounts for
his men without advance payment, Jingo supplied the necessary horses from his Military Colonial Ranch. When
saddles were not forthcoming from the east, he arranged for

them to be made by a local saddler, Cottingham's in Calgary, working night and day. When a large supply of ammunition arrived at Gleichen, Jingo was thunderstruck to find
it was consigned to a local Métis trader, for sale to Indians,
while his own force was still without. Ottawa would do
nothing, Dewdney could do nothing, so Jingo simply seized
the consignment, along with all the ammunition in the
trader's store for good measure.

But there was some progress. When the news of the Frog
Lake massacre arrived in Ottawa, a note of emergency could
be detected in government responses. The first of the long-
promised rifles arrived. The weapons were fifty long-barrelled
Sniders, of little use to mounted men, and the ammunition
was an old condemned batch, but it was a beginning at least.
As Jingo noted grimly in his journal, "There is nothing like a
massacre to stimulate the official mind."

Other assistance resulted from a quirk in another official
mind. Middleton wanted none of the French-Canadian
units foisted on him by careful government ploys; he was not
bilingual, and he distrusted the fighting value of French-
speaking units against French-speaking rebels. Consequently, when the first of the Quebec regiments reached the
West, he passed them on to Jingo's column. Moreover, he
had no patience with untrained units and was thus happy to
pass on to Jingo the raw militiamen of the Winnipeg Light
Infantry recruited only days before from willing youngsters,
fresh from the plough.

But by far the greatest benefit resulted from Middleton's
running feud with the North West Mounted Police, stem-
ming originally from his vain attempts to have the force
placed under his Ottawa department, the Ministry of Militia. Middleton constantly denigrated the force, referring to
them on occasion as "gophers" and accusing them of "hol-
ing up" in Prince Albert instead of taking the field on their

own against Riel. As a result, Jingo was able, after much badgering of numerous Ottawa officials, to have a detachment of twenty-five mounted policemen, together with a rifled nine-pounder field gun, join him from Fort Macleod.

An even greater plum fell into his lap. The man Jingo most wanted, the only person he specifically went after, was Sam Steele, the prodigy he had admired in the days of the gunnery training schools, who was now an inspector in the North West Mounted Police. After much writing and telegraphing, Jingo was able to secure his release from his policing duties with the strike-bound Canadian Pacific Railway and Steele became Jingo's cavalry leader. A born leader of men and an experienced plainsman, he was the new force's single greatest acquisition. He and Jingo hit it off from the beginning, being two of a kind, and they were to work together in closest harmony throughout the campaign.

Steele was as pleased as his commander on joining the force. In his journal for April 1885, he noted: "Gazetted Major in Canadian Militia. Raised a mounted corps which the General did me the honour to name 'Steele's Scouts.' "

The arrival of the Winnipeg Light Infantry, raw but red-coated and therefore invested with all the majesty of the Queen, and of the 65th Quebec Carabiniers (instantly re-named voltigeurs by Jingo) smart in their uniforms of dark green, marked a turning point in civilian attitudes in Calgary, and indeed throughout the region. Gone was the air of panic, the dark intimations of massacres and rapine; here were troops, two regiments of them, sent from the east by a federal government which seemed, at last, aware of the predicament of its western citizens. Few of the redcoats marching so bravely up Calgary's main street could fire the rifles they carried, and the French Canadians might have difficulty keeping in step, but they carried themselves with confidence. The Army had arrived, and now even the mayor raised no objection to Jingo's feverish preparations for the march to the north.

Getting his untrained soldiers and volunteers licked into some sort of shape, able to march in coherent order and to load, aim, and fire their weapons was his principal preoccupation. For officers, he had a somewhat mixed bag to choose from. George Hatton, his old ranch foreman, was appointed to command a new militia unit, the Alberta Mounted Rifles. He was fortunate to find a number of former gunner NCOs to assist and a sprinkling of officer graduates from the Royal Military College and from the military training schools he had run, as well as a few ex-Imperial Army officers. Some of these could be a trial at times. One, whom he had made his brigade major, constantly inveighed against the standard of drill of militiamen in general and French Canadians in particular; it required all Jingo's tact to point out that what the voltigeurs might lack in parade-square precision they more than made up for in their skill with axe and spade, skill they were to demonstrate time and again on the long march ahead.

To stabilize his base, Jingo sent garrisons to Gleichen and several other hamlets which considered themselves threatened. He left an effective garrison for the Calgary region under the command of Major Walker, but he never had the slightest fear of any sort of Indian assault upon the town itself. Indian warfare was a matter of individual raid and rapine, of sudden ambush and quick escape; protracted sieges or frontal assaults upon large settlements held no attraction for warriors intent on glory, scalps, and booty. Old Crowfoot had explained the native style of warfare to Jingo long before. However, the dread of towns being torched and their inhabitants butchered still affected civilian thinking in Edmonton, Prince Albert, and Calgary, and had to be borne in mind when arranging troop distributions.

Indeed, throughout Canada there was widespread exaggeration of the magnitude of the threat posed by the rebellion, and of the military effectiveness of Métis and Indians. Once the first troops began to arrive from the east, however inadequately outfitted and trained, and the rebellion failed to spread southwards, its suppression was only a matter of time. Both Indians and Métis fought as individuals, and not even Dumont's tactical genius could consolidate them into a force capable of fighting a pitched battle, let alone undertaking a siege. But the shadow of the Little Big Horn still loomed large in the minds of Canadians, both soldiers and civilians. If the Sioux under Sitting Bull could wipe out an entire troop of United States cavalry, what might the turbulent Cree warriors of Big Bear not do?

It was at this point that some well-wisher sent Jingo a book describing the bloody demise of the Seventh United States Cavalry, which led him to promise, over and over, never "to commit Custer." That general's impetuous attack on a Sioux encampment, without any prior reconnaissance to establish the strength of the native warband, had led to his encirclement and massacre. Jingo did not intend to repeat the mistake.

At their camp on the outskirts of Calgary, his little army was taking shape, as militiamen and local volunteers spent long hours on the rifle ranges Jingo had extemporized. There were sessions of "square bashing," too, on the grassy parade ground, but the emphasis was more on the learning of formations and the handling of weapons than on mere parade precision. Jingo wanted a force that could quickly form a column and march, and even more quickly be deployed into skirmishing line and open fire. His youngsters might lack the drill-square precision of the Brigade of Guards, but they were willing to learn and eager for battle. Weapons and equipment continued in short supply. When the long-promised shipment of rifles and ammunition from the east still failed to arrive, Jingo telegraphed Ottawa threatening to disband his force unless arms were shipped immediately. It was this last gesture that finally brought response; rifles and ammunition for his men arrived at last. Their issue gave the little army a sense of pride and purpose; each man now had his own weapon and felt capable of using it effectively.

The French-speaking Catholics of the voltigeurs and the Protestant farmboys of the light infantry had managed to get along together without any of the frictions anticipated by Middleton. Jingo himself, with the assistance of several of his bilingual former gunners from "B" Battery days, saw to it that both units received equal treatment, and a healthy rivalry on the ranges and parade square soon developed. The original commanding officer of the voltigeurs, Lieutenant-Colonel J. A. Ouimet, a Quebec MP, no sooner arrived with his men than he sought Jingo's permission to depart. He was needed, he said, in the House at Ottawa. He was also very ill, he assured Jingo, and in any case he would be more useful back east where he could hurry up needed supplies. Such a disheartened and disheartening officer could only prove harmful in the tough campaigning that lay ahead, and Jingo was glad to give him leave to depart. Having arrived on one train, the reluctant colonel therefore was able to leave on the next one without ever having quit the safety of the railroad station. A furious Caron however, shipped him back west, where he was installed as base command officer in Edmonton and did much useful work in expediting men and supplies to the little army in the field.

Discipline in the growing force was always a concern, especially as Jingo's own military status was not officially defined. It was essential that the power to punish when required be given him, and that this authority be extended over all militia soldiers, ranch hands, and mounted policemen in his complex little army. Dewdney was of no help, and Ottawa was too remote to appreciate the problem. It was only when a drunken constable threatened to shoot the officer of the guard that matters came to a head, and Caron wired Jingo: "Every man on active service must be under military discipline. You will be supported." It was all that was needed. Jingo and his old soldiers soon had matters under control, and militiamen, cowboys, and constables began serving a common purpose under a common discipline.

As the force rapidly took shape, transport for the campaign became the next concern. None was available, and none, Jingo soon learned, would be supplied from official sources. Left to his own initiative, he resolved the problem in his usual forthright manner.

An energetic Sergeant H. Hamilton of the NWMP was appointed supply officer, and armed with Jingo's authority, he scoured the neighbourhood for anything on wheels. A number of two-wheeled carts, left over from government survey operations, were appropriated, and then an intensive campaign was launched to recruit both district farmers and their wagons, for the vehicles would be better looked after by their owners than by any hired carter. Wages would have to be high to compensate the farmer for the loss of a crop, but the need was urgent. By paying from five to eight dollars a day for wagon and driver, all found, Jingo was quickly able to get his column mobile, thus resolving what had appeared to be an insuperable problem.

Clothing needs were not so pressing as anticipated. The militia soldiers had arrived with their own changes in addition to the uniforms they wore. The police were completely equipped, and the few needs of the cowboys were quickly filled from Calgary stores. Jingo was unhappy with the scarlet coats of his police constables, however, and wanted something less conspicuous for his scouts who, as his column's eyes and ears, would have to be able to shadow the enemy while remaining unseen. Accordingly, they wore brown canvas campaign jackets for the duration of their army service. The cowhands who formed the remainder of the scouts were similarly outfitted. Only Steele, as their commander, remained resplendent in red coat and white helmet; he drew enemy fire like a magnet, but was completely oblivious to it and led a charmed life.

Jingo's major change in the appearance of his men concerned their headgear. The little braided pillbox caps of the two militia regiments, however smart on parade, were supremely impractical in the field. Jingo had every soldier issued with a wide-brimmed soft felt hat, traditional western cowboy wear, which provided shade for the eyes and protection from the rain, and could be rolled up and used as a pillow at night. To impart a distinctive appearance, he had them worn rolled up on one side and pinned with the regimental button, in the fashion of the Bersaglieri,the famous Italian light infantry regiment. When the Alberta Field Force paraded as a unit for the first time, marching in review past their commander before taking the field, they did so with a distinctive swing and swagger that betokened the confidence of men who felt themselves part of an effective fighting force. The collection of human odds and ends of only a few days ago had become a coherent military unit, knocked into shape by the concentrated effort of a few old soldiers and given a distinctive *esprit de corps* by their unshakable faith in their unique leader.

From the beginning, they took enormous pride in the colourful figure who led them. Because of the buckskin cowboy jacket he always wore, they called him "the buckskin brigadier," and he was as much their totem as their leader, with his beard, his eyeglass, and his great voice, to say nothing of his vocabulary, for he left no one in doubt as to his opinion of their performance. His own costume was as distinctive as the one he had devised for his men. He had managed to find an old pair of blue police trousers, striped with gold at the sides, which he wore stuffed into the tops of his riding boots, and on formal occasions he substituted a blue frock coat for his usual buckskin jacket. As an indication of rank he wore three twists of gold braid, taken from a NWMP jacket, around his pinned-up cowboy hat; corps commanders wore two twists, and captains, one.

Of more importance than the jaunty appearance of the Alberta Field Force were their arms and equipment. Jingo's scouts were armed with the short carbine, ideal for mounted use, and carried a woollen blanket rolled up with a change of clothing behind their saddle. These sixty men, made up of police constables and cowboys and led by the redoubtable Sam Steele, were all tough, experienced horsemen and formed the elite corps of Jingo's little army.

His two regiments of infantry, consisting of 320 men, were now competent riflemen, their old Snider rifles giving them an effective range of about 600 yards.

As an old gunner, Jingo was especially proud of his "artillery," a rifled nine-pounder gun on a wheeled field carriage, complete with limber and a small supply of ammunition, and manned by a special unit of police gunners, all trained at the artillery school at Kingston once commanded by Jingo.

His "transport corps" included 175 wagons, with good horses and driven by their owners. They were to prove both expensive and troublesome, but their assembly was nonetheless something of a minor miracle, and Jingo felt himself fortunate to have obtained them.

He was impatient to be off, but in April, before leaving for the north, he moved his family to Calgary for safety's sake, installing them in a house he had rented. The ranch house and outbuildings, all in a good state of defence, he left in the care of his younger son, Alec, with half a dozen cowboys to keep an eye on the stock. His elder son, Harry, now a Royal

Military College graduate and holder of a militia commission, accompanied him as his aide-de-camp, for Jingo did not intend, as he said himself, to put all the Strange eggs in one basket.

News of a fresh disaster from the north spurred final arrangements for departure. On April 15, at Fort Pitt, another of the indefensible, poorly sited "forts" inherited from the fur-traders by the Mounted Police, Inspector Dickens, the ill-starred son of the great novelist, had been outfaced and humiliated by Big Bear's Cree warband, yielding up all the post's white civilians as prisoners and abandoning the fort under cover of darkness. The unfortunate Dickens, a dwarfish, driven little man, psychologically unsuited for a police career, was the victim of circumstances beyond his control and should never have been left in such a responsible post by superiors dazzled by a famous name. He and his men were now safe at Fort Carlton, but the release of the Fort Pitt prisoners now became another priority of Jingo's little army.

On April 20, 1885, it took the field, marching north in two columns. A detachment of Mounted Police under Lieutenant Coryell was far in advance, checking out the route to Edmonton, followed by Steele and his scouts, and half his infantry, a total of about 200 men. A further 160 men and the field gun, under the command of Inspector A. B. Perry, NWMP, marched in a second column three days later, leaving behind sufficient garrisons to stabilize communications and defend the area.

The period from the arrival of Caron's telegram asking Strange to raise a corps to the beginning of that corps' march was just under three weeks!

There was nothing showy about the members of the rough-and-ready little force that followed their Buckskin Brigadier, but they had an air of purpose as they swung along on the long march north.

FOURTEEN

Quick March!

They camped that night in swirling snow—huge, wet flakes driven by a cruel north wind, and so thick at times that the world was blotted out in a whirling maelstrom of white. The blizzard had caught them towards the end of their first day's march. Tired and footsore as they were, this seemed the final, crushing blow.

The march, begun so cheerfully, had changed with every passing hour into an ordeal. Nothing in all their experience had prepared them for this, the weary plodding over endless miles of blackened prairie, for the Indians had fired the grass ahead of them to deny any grazing for their horses.

There were bogs and quagmires and morasses of the thick black prairie "gumbo," and the wretched carts, loaded with tons of supplies and equipment, sank axle-deep into them, and had to be extricated by dozens of cursing soldiers labouring in the mud beside the frightened, hard-pressed horses. This was not soldiering, this was not what they had volunteered for. They had given up their comfortable lives back home to fight Indians and rebels, not to labour in mud like gangs of slaves. And they got no thanks from the drivers, the carters who were being handsomely paid for simply sitting up top, away from all the mud, while they, the underpaid soldiery, had to walk. Already, on this very first day of what promised to be an interminable journey, there were dark looks, and mutterings in both French and English. The Alberta Field Force was showing signs of disintegrating before its first campaign could get under way.

It was Jingo who kept it going. It was Jingo who showed the carters how to unhitch the teams from unhindered wagons to assist the labouring animals of bogged carts. It was Jingo who showed toiling soldiers how to use poles as levers to aid in freeing heavy wagons from the clinging gumbo, and it was Jingo who directed the teams of husky young men tallying on to the ropes, turning the brute work of hauling into competitive tugs of war. It was Jingo who showed them how to ease the burden of their packs, and how to sling their rifles in the most comfortable way, and who started the songs that lightened their weariness towards the end of the long day's march. He was everywhere, cheerful and knowledgeable, full of the lore of the old soldier, the age-old tricks and notions that have eased the lot of marching men since the legionaries of ancient Rome walked their way around the known world.

And now, in the blinding blizzard, it was Jingo who made the surly carters form their wagons into a huge ring, nose to tail, before picketing their tired horses inside. It was Jingo who made the weary soldiers sweep the snow from the ground inside their tents before spreading their bedrolls and collapsing on them, thus ensuring a dry, less uncomfortable sleep.

Next morning the sun shone, the melting snow had vanished by noon, and soldiers and carters had grown more wary of the boggy bits in their path, having learned to detect them in the subtle variations of the grass and ground. Heartened by a night's rest and a good breakfast, the men swung along cheerfully, although as the day wore on the column tended to stretch out even longer.

It was, of course, mostly a baggage train, with the soldiers there simply to protect it and overawe any Indians encountered en route. Jingo wished not only to put some military presence into Edmonton, but to build, supply, and garrison three small forts on the way, to ensure a safe, reliable communication route to his base in Calgary. He was also determined to carry enough supplies with him to make his little army independent of local sources. He had learned, long ago in India, the dangers and difficulties of attempting to live off the land in hostile country. The burned-over grazing land of the first day had not daunted him in the least.

It did not take long for the skills of the French-Canadian woodsmen among the voltigeurs to be put to the test. The Bow River and, further on, a large tributary, had to be forded while in spate. Jingo's mounted men were able to splash across, but large rafts were quickly prepared by expert axemen to carry the carts and, in the second column, the force's precious field gun. With the aid of ropes secured to the upstream banks, the rafts were piloted across, the force of the current carrying them quickly over. A party of voltigeurs was always in advance of the main body, clearing brush and building small bridges, when required, over awkward bits of terrain. They were perhaps the finest natural sappers and pioneer troops in the world, and Jingo made a point of telling them so.

Far ahead of the main body of the force, Lieutenant Coryell and his police patrol were encountering their own problems. Coryell and seven constables suffered severely from snow blindness, and their horses had to be led by others whose vision was unimpaired. Travelling with them was an indomitable clergyman, the Reverend John Mac-Dougall, one of the great pioneering missionaries of the West and a trusted friend of the Cree and Stoney tribesmen of the northern woods. He had volunteered to accompany the force, both to reassure white settlers and friendly Indians along the way, and to promise the people of Edmonton and nearby tribes that a major military force was on the march and would soon arrive. News that the army was coming would, it was hoped, forestall any moves by restless tribesmen who might be considering joining the uprising.

Despite the heavy going in the slush and slop left by the melting snow and the inevitable problems entailed in moving such a large number of heavily loaded wheeled vehicles through difficult country, the column made remarkably good progress. The militiamen swung along like seasoned infantry, averaging twenty miles a day. Towards the end of the march, the toughened voltigeurs covered thirty-five miles in a single day. Curiously it was the carters, who rode, rather than the soldiers who walked, who gave occasional trouble. There was always tension between these hired contractors, as they considered themselves, and the cowboys and militiamen who made up the military component, a tension exacerbated by the differences in pay. Jingo was at pains to ensure that wagon drivers, like the soldiers, were subject to the common discipline of the force. When a sergeant's rifle fell into a stream from one wagon and the driver of the cart behind deliberately drove his team over it without stopping, Jingo broke up the resultant near-fracas by dismissing the driver on the spot and confiscating his wages to pay for the damaged rifle. But when a soldier carelessly allowed his rifle to fall into a small stream, he was made to strip and go in after it, groping about in the icy water until he had recovered it.

Day by day, as the men fell into regular marching routine and the weather improved, morale rose steadily. When columns of smoke by day and signal fires at night indicated that the column was being shadowed by hostile Indians, the first sign of any "enemy" activity most of the soldiers had ever seen, the whole undertaking became the great adventure they had originally hoped for. At night, sitting around the bright campfires within the sheltering shadows of the tight wagon ring, the young men, soldiers and cowboys alike, raised their voices in song, partly to keep the vastness of the silent wilderness at bay, but mostly in sheer exuberance of spirit. The voltigeurs sang their habitant folk songs or the canoe songs of the old voyageur days—"En Roulant ma Boule" and "Vive la Canadienne." The cowboys responded with "The Old Chisholm Trail" or "The Dying Cowboy's Lament." "I had not the heart to stop them, though they might have attracted the attention of a prowling Indian scout," Jingo admitted. "Still, it cut both ways, raising the confidence of my men, while it showed the Indians we had no dread of what they could do."

He himself was relieved to be in the field, away from the frustrations and delays of his Calgary base and the endless procrastination from the east. Dewdney had become tiresome, alarmed lest his hopes of appeasing the southern tribes should be upset by Jingo's peremptory attitude towards cattle rustlers. Middleton robbed the Calgary column to strengthen his own; any problem people, though, he quickly passed on to Jingo. And Lieutenant-Colonel Guillaume Amyot, who had been commanding the 9th Quebec Voltigeurs in garrison at Winnipeg, a safe, though boring, berth, had been passed on to Calgary after making himself unpleasant to every Manitoban within earshot. Jingo was glad to have his regiment garrison the Calgary area and release the Winnipeg Light Infantry, after weeks of training, for campaigning in the north. But its commanding officer was a different story.

A Quebec MP, whose military role had been a mere adjunct to his political career, Amyot was a born fomenter of trouble. Already Jingo knew that he was corresponding with newspapers in Quebec and with the Minister of Militia, contrary to military regulations, complaining about everything and everyone and claiming that Calgary was in a state of panic and required immediate assistance from the east. Jingo was glad to be clear of him, and of the glowering voltigeur paymaster, Charles Bosse, who accused Jingo of harbouring a deep hatred of all French Canadians.

Out here on the open prairie there were no such animosities. Major Georges Hughes, now commanding the 65th, and Lieutenant Starnes, his acting adjutant, had proved themselves loyal and active officers. The muddle and mess of previous weeks was left behind, too: the rotten saddles from the east, which had had to be rebuilt by his own men; the Winchester rifles, so long promised, which never arrived; the customs officers who refused to release vital supplies without authorization; and the bureaucrats who would not give such authorization. By comparison, Big Bear and his warriors posed only straightforward problems, and Jingo retired each night with an easy mind, his slumbers undisturbed by the clashes and clamours of the telegraph lines.

The only alarms encountered on the long march north were furnished by a handful of medical officers, attached to the column's improvised field ambulance unit. Having nothing better to do, since the men were all in good health, these gentlemen enlivened their days by shooting at any small game encountered on the march. Their gunshots alarmed the scouts deployed far from the column. Suspecting Indian raiders, they would gallop to investigate. Steele grew so annoyed at this repeated nuisance that he contemplated peppering the doctors with birdshot, but cooler counsels prevailed. Jingo simply confiscated the doctors' guns.

The only other gunfire heard by the force on its long march was the welcoming salute from the two old brass guns at Fort Edmonton, one of which, fired in haste, sent its rammer high in the air to land in the midst of the startled column. Jingo rode into Edmonton to a tumultuous welcome on May 1, his little army having established a defended line of communication with Calgary and having marched 200 difficult miles in just ten days. He found the fort crowded with settlers who had been called in from the whole area by the Mounted Police to the shelter of the log stockade.

In this isolated region, in the heart of Indian country and with only a few farms scattered about the river, fears of a native uprising were very real. The Reverend Mr. Mac-Dougall's assurances that relief was on its way had been received with some scepticism. The arrival of the force was therefore greeted with wild—Jingo thought excessive—jubilation, and everyone turned out to welcome the little army marching up the riverbank. Sam Steele, bright in scarlet and pipeclay, was an imposing figure as he led his scout cavalry at the head of the force. He was followed by Jingo, arrayed for the occasion in his "best" blue coat, at the head of his voltigeurs, all cleaned up and smart in rifle green.

Led by a cart flying a sixpenny tea towel printed with a bright Union Jack, the column's own proud banner, a long line of wagons, piled high with supplies, stretched for more than a mile behind, solid evidence that this was no fly-by-night force dependent for sustenance on the meagre resources of the fort. Here, indeed, was true relief, and the population of the little settlement set out to make the newcomers truly welcome. The highlight of the proceedings was a review of the troops, held just outside the fort gate and addressed by Jingo himself.

"You have now proven yourselves to be real soldiers, capable of marching anywhere and fighting anyone," he told them. He went on to praise their endurance, their high spirits, and their remarkable ability to build roads, ford rivers, and contrive bridges and rafts. It was an unusual tribute from an exacting and demanding commander, and was consequently much relished by the men.

There was little rest for them here, however. Once the welcoming festivities were over, everyone was put to work getting Fort Edmonton into a state of defence. Like so many western communities, it had grown up around a trading post of the Hudson's Bay Company, whose faded banner, flying above the stockaded citadel, aroused the curiosity of a young soldier.

"What's HBC mean?" he enquired of an older companion.

"Here before Christ," was the old stager's reply.

After the log ramparts had been strengthened and shelter trenches dug to cover the approaches to the fort, Jingo resorted to an old artilleryman's trick for defending a permanent position. He had accurate measurements made of the distances from each of the bastion gun positions to various local features in the surrounding landscape, and the distances noted on lists posted inside each tower. By thus knowing the exact range, a devastatingly accurate fire could be instantly opened on any attacking force.

The marksmanship of his own men was a continuing obsession, and all day half of the little army was kept blazing away on the rifle range set up on the flats below the fort. During the march north, Jingo had used rest periods to get his soldiers to estimate the distances to various features on the prairie about them, so that they could become proficient at adjusting the sights on their rifles before opening fire. Now this experience was put to good use, as great emphasis was put on the men dropping to the ground on the word of command, and opening an accurate fire on the nearest target.

The scout cavalry was also involved in the constant rifle practice. Jingo adopted an old cavalryman's trick for getting the horses, all half-broken "cayuses," accustomed to gunfire, by moving them steadily closer to the firing until the noise was accepted as harmless. Revolver shots were used as the signal for feeding time, and soon the animals were so habituated to the banging of small arms that their riders were able to steady their rifles on their saddles before opening fire across their backs.

While half the troops were on the ranges, the other half were kept busy practising skirmishing action, learning to deploy quickly and take cover, and to advance and retreat without exposure to an unseen enemy. This was the sort of fighting that could be anticipated against Indian and Métis woodsmen, and Jingo was determined to make his force as proficient as possible in such an encounter.

There were drill sessions on the parade ground, too, intended to accustom the men to thinking of themselves as members of a unit with a cohesion and purpose of its own, rather than as a mere huddle of individuals. In the days that followed, the Alberta Field Force, already a hardened and accomplished marching unit, became a fighting force to be reckoned with.

Leaving the direction of these drills to his subordinate officers and NCOs, Jingo continued the frustrating business of administering, supplying, and reinforcing what was still a sort of private army. It had little official standing and its commander seemed to lack official authorization in every field. His wagon drivers were giving trouble again; hearing that those employed in Middleton's column were all supplied with rifles, they refused to move again unless so armed. Jingo promised to try and get arms sent to Fort Victoria, the next stop downriver, and the drivers grudgingly agreed to move so far but no further without their own weapons. In the meantime, it was hoped that the long-promised rifles might arrive any day. Hopes were raised by the arrival of several wagonloads of long, flat boxes. They were quickly dashed when the boxes proved to be filled with young trees, ordered long ago by Jingo for planting at the ranch and now forwarded by an over-zealous freight agent in Calgary.

Edmonton's townspeople were proving difficult, too, urging the force to remain in permanent garrison. They had discontinued their own local defence force upon the army's arrival. But when they learned that it would shortly be

marching on, leaving only a small garrison of French-Canadian voltigeurs behind, they promptly reformed their "home
guard," greatly to Jingo's satisfaction.

A voltigeur officer added to Jingo's troubles when he
complained that the ammunition issued was of poor quality,
so that rifle fire was unable to reach the thousand-yard range
it was supposed to. Jingo knew that the cartridges issued
were over twelve years old, but he also knew that no soldier
could be trusted to hit any target at a range of much more
than two hundred yards.

"Tell your men to hold their fire until they can see the
white of the enemy's eyes," he advised the worried lieutenant. "After that, they can charge with the bayonet!"

The precious field gun, with its complement of police
gunners, arrived in camp together with the balance of the
65th Voltigeurs, and shortly thereafter the Alberta Field
Force reached full strength with the arrival from Calgary of
the remainder of the Winnipeg Light Infantry under Lieutenant-Colonel Osborne-Smith. All the new arrivals were
immediately included in the intensive training program, the
performance of their "artillery" section under Inspector
A.B. Perry receiving special attention. The unit was short of
ammunition and the case-shot (the anti-personnel shells
most effective for use on widely-spaced targets such as the
rebels were likely to offer) was of inferior quality. Accordingly, Jingo had a supply improvised, using bags filled with
trade bullets from the Hudson's Bay Company store.

Meanwhile preparations for the advance went ahead.
Supplies for the army were moved to the riverbank ready for
embarkation, after a sufficient quantity had been stored
within the fort for the use of the civilians and the garrison.
The plan was for the force to strengthen and supply Fort
Victoria before moving downriver to rendezvous at Battleford with the columns led by Otter and Middleton. The
entire force would thus be concentrated in the very heart of

the rebel country, with the areas in the rear of each column stabilized with a chain of garrisoned forts.

Middleton's strategy was excellent, but his tactics were another matter. Communications with the other two columns were poor. Jingo was forced to rely for news upon captured rebels, rumour, and out-of-date newspapers. What news did get through was all bad. Middleton had experienced a setback in his first encounter. He had been fought to a standstill by a small force under Dumont at Fish Creek and forced to withdraw with a loss of six dead and forty-nine wounded, four of them mortally. The Métis, according to newspaper accounts, had four dead and one wounded but had lost fifty-five horses, their most significant casualty. Middleton's fifty-five men represented a heavy casualty list for a force of some 350, but the worst loss seemed to be to the general's confidence. His brief, disjointed dispatches to Jingo thereafter reflected the outlook of a badly shaken commander.

Hot on the heels of this disturbing setback came the news of another reverse, contained in a letter in the pocket of a Métis captured by one of Steele's scouts. Written by a relative of the captured man, it was an eyewitness account of a shocking defeat suffered by Colonel Otter's column at a place called Cut Knife Hill. Hearing that some of Poundmaker's men had sacked and burned a little settlement there, Otter had marched directly for the main Indian encampment which, he had been told, lay on the eastern slope of the hill. Advancing without prior reconnaissance, he emerged on an open hilltop to find that the encampment had moved to the west of the hill. His force was thus exposed without cover and quickly encircled by Indians screened in wooded ravines. He was fortunate to escape with only eight dead and fourteen wounded. Had Poundmaker's warriors been more aggressive, it could easily have been a massacre, a sort of Canadian Little Big Horn. Indeed, both of his fellow commanders had committed the same fatal error, giving battle without reconnaissance under circumstances of the enemy's choosing. More than ever, Jingo was determined not to "commit Custer" when his own encounter with the rebels came.

FIFTEEN

Inland Admiral

Edmonton had never seen such a sight before! Everyone in the crowded little settlement turned out to enjoy the spectacle as the fleet cast off its lines and moved out into the stream, led by its flagship, which the troops had irreverently christened *Big Bear*. She seemed immense, towering above the other five vessels, with her cannon projecting from her bows and her flag—the same sixpenny tea towel that had marched with the force from Calgary, now sadly faded— fluttering bravely from the stern. The soldiers manning her sweeps heaved lustily on their long poles, directed by the local pilot who had undertaken to navigate the ponderous vessel and her flotilla among the mudbanks and swirling currents of the North Saskatchewan River, now in full spate. The small boys along the riverbank raised a ragged cheer, while women in the crowd behind waved handkerchiefs. The soldiers crowded aboard the scows, scarlet-coated Winnipeg Light Infantrymen, waved in reply. As the last scow left the wharf and the current caught their heavy craft, the whole force, led by a young captain, gave three cheers, waving their hats in the air as the sound echoed from the low bluffs across the river. The first war fleet Edmonton had ever seen was now afloat, and the townsfolk meant to make the most of it. Already boys and dogs were running along the bank, their shouts—and barks—adding further animation to the general excitement as they sought to keep pace with the fleet.

It was May 14, 1885, and the Alberta Field Force was embarked for its voyage down the North Saskatchewan River to Fort Victoria and whatever fate lay beyond.

From his commanding position in the bows of *Big Bear*, Jingo watched the proceedings as his flotilla got under way. He had commanded units of horses, elephants, even camels, before, but had never exercised command of a fleet afloat. A veritable prairie admiral, he relished every moment of it.

The fleet he now commanded—five scows, including the "flagship," largest of all, and a ferryboat—had been planned long before and had not materialized without much hard work and acrimonious argument. He had instructed the Reverend Mr. MacDougall, sent ahead from Calgary when the march began, to organize the building of the scows upon arrival in Edmonton. MacDougall, among his many other accomplishments, was a veteran riverman who knew all the branches of the Saskatchewan River well and understood exactly the type of craft required to move heavy loads on it. From the beginning, Jingo had planned to rendezvous with the other columns at Battleford by using the favourable current to move his men quickly.

The missionary had done his work well. Immediately on arrival, he had organized the building of typical river scows, unwieldy-looking, flatbottomed rectangular affairs, lightly framed and planked and held together by wooden dowels. Four of them had been completed soon after the arrival of the force, and Jingo had then appropriated the Hudson's Bay Company barge, a much larger and heavier vessel, to serve as his gunboat, armed with the force's only artillery, the police field gun. The gun was installed on a strong platform built into the bow and lashed securely in place, so that the whole barge would absorb its recoil. The undecked barge had a narrow platform running down both sides at gunwale level for the use of the men at the sweeps, and Jingo had a parapet built up on this with beef and pork barrels, alternating with bags of flour. The sides of the barge below the platform were similarly strengthened. These protective walls were suitably loopholed, so that the barge crew had more protection against plunging rifle fire from the banks than could be provided by the thin planking alone.

In an age when the new "ironclads" were the pride of the world's seagoing fleets, Jingo thought it appropriate to call his own "armoured" vessels "flourclads." The barge carrying hay for the horses rather than flour for the men, he termed a "hayclad." His men appreciated having their supplies arranged as defences rather than piled in as mere cargo.

But from the first the barges had been a problem. Being new-built, they leaked like baskets, and Jingo had been forced to discharge the civilian crews he had first hired because they refused to bail and allowed their craft to sink alongside the wharf. In the end, soldiers had been recruited, with a few Métis familiar with the river, to act as pilots and to instruct the green crews in the unusual technique of poling and sweeping their clumsy craft through the swift and shallow turbulence of the river.

But the most difficult hurdle had been the obstruction of one of his own officers. Lieutenant-Colonel William Osborne-Smith had refused to allow his men to embark in craft which he claimed, in a formal written protest to Jingo, were clearly unsafe. They were too lightly built to carry heavy loads, he said, and he refused to embark his regiment. Furthermore, he demanded that a board of officers be convened to judge the safety of the craft, and to check whether the defensive walls of floursacks and barrels would keep out rifle fire.

But Jingo was too old a soldier to be foxed by any mere
militia commander, however senior. Adopting the techniques used, as he put it, "to empanel an Irish jury to convict
a prisoner," he convened a board composed of the construc-
tors who had built the barges and the expert rivermen
accustomed to them, who quickly dismissed the charges
and declared the craft both sound and safe. As for the ability
of the improvised parapets to stop rifle bullets, Jingo proposed to leave that test to enemy marksmen and dissolved
the board. Osborne-Smith could only acquiesce, which he
did with admirable grace. "It was straight obstruction," Sam
Steele wrote in his journal, "which General Strange disposed
of in characteristic manner."

In fact, the doubts had arisen because of the light construction used for all river craft, unlike the heavy-framed
hulls common elsewhere. Riverboats were flexible so as to
be able to take the ground, as they frequently did, without
damage; they could be poled off banks where more rigid
craft would stick. In the event, they proved highly successful, although they were leaky and required constant bailing.

Paddling in advance of the fleet was a flotilla of canoes,
checking for any obstructions in the river or for signs of
enemy activity. Even further ahead were Steele's scouts, who
had left the camp two days previously, along with the hard-
marching voltigeurs of the 65th Regiment, to proceed along
the north bank of the river and rendezvous with the fleet at
Fort Victoria.

Once the barges had left Edmonton, Jingo took steps to
put his force in the first degree of readiness for an attack, for
they were now proceeding through a region already ravaged
by hostile Indians, abandoned by all white settlers, and used
as a home base by tribes associated with Big Bear and Poundmaker. Steele's reports noted that the scattered farms he had
encountered were all empty, plundered, and sometimes
burnt. The fate of the inhabitants was unknown. But it was

other intelligence, learned from Métis prisoners captured by his scouts, that led Jingo to anticipate an attack. The Métis told him that the Indians intended to assault his column rather than Otter's or Middleton's. They believed the French-speaking voltigeurs, clad in dark uniforms, would not fight like "real" soldiers, who wore red coats like all who served in the Great Queen's invincible army. Besides, these oddly clad men spoke the language of the Métis; surely they would not kill their brothers?

Jingo made sure the 65th learned this assessment of their fighting abilities and promised to give them every opportunity of proving it wrong. In the meantime he would use his voltigeurs as bait, and to confuse the watching Indians who shadowed his force he intended to switch the 65th from ship to shore and back again without warning to anyone, so that the enemy would be uncertain as to the unit's whereabouts.

The troops on the barges were divided into three watches, like a ship's company at sea, and all bugle calls and other unnecessary noises were curtailed. Jingo eased this last restriction during the day to allow his soldiers to vent their high spirits in song, especially in the voyageur songs learned from their Métis pilots. Once ashore and encamped for the night, however, a close and silent sentry watch was maintained, and Jingo himself ensured that his pickets were always vigilant.

A notable feature of the little river-borne force was the number of clergymen who had attached themselves to it. The Reverend J. MacDougall, of course, was of the greatest use, travelling with the scouts, where his knowledge of Indian languages and ways was put to best use. He was relieved from time to time by an Anglican clergyman, Canon John McKay, thus allowing MacDougall to enjoy the easier travel aboard a barge. McKay showed himself to be utterly fearless, and later exposed himself to the greatest danger by attempting to negotiate a truce with hostile and threatening

Indians. McKay was the son of a Hudson's Bay Company official and a master Indian linguist.

Yet of all these representatives of the "church militant," none was to show greater bravery than the young Roman Catholic priest who acted as the chaplain for the 65th Regiment and accompanied the ambulance unit. Armed only with his crucifix, Father Prevost went under fire to administer the last rites to men mortally wounded, an act made doubly noble by the stark fact that the only churchmen murdered by rebels were Roman Catholic priests.

Fort Saskatchewan, a few miles downstream, was reached in a violent snowstorm on May 15, and was found crowded with refugees from the ravaged countryside. They included the family of Major Butler, together with their governess, the daughter of an old friend and brother officer of Jingo's Indian Army days. Butler pleaded to join the force, and as he was an expert axeman as well as soldier, he was put in charge of the road-repairing party of the shore contingent. His wife and daughters, who had thrown their valuables and finery down their farmstead well and then watched from the woods while their house was ransacked by Indians, volunteered to join the force as nurses. But Jingo, wary of adding four women, three of them young and pretty, to an army of young men, declined the offer, tactfully adding that they "were too attractive for the position."

The plight of the Butlers and of other families at the fort who had lost everything to marauding natives prompted him to write to his wife and warn her not even to consider returning to the ranch, which he thought might well be burnt by vengeful tribesmen.

While completing an inspection of the fort, Jingo was pleased to be joined by an old army friend, Captain Edward Palliser of the 7th Hussars, who had secured ministerial permission to leave his Ottawa post to serve with the Alberta Field Force. A giant of a man, standing six foot six and weighing two hundred pounds, he had made his own way to the front, by horse, by canoe, and on foot, and was to prove a loyal and stalwart member of the force as assistant quartermaster general.

As the fleet cast off early on the morning of May 17 to continue its voyage downriver, the "hayclad," the leakiest of the barges, sank near the shore, and horses and men had to swim for it. Fortunately, some of the drivers were able to guide the leading horse to the bank; the rest followed and all were secured and joined the shore party. The sunken barge was speedily pumped out and rejoined the flotilla, being taken in tow by one of the others for safety's sake.

The force was now in daily contact with the enemy and occasionally came under fire from scattered Indian scouts or pillaging parties. The order of march was found to be most successful. Steele and his mounted men, scouting far ahead, were followed by the shore contingent, which alternated day by day with the troops embarked in the barges. The ferryboat would allow men to be swiftly moved from one bank to the other as required, should opposition be met, so that the column was always kept flexible and could adapt to any situation that might arise. Progress was surprisingly rapid, and Fort Victoria was reached on the afternoon of May 17.

The conditions here and in the surrounding area were described by Jingo in a letter to his wife—conditions which prompted an uncharacteristic expression of his feelings of anger and frustration.

This is a very lovely place, an old H.B.C. fort I am trying to repair and garrison with settlers; poor people, who have been hiding in the woods, return when they see the troops. The young children look especially miserable, and many have died. I shall try and get food for them, and get them all into the fort. The country is in a terrible state—no food—and

ravaged by Indians and Riel emissaries. I can't be
everywhere at once. If the damned government would
only send arms for settlers they could defend
themselves. General Middleton seems to be well
supplied with regular troops, artillery and a steam
flotilla. I wish you saw my flotilla of flour-clads
floating down the Saskatchewan! If it were not for the
amazing delay of the Militia Store Department in
sending arms, etc., and opposition from almost every
source, excepting the enemy, I would have been
through this business a fortnight ago, or at any rate, a
good way through it.

At Fort Victoria, Jingo was at pains not only to rebuild
the dilapidated defences but to organize the local settlers
into a proper garrison, which he stiffened with half a company of his voltigeurs. He put the Methodist minister, an
able and intelligent young man, in command and sketched
out a plan for a projecting bastion to be built to command a
vulnerable section of wall.

By thus establishing these garrisoned strongpoints, Jingo
sought to ensure the safety and confidence of the civilian
population, as well as to secure his own communications.
He looked upon the re-establishment of the civilian popula-
tions in this "war zone" as a prime part of his campaign. The
garrisons left behind weakened his main force, but it was
still sufficient for the purpose, and he knew that he would be
joining the powerful columns of Otter and Middleton somewhere up ahead.

At Fort Victoria there came the first indications of a
weakening in the resolve of the rebel forces. Peccan, chief of
a Cree tribe whose young warriors had been ravaging the
countryside and who was known to be about to throw in his
lot with Poundmaker and Big Bear, sent an emissary to treat
with Strange's column. With the Reverend Mr. MacDougall

as interpreter, the messenger explained that Peccan had
resisted both the blandishments and threats with which Big
Bear had tried to induce him to join the rebellion. One of
Peccan's Crees had killed a warrior of Big Bear's, and Peccan
sought Jingo's help in escaping retribution. Whatever the
truth of the claim, it indicated a wavering of rebel support in
the area, and Jingo intended to make the most of it. He had
MacDougall ask if Peccan would, in turn, supply scouts for
the column in this unfamiliar region. The troops then encamped for the night to await the chief's reply. Next morning brought Peccan himself to the camp. Bland and
imperturbable, he assured Jingo of his own good intentions,
but regretted that none of his warriors was willing to scout
for the soldiers. After an exchange of civilities, the two
leaders parted, not without some sense of satisfaction on
either side, Peccan confident that the soldiers would not
ravage his encampment, Jingo assured that Peccan would
give no further trouble in the area. Leaving some supplies of
food to sustain the half-starved civilians in the little fort,
Jingo pressed on downriver.

Up ahead, Steele's scouts were coming into increasingly
frequent contact with Indian warbands, and some sharp
exchanges inflicted casualties on both sides. Like all good
cavalrymen, Steele pressed hard on the heels of his retreating
enemy, and Jingo grew increasingly anxious to support his
tiny mounted contingent. Middleton, he knew, had a large
cavalry force with him, completely unused, but the general
seemed out of touch with his isolated columns. At Victoria,
Jingo had received a message from him, but it was a month
old and told him nothing of his senior officer's intentions.

Exasperated at his general's failure to communicate either
his own location and intentions or orders or instructions for
his subordinates, Jingo took it upon himself to get in touch
with Middleton, last heard from on the march for Batoche.
He dispatched two volunteers, Sergeant Borrowdale and

Scout Scott, to travel by canoe downriver to Battleford to convey news of his own situation and to enquire after Middleton's intentions. The intrepid pair, travelling through enemy-held territory, were to paddle by night and lie up under cover by day.

The two arrived safely at Middleton's camp, with no loss beyond Borrowdale's revolver, only to be cut to the quick by the general's reception. Far from appreciating their enterprise and effort, Middleton refused to replace the lost revolver from his large store of arms and contemptuously observed that he could have walked through the country the pair had traversed armed only with a walking-stick. And this from a commander, as the pair soon learned, treated with open contempt by his militia officers and viewed by his own soldiers as a coward after his abysmal display at Fish Creek and Batoche.

Contempt was met with contempt. When Scott and Borrowdale returned to Jingo's camp, they wore, printed on the upturned flap of their hats, the notice: "I was *NOT* at Fish Creek. I was *NOT* at Batoche." And indeed, as Jingo learned in detail from his two messengers, Middleton's encounters with the rebels had been sadly inglorious affairs. After being soundly beaten by Dumont at Fish Creek, Middleton seemed traumatized. His advance on Batoche had been reduced to a sort of crawl, giving the Métis ample time to fortify their capital with skilfully sited rifle pits. On arrival at the village in overwhelming force—850 men, 170 wagonloads of supplies, and all the supporting cast of artillery, steamers, and staff—he seemed absolutely nonplussed by the rebel defences, without the least idea as to how to deal with them. His force was the finest the country could produce; Middleton had had his pick of the best-trained militia regiments in eastern Canada, together with tough professionals of the regular army from the training schools, all armed and equipped with everything the nation could provide. Yet in a series of half-hearted attacks, he had managed to expose his men, deployed without shelter on open ground, to the galling fire of an unseen enemy screened by bush in a secure defence perimeter.

After incurring the inevitable heavy loss in killed and wounded, the troops had been marched back to their nearby camp without ever having had an opportunity to make any effective reply, let alone the full-blooded attack on the thin defensive line for which they increasingly longed. Though at first inclined to panic under fire, the raw young regiments had quickly steadied, and after three days of this charade they had become exasperated and almost mutinous over their leader's lack of enterprise. Prompted by their mutterings, and the open contempt of their officers, Middleton had finally summoned the resolve to make a determined assault.

Despite the farcical display of a riverborne force, which began its attack an hour late and sent the steamer *North-cote*, its masts, funnel, and wheelhouse sheered off by a wire stretched across the river, careering helplessly downstream, the attack quickly overran the defences and the rebel capital was captured. The highlight of the four-day siege, the soldiers had informed Jingo's messengers, had been their intrepid general's capture of a Métis prisoner. While out on horseback, Middleton had encountered an aged Métis, unarmed and alone, wandering in search of his missing cow. He had proudly returned to camp with the old man walking, hands aloft, in front of him, prodded along by the general's pistol. Dubbed "Middleton's Métis," the toothless old man had been adopted by the troops as a sort of mascot, a symbol of their leader's ineptitude.

Notwithstanding this scornful levity, the fact remained that Middleton had captured Batoche. He subsequently accepted the surrender of Riel, who gave himself up, hoping for a state trial that would provide him with the national

audience he sought. Middleton was thus free to join with
Otter and Strange in pursuit of Big Bear and Poundmaker,
whose warbands now constituted a purely Indian threat.
Jingo accordingly pressed on downriver to join up with
Middleton. He did his best to suppress any criticism of the
general among his men, although he noted grimly in his
journal that Middleton, approaching the country he declared he could walk through with only a cane in his hand,
took good care to come equipped with cavalry, infantry,
guns, and steamers.

SIXTEEN

Frenchman's Butte

Hatred, like a thief in the night, crept into the cheerful encampment on May 24, the Queen's birthday. The hatred was born of horror of the terrible things discovered by a party of soldiers wandering about the blackened ruins of the Frog Lake fort a mile from the campfires of the Alberta Field Force. The soldiers knew that Big Bear's warriors had killed nine settlers at the old HBC post at Frog Lake before setting fire to the buildings, but they had heard few details and were quite unprepared for what they would find on their idle stroll about the ruins.

After breakfast that morning at five o'clock, Jingo had addressed them, an unusual procedure, and informed them that it was Queen Victoria's birthday. They had stood there in the pouring rain, while he praised the way in which they had marched and told them he was proud of them. "This is the Queen's birthday, without the Queen's weather," he said, "but we cannot have any fireworks today unless Big Bear cooperates. We are close on his heels, and I know you will soon have the opportunity of staging some fireworks of your own." He had led them in three cheers for the Queen and then, since it was Sunday, they had sung a verse of "the Old Hundredth" hymn before swinging off in the rain on their downriver march. That night, they had camped on the bank near the site of the old Frog Lake post and, the weather having cleared, the ruins beckoned the curious.

The buildings—the Roman Catholic Mission, the trading post, a mill, and nine or ten houses—were mere blackened heaps, and their furniture and contents, strewn about the site, added to the sense of ravaged desolation. Over all hung the frightful stench of death, and it was this smell that led to the full revelation of what the ruins concealed. In the basement of the parsonage the soldiers found four headless bodies thrown into a corner. Two of them were identified by the beads in their pockets as the remains of Father Fafard and Father Marchand. Elsewhere in the wreckage were the bodies of Delaney, Quinn, and Gilchrist, all well-known members of this little settlement, badly mutilated. The heads of some, scalped and charred by fire, were found separately, and the body of a woman, with legs and arms cut off, was found at the bottom of a shallow well.

The young soldiers were stunned. The butchery of unarmed men and women was dreadful in itself, but the sadistic mutilation was revolting, and the news of the find set the entire camp abuzz with anger. Next morning the dead were buried as decently as possible, the men looking on with pale, set faces. When the march began, a new air of grim determination was evident throughout the column. The soldiers were bent on one common purpose: to punish the men of Big Bear's band who had done this thing. For Jingo, however, there was another and graver concern. More than thirty white prisoners, mostly women and children captured at Fort Pitt, were still held by Big Bear; he must somehow contrive to liberate them before they were slaughtered by increasingly desperate warriors. The ghastly remains at Frog Lake showed how terrible their fate might be.

The new mood of the Alberta Field Force soon manifested itself in an unexpected way. Jingo himself, coming upon the body of an Indian killed in a skirmish with his scouts, was astounded to find that it had been scalped, Indian-fashion. Revolted and angry, he issued an order through his brigade major that any further mutilation of the dead would be instantly and severely punished. But in his journal he was more philosophical. "A la guerre comme à la guerre," he wrote.

Together with the warning to his troops against ill-treatment of the dead went another expressing concern for the living. In view of the fact that the column might soon expect to have a considerable number of freed captives to feed, including half-starved women and children, anyone taking more than his fair share of supplies would be treated "as a brute devoid of human feeling," and punished accordingly. The troops appreciated the need to conserve supplies, and there were no further incidents of the old soldier's game of pinching extra rations whenever possible.

For days now, the column had been making its way through tangled scrubland drenched with heavy rains and full of bogs and marshy inlets along the riverbanks. It had been brought up to strength by a company of the Alberta Mounted Rifles under Major George Hatton, who joined the column at Frog Lake, and the men marched in good heart, the brush-cutting section under Major Butler playing a vital role in helping maintain a good rate of progress through the difficult terrain. Despite the deep, black, clinging mud and the swarms of pestilential mosquitoes, even the surly wagon drivers made few complaints, since the rifles they had demanded had arrived at long last, brought in by the Alberta Mounted Rifles.

Vermilion Creek was passed, as were Dog Rump Creek and Saddle Lake and half a dozen other landmarks with curious names that marked the column's progress downriver. As they pressed on, caught up in the passion of pursuit, the scouts increasingly reported signs of the enemy just ahead. Near Fort Pitt, a message arrived from Captain

Oswald, who led the most advanced party of scouts. It electrified the eager soldiers: Indians were in sight, and in force, among the ruins of the fort, still smoking after its devastating sack more than a month ago.

Jingo, eager to catch up with the enemy as quickly as possible, wasted not a second in giving his orders. He and Major Steele would gallop ahead with the Mounted Rifles and the scouts, together with the Mounted Police's horse-drawn field gun and a company of the light infantry in the swiftest of the wagons. The remainder of the Winnipeg Light Infantry and the supply train would follow at best speed under the command of Colonel Osborne-Smith. Orders were sent to Colonel Hughes and his 65th Voltigeurs, embarked in the flotilla, to drop back and keep abreast of the shore force so that it could be reinforced quickly if necessary.

The message had arrived at noon, and within minutes the "flying column" was on its way. By early evening it arrived on the scene, having covered thirty miles of most difficult country in record time. Jingo found Captain Oswald and his troop of scouts posted atop a poplar bluff, where they could observe the low country below without revealing themselves. With them was the pioneer party of Major Butler, which had caught up with the horsemen.

The Indians had left the fort, having evidently been pillaging its few remaining buildings. With darkness closing in, they must be encamped close by, and there was every possibility that they might be brought to action next morning. In the meantime, Jingo's little force camped where it was, after posting a strong picket to guard against any surprise night attack.

A reconnaissance at first light brought disappointing news. Far from camping nearby, the Indians had melted away in the night, and it was up to Jingo, seeking to maintain a hot pursuit, to judge in which direction they had gone. The established trails forked here, with routes leading off in three directions. In a fever to pick up the trail, Jingo sent scouts to investigate each path, and a detachment of Mounted Police under Inspector Perry with the column's best trackers, Canon McKay and the Reverend Mr. Mac-Dougall, was ferried across the Saskatchewan. They reported signs that showed that a band of Crees, accompanied by white women whose slippered footprints were clearly identifiable, had crossed the river opposite the fort. It had been a large band, accompanied by wagons, and was heading for the trail junction. Jingo immediately sent Perry and his policemen on ahead to determine which of the three routes the Indians had taken. He then set another party to work stretching a wire across the river, to which the ferryboat was attached by rope and pulley, so that the force could be transported from one side of the river to the other.

In the meantime, a fatigue party of light infantrymen was given the unpleasant job of cleaning up the remaining buildings of Fort Pitt and putting them into a state of defence, for Jingo was determined to make the vital junction point as secure as possible. The whole of the settlement site was littered with debris cast aside by pillaging Indians after the fort had been abandoned by Inspector Dickens and its civilians taken hostage. Many books, including Bibles and religious tracts in the Indian sign language, were scattered about, their pages blowing in the breeze. Their missionary message of mercy and a gentle Jesus had not penetrated far, Jingo reflected grimly; among them lay the mutilated corpse of a mounted policeman, his heart, cut out of his body, stuck on an upright stick.

In the midst of this work, a violent storm engulfed the force, and blinding rain and gale-force winds made all movement difficult. Hunched in slickers, the rain streaming down their horses' flanks, little parties of horsemen received their orders from their oil-skinned general. Steele was to reconnoitre the tracks on one side of the river and determine

whether Big Bear had gone north or west. Another party of
scouts was to examine the trail on the opposite river bank.
Perry and his clergymen-trackers were to scout ahead. More
than one band of Indians was involved; Jingo had to learn
which one was travelling with the prisoners.

To the waiting troops, it seemed that reports from the
scouts would never come in. Minutes, hours, dragged by
interminably. Inspector Perry and his police detachment
were never heard from at all. It would be nine days before
Jingo, having given them up as dead or prisoners, would
learn that Perry, for some unaccountable reason, had ridden
straight on to Battleford, a distance of some ninety miles,
without sending any word of his intentions. By thus abandoning the force on the eve of its major confrontation with
the enemy, Perry, whose detachment included the gunners
who manned the all-important nine-pounder, had robbed it
of its only trained gun crew.

But Jingo, an old gunner himself, was equal to the challenge. When he realized that Perry's force, for whatever
reason, had vanished, he formed a new gun crew under the
leadership of his son Harry, a trained artillery officer who
had once won the Dominion prize for artillery marksmanship. With Sergeant O'Connor of the Mounted Police to
help, a detachment of the Winnipeg Light Infantry was
quickly enrolled as gun's crew, and after several hours of
brisk training they were adjudged able to hit any target
within the gun's range.

They would soon be put to the test. One party of scouts
reported no trace of the enemy, but from Steele came exciting
news: a very large body of Indians, including carts and
"travois"—a device used by Indians to move a teepee and all
its household belongings—had moved west and then north
along a heavily congested trail. He and his little force was hot
on their heels and intended to follow at best speed. Jingo
wasted not a second in setting out in support. It was essential

to maintain contact with this elusive enemy, and Steele's little unit must receive instant reinforcement if it was not to be mauled by an encounter with so formidable a force.

Leaving behind a company of the 65th to fortify and garrison Fort Pitt under Captain Giroux, Jingo marched with all the troops at his disposal. In order to move as quickly as possible, they took only essential supplies, leaving behind all unnecessary wagons. The men marched with three days' rations in their haversacks, together with arms and ammunition. Even tents were dispensed with, a serious decision in such wet weather. The striking force consisted of 197 infantry, rank and file; 27 well-mounted cavalrymen; and the field gun and crew, with a full ammunition limber and an excellent gun team of horses. After sending word to Major Hughes in the barges to join him with the 65th Regiment as soon as possible, Jingo led his men out of camp on a forced march to the support of his scouts far ahead.

A trooper brought fresh news: Steele had fought a sharp skirmish with a rearguard of the enemy, which had laid an ambush in the growing dusk of the previous evening. Challenged sharply in Cree, a scout had replied in the same language, but the Indian had glimpsed Steele's white helmet in the darkness and had opened fire. The bullet just missed the burly policeman. Whipping out his revolver, Steele shot and killed his assailant before he could get off a second shot. A wild encounter had followed. Mounted Indians, yelling their warwhoops, poured out of the surrounding bush. A flurry of shots was exchanged, but in the confusion and the darkness no results could be observed. The Indians galloped off, leaving two of their horses behind; the scouts were unhurt.

After bivouacking for the night, Steele, as a good cavalryman should, set out to follow up his enemy, who seemed to be circling back towards the river. He reported to Jingo that he had come upon the enemy's main camp in a position of great natural strength, and had kept it under observation without himself being detected. There were no fewer that 187 lodges, and large numbers of mounted warriors could be seen milling about among the teepees. It was a very large force indeed.

On reaching Major Steele after a rapid march through difficult country, Jingo formed his few wagons into a defensive corral and left them under the care of their armed drivers, while he pressed forward with the remainder of his force. Steele led him through a narrow ravine, so thickly wooded with small saplings that it was difficult for a man to walk, let alone ride, and so to a knoll where the enemy position could be watched unobserved. Steele, who had been here in 1876, remembered it as bald prairie; now the entire site was thickly covered with brush.

The scene before him fairly took Jingo's breath away. From the ravine at its foot, a great ridge raised itself high against the sky. Its lower slopes, bare and steep, rose up to precipitous bluffs fringed at the top with woods. Above these was a sloping open area, now filled with the teepees of a large Indian encampment, and alive with warriors, many of them mounted. Here at last was the enemy so long pursued, the object of so many weary days of hard marching.

It was the strength of the position that immediately impressed Jingo. The hill was encircled by the Red Deer River, which ran around its northern and eastern flank before emptying into the Saskatchewan. A sluggish, marshy tributary at the bottom of the narrow ravine bordered the western and southern slopes. The only practicable approach, unless one attempted a direct climb up the steep bare slopes, was a trail that led diagonally up from left to right, crossing the front of the position and commanded for its full length by any riflemen on the crest. With his field glasses Jingo could see that this trail had been marked out by pieces of red and white cloth, obviously cut from calico looted from Fort Pitt and tied to branches. Their only function seemed to be to make this easy access to the hilltop abundantly clear to any attacker. The cleared spot at the foot of the hill, where the soldiers were now taking position, was obviously an Indian ceremonial centre, and numerous burnt-out fires and sapling frameworks showed that it had recently been used for a sun dance or thirst dance, in which young warriors underwent self-inflicted ordeals to demonstrate their courage and endurance.

Jingo estimated that there must be a force of some 500 warriors on the hilltop; obviously Big Bear's band had been joined by those of other chiefs. The size of the enemy force and the strength of its position were daunting enough, but it was something else that impressed itself on Jingo's subconscious as he examined the place, identified on his map as Frenchman's Butte. The mounted warriors, openly displaying themselves in the encampment, the gaily marked trail revealing the only approach to the position—all this was entirely at odds with traditional Indian practice. As his men filed past, deploying in extended order along the whole length of the ravine at the foot of the hill, Jingo again studied the wooded crest. Surely there was something odd about part of that growth; looking closely, Jingo could see that branches had been stuck into the ground here and there, their wilted leaves contrasting with the fresh green of the natural undergrowth. They could only be camouflage for defences of some kind—almost certainly shallow rifle pits of the sort dug by natives in other engagements. They seemed to extend right along the entire front, giving complete command of the bare slopes, which served as the glacis for this natural fortress. To climb the trail, any attacker would have to traverse an open hillface swept by enemy fire.

Jingo had seen enough. This was no position to be taken in one swift assault. Orders were passed to halt the deployment of the force, and it was withdrawn instead to the relative shelter of the wagon corral, where it spent a quiet, though not necessarily restful, night. The men sheltered as best they could beneath the wagons. The voltigeurs, who had marched in haste from the barges without rations or greatcoats, shared those of the light infantrymen.

Next morning, after a meagre breakfast, their teeth chattering from the early morning chill and nervousness, the men were marched off to positions Jingo had chosen the day before. They were deployed left and right from the ceremonial clearing along the narrow ravine to take what cover was available in the sapling thickets along the course of the boggy creek. They were intended to contain the enemy, rather than to assault. The Indians were to be attacked by artillery shelling, not by infantry, up those appalling slopes.

Jingo had read the whole position as one vast trap, an ambuscade on an enormous scale. It was the way Indians traditionally fought, after all, catching their opponent exposed in the open while they remained concealed. And it had proved successful, too, time and again. At Duck Lake, at Cut Knife Hill, at Fish Creek and Batoche, they had caught white forces in the open. All the commanders—Crozier, Otter, and Middleton (twice)—had allowed themselves to be put at serious disadvantage by natives firing from under cover. Jingo was certainly not going to allow his name to be added to that list.

He considered that the enemy would be most vulnerable to artillery fire, since the open rifle pits afforded little shelter from shrapnel bursting overhead. Accordingly, he positioned his field gun, with its new crew, in the central clearing below the hill while his force took up position. He put the Winnipeg Light Infantry on his extreme right, the Alberta Mounted Rifles in support of his artillery in the centre, and the 65th Voltigeurs to his left, to determine the extent of the enemy defences and to see whether their flank might be turned.

The field gun opened fire, dropping its first shell directly on its target, a line of rifle pits exactly 600 yards away. After the shell burst, activity could be detected in the enemy camp as men scrambled for cover. The Indian response was prompt: a general fire was opened from the hill crest on the long line of troops in the valley beneath.

The soldiers, taking what shelter they could find in the sapling thickets, returned the fire as best they could, but as they were firing up a steep slope at an enemy they could not see, their shooting could hardly have much effect. Jingo rode along the line, providing encouragement to his soldiers, some of whom had had to flounder through mud and water to reach their positions and might be feeling a few qualms at being fired upon by an invisible enemy. As the only mounted man in sight, Jingo drew a good deal of fire, and he soon dismounted, finding it easier in any event to walk through the tangled scrub than to ride. He was experiencing some qualms himself after finding how confining the ravine was proving to his deployment; some of the boggy meanders of the creek were proving impassable, so that he was unable to encircle as much of the hill as he had wished.

Jingo's object had been to pen Big Bear closely enough to force him to make his escape towards the Saskatchewan River, where Middleton's steamers were hourly expected, loaded with troops and supplies. Now Osborne-Smith's light infantrymen had found themselves unable to move much beyond the front of the position. A message from Steele, searching to the left to find the flank of the enemy position, reported no end after more than a mile. It would not be until after the battle that he would learn that the Indians had deceived him by sending a party of riflemen to keep opposite his party and maintain a steady fire, so as to give the impression of a continuous line of defence.

Young Harry Strange's artillery fire seemed the only effective weapon against this almost invulnerable position, and its gunners were proving impressively accurate.

A young militia subaltern, Lieutenant R. G. MacBeth of the Winnipeg Light Infantry, later recorded in his journal an exchange overheard during the height of the bombardment. An Indian warrior, with a distinctive war bonnet and mounted on a spirited pony, presumed to be the tribal war chief, Wandering Spirit, was galloping back and forth along the line of the enemy position, waving a coloured blanket from an improvised flagpole and obviously encouraging his tribesmen. He seemed a person of importance, probably a war chief, and Harry Strange pointed him out to his gunners as a possible target. "Do you think you can hit that mounted man?" he asked his gun's crew.

"Bejabbers," responded a grinning Irish gun captain, "Oi'll ate what's left of him!"

The gun was traversed, the eager Irish gunlayer took careful aim, and a shell fired which, bursting right over its target, blew him to bits.

The victim was not, however, Wandering Spirit. MacBeth later noted that the war chief was shouting down at the red-coated infantrymen below him: "Tan at eee! Tan at ee!" Apparently the chief had overheard soldiers at drill and was attempting to shout "Stand at ease!" in the hope that the redcoats would then relax into immobility and cease any martial activity.

MacBeth was equally amused at another order, this one from Steele, who ordered the infantrymen about him to "Keep down, keep under cover!" while he himself, resplendent in red coat and white helmet, sat on his horse in plain view of enemy snipers.

Watching the effects of his fire, Harry Strange thought the anti-personnel shrapnel was having little effect, as the screen of branches over some of the rifle pits sheltered the enemy from the small projectiles; so he reverted to ordinary shell, fused to burst above the ground, as being the most effective. The gun and its crew, necessarily sited in the open central clearing, was now drawing most of the enemy's fire, and its crew either knelt or lay down to avoid it. Only Lieutenant Strange, as its directing officer, remained on his feet.

As the day wore on, with no sign of Middleton pushing upriver and both Smith and Steele reporting no hope of a flank being turned, Jingo came to a decision. His artillery fire must now have done what execution it could, and the enemy had managed to shelter from its further fire. There seemed little point in exposing his men in positions dominated by an unseen enemy, where their morale could only suffer. Many were now cold and wet, they had had nothing to eat since daybreak and little enough then, and since no vulnerable flank had been found there was no possibility of an infantry assault in which they could come to grips with their elusive enemy. Jingo refused to send them up that murderous glacis, although some of his officers seemed eager to try. Time was on his side. He would wait until Big Bear either resumed his march and could be brought to action by a close pursuit, or until the arrival of Middleton with all the guns and men necessary to storm the position. A glance at the gun limber confirmed his decision; there were only twenty-two rounds left, too precious to waste here. Jingo gave orders to retire and reform at the wagon corral, and as the weary soldiers filed by, the Battle of Frenchman's Butte came to an end.

Or nearly so. Three of his men—Constable McRae of the police and Voltigeurs Lemai and Marcotte of the 65th—had been wounded, but Jingo noted that only two men had been carried past him on stretchers. Enquiry revealed that Private Lemai had been left behind in a position exposed to enemy fire. An officer of the 65th, confronted by Jingo, simply shrugged the matter off: "He's going to die, anyway!"

A furious Jingo pointed out that, as an officer, he was responsible for his men, only to receive the reply: "General, I have been shot at quite enough today, and I am damned if I go down there again!" As his subordinate slunk off, Jingo quickly beckoned a stretcher party to him, together with a surgeon of the 65th, Dr. Paré, and the chaplain, Father Prevost. They were eager to assist. They found Lemai lying in full view of the enemy, badly wounded but conscious, and Father Prevost, crucifix in hand, knelt to administer rites of the Church. The enemy now opened a hot fire, and as the bullets whistled about them, Jingo confessed to becoming somewhat impatient at the formal confession of sin, and asked the chaplain whether he might not "lump the lot" for the purposes of granting absolution. In the circumstances, Father Prevost was able to see the sense of the suggestion, and quickly concluded the ritual, whereupon the wounded man was bundled into the stretcher, under the direction of Dr. Paré, and borne off. Jingo brought up the rear, carrying the man's rifle.

Enemy fire now became intense, and the rear stretcher bearer panicked and dropped his end of the stretcher. Jingo promptly picked it up and Lemai was borne safely from the field by his general, who afterwards noted in his journal that "Jingo, having finished his first fight by kicking his general, met a just retribution in having to carry his wounded off his last field."

With Major Hatton's Mounted Rifles and Steele's scouts as rearguard, the force retired to Fort Pitt to regroup. The 65th's tents and rations had departed on the barges which, having moved downstream to avoid enemy fire, were unable to return against the strong current and had elected to proceed on to Battleford. A supply train from Edmonton, escorted by a detachment of the Winnipeg Light Infantry under Captain Dudley Smith, arrived next morning, however, and the troops, now rested, clothed, and fed, were given a day of leisure to recover from their exertions.

Their mood, while confident, did not reflect any particular jubilation. The battle they had fought, it seemed to them, had been inconclusive. They had been shot at and had suffered only three men wounded, but they had no way of knowing what casualties, if any, had been inflicted on the enemy.

It was only when five white men, prisoners who had been released by the Indians, were led into camp by scouts that they realized what a shattering blow had been dealt the rebel cause by the fight at Frenchman's Butte. Their fire had driven the Crees from the hilltop even as they themselves were withdrawing to Fort Pitt. All unaware, they had won a decisive victory, at the cost of three men wounded.

For Jingo, it was a victory won not so much by what he did as by what he did not do. By not charging up those slopes, by not following that enticing upward trail, he had reduced the whole elaborate trap to a costly and humiliating failure. Jingo, whose reputation had been founded on aggressive, daredevil tactics, had won his most notable success through the exercise of cautious prudence. Gunner Jingo had matured into General Strange!

Four of the released prisoners had been captured by Big Bear at Fort Carlton; the fifth was W. B. Cameron, a Hudson's Bay Company agent and the sole male survivor of the massacre at Frog Lake. The eager soldiers flocked around them to hear their story. After his successes at Frog Lake and Fort Carlton, they learned, Big Bear and his band of Plains Crees had remained in the district. They hoped to persuade their cousins of the more numerous Woods Crees to join forces with them and to combine with Poundmaker at Battleford in armed rebellion against the white settlers and the government's plans to confine Indians within the limits of "reservations." But the Woods Crees had been reluctant to join the rebellion. They had delayed and temporized. They had also resisted the urgings of some of the more militant Plains Cree warriors to butcher the white prisoners, more than thirty in number, mostly women and children taken at

Fort Pitt. They would be valuable as hostages, the Woods Indians claimed, and the Indian women had protected the captive women from the overtures of a few brash young warriors. Indeed, the captives had been treated more like guests than prisoners, and had been fed and sheltered on the friendliest terms with the native families they lived among.

The warmth of this care and kindness contrasted with the ferocity the warriors had shown at Frog Lake. Cameron told his grim-faced listeners some of the details of that terrible scene, when the congregation had filed out of the little church, to be set upon by Wandering Spirit and his young followers, fearsome in their warpaint and crazed with bloodlust. Big Bear, who had been inside the church, was unable to restrain them: Wandering Spirit, Miserable Man, the Worm, Ugly Man, Bare Neck, Little Bear, He-Who-Wins, and half a dozen others had killed and butchered until their passion was spent.

The ineffectiveness of Big Bear's efforts had robbed him of his prestige in the eyes of his people. Now, in the loose tribal system, they were dominated by Wandering Spirit, the leading buffalo hunter and warrior of the Plains Crees, and their war chief. It was Wandering Spirit who had selected Frenchman's Butte as their base and had persuaded his warriors, against their natural inclinations, to undertake the laborious task of digging its elaborate fortifications. Their toil would be rewarded, he assured them, when the tall black-bearded one on his red horse would lead his soldiers up the clearly marked trail, to be exterminated by the carefully concealed warriors lying in wait. It was Wandering Spirit, too, who had organized the ceremonial war dances to whip up tribal spirits, interrupted by news of the soldiers' unexpectedly early arrival at Fort Pitt.

Success at Frenchman's Butte was crucial to the Indian cause. Wandering Spirit had staked everything on the success of his carefully prepared ambuscade. An able tactician, he knew of the propensity of white leaders to lead their men forward in a frontal attack, and the black-bearded one was known for the aggressiveness and rapidity of his marches.

The artillery fire, which had killed one man and severely wounded six others in the first few minutes, had unnerved the Indians in their rifle pits. Even after they had taken cover as best they could, the experience of being under fire from shells bursting overhead had been a trying ordeal. But it was the long wait, hour after hour, for an attack which never came that had completely unsettled them. They saw their long hours of arduous toil going for naught, their whole carefully laid ambuscade wasted on an enemy content to encircle them, under cover and out of reach. This whole plan of Wandering Spirit's had been madness from the start. What were they doing, warriors accustomed to roam and raid wherever they wished, cooped up in holes in the ground on this forsaken hilltop?

Wandering Spirit strove to keep them in their places, but his magic had failed. Even as desultory firing continued from the distant soldiers, the hilltop's defenders began to melt away. Soon the movement became general; by nightfall the hill was deserted. The disillusioned warriors, with their women and children, abandoned their loot and any unnecessary impedimenta and streamed away to the north. They were leaderless now, bent only on escaping from the remorseless blackbeard who, they knew, would soon be on their trail. A broken man, their war chief rode silently in their midst, all dreams of glory vanished, a Wandering Spirit indeed.

SEVENTEEN

Victory

As poignant and sharp as a child's cry, it had come to Jingo as he paced about the pitted top of Frenchman's Butte, cluttered with wagons and littered by loot abandoned by Big Bear's fleeing warriors. It was a message from the prisoners, the little band of frightened women and children whose safety was now the only object of concern to every man in the Alberta Field Force. One of Steele's scouts, a Montana cowboy and a veteran of the American frontier wars, had found the scrap of paper and brought it over to Jingo, as he and a group of horsemen had inspected the hilltop fortifications which had made the Butte so impregnable.

"Reckon you should see this, General," he had said. "I picked it out of the bottom branch of that tree, there."

The message had been brief, reflecting the urgent haste with which it had been written: "Look for us up the hill northwest of here. W. J. McLean and family. All well. May God protect us."

It was a cry for help, an appeal that struck to Jingo's heart, but what added pathos to the note was the paper on which the pencilled message had been scribbled. It was a page torn from a child's copy of *Robinson Crusoe*, and on that wind-ravaged hilltop it spoke, more eloquently than any words, of the cosy domesticity of a family circle, now rent apart by war and bloodshed. To reach and free that frightened family was all that mattered to Jingo and the horsemen, whose faces were now turned expectantly towards their leader.

He was angry, now, they knew, and they sensed a new urgency in the stream of orders he issued, an urgency which was swiftly communicated to every man in the force. The saving of life, not the taking of it, had become the primary purpose of the little army, and speed the first requirement.

Major Steele, shaven and immaculate as ever in his scarlet tunic, was called over. His white-helmeted head nodded understanding as Jingo poured out his instructions, ending with a clap on the shoulder and a hearty: "Off you go!"

Within minutes Steele led his scouts, some sixty in all, out of camp, trotting northwards on the trail of the largest party, for the Indians had now separated into two distinct groups. The Hudson's Bay factor, McKay, who knew the region better than anyone, was sent with a mixed detachment of scouts and Mounted Rifles to follow the other trail, every trooper in the two forces carrying only the barest essentials in his saddlebags: ammunition, tinned meat, and biscuits.

Once the cavalry had left, Jingo set about organizing the remainder of his force. He proposed to move his infantry and artillery as rapidly as possible on a route parallel to that taken by his horsemen but to the west, heading for Beaver River, and the Hudson's Bay Company post there. All indications were that Big Bear would head for this small post, the last trading depot where he could hope to obtain the provisions he desperately needed. His band had abandoned large quantities of food supplies, including tinned provisions as well as much bacon and flour, in its haste to evacuate Frenchman's Butte, and Jingo now proposed to head it off before it could be re-supplied. With Steele following closely on its heels and Jingo's infantry, with despatch and luck, ahead of it, Big Bear's band would be caught between two fires. Dominating every aspect of this plan, and emphasizing the need for speed, was fear for the safety of Big Bear's prisoners. As food grew short and conditions desperate, his surly warriors might well kill their captives, both as revenge and as a means of easing the burden on food supplies and the speed of travel.

But before Jingo could set out with his infantry, a message arrived from Middleton. The general himself, together with a considerable army, would arrive in Jingo's camp next day. For weeks, there had been no word from him, no reply to the messages and reports sent him. Three times Jingo had sent messengers, but none had returned. The help, the supplies, and above all, the reinforcements so long and eagerly awaited were to arrive at last, now that they were no longer needed. Worse than that, word that his superior officer would shortly arrive deprived Jingo of the authority to make decisions in the interim. He must now remain in camp and await Middleton's arrival.

But the same day brought more welcome developments. Scouts arrived from both parties, leading with them a number of prisoners released by the Indians: first a group that included two women, Mrs. Gowanlock and Mrs. Delaney, accompanied by a number of Woods Crees as escort, and later a mixed group that included Mrs. Quiney, five Métis families who had not been held hostage but wished to leave Big Bear's doomed band, and three white men.

In a fever of impatience to release the remainder, Jingo still found time to write in his journal: "The chivalrous treatment of their lady prisoners speaks volumes in favour of the Canadian Red man, as compared to his brother across the boundary, perhaps because neither the government of King George nor of Canada has ever broken faith with the Indian. Pity it was that the land claims of the French half-breeds were ignored until discontent grew into rebellion."

But the scouts also brought a report on the darker side of the Indian mood. Hanging from a tree at the side of the well-marked line of retreat, they had found the body of a young Indian woman; dangling from another rope nearby hung the body of a dog. This gruesome find represented the final chapter of a tragic story which Jingo later learned from one of the released hostages, and which had played a part in the grisly massacre at Frog Lake.

Apparently the government's Indian agent there had had a young warrior from the local Cree band arrested for stealing a quantity of beef—meat which, gossip had it, the agent had deliberately left in the Indian's way. The brave had been jailed, and in his absence the agent had taken up with the man's wife. When the husband returned and learned of his wife's infidelity, he took the opportunity afforded by the Indian occupation of the white settlement at Frog Lake to hunt down and kill the agent. This killing, so the hostage maintained, had helped trigger the massacre of other white settlers there.

The erring wife had accompanied the band during its campaign. But when the defeat at Frenchman's Butte put an end to any hopes of Indian success, the embittered tribesmen had executed both her and the agent's unfortunate dog, and had left them hanging as a sign that the guilty parties had both paid in full for their actions.

Middleton duly arrived and pouted with annoyance to learn that Steele's scouts were already on Big Bear's trail. He refused Jingo's request for his cavalry to be sent on in support. "Not a man! Not a man!" he exclaimed. "Who is this Major Steele?"

A heated exchange then took place, which resulted in a sullen Middleton eventually agreeing to send 200 of his horsemen in support. He delayed their dispatch until next day, however, and thereby missed a golden opportunity to bring the campaign to a quick and triumphant end.

For Steele had caught Big Bear. His leading troopers had overtaken the Indian rearguard, and in a furious, swirling action fought out in a tangled scrub, had killed several warriors and put the rest to flight. In this desperate encounter, one scout was wounded, and a prisoner, Quiney, managed to elude his captors and join Steele's party. He informed them that Big Bear had only fifty warriors with him, the rest having returned to their various reservations, but was still holding hostage the McLean family—two parents and nine children.

After camping briefly in the hours of darkness, Steele marched at first light, anxious to press his advantage. He had come up with Big Bear's group as it was crossing a ford at the narrows of a small lake to reach a long, wooded peninsula, a strong defensive position surrounded by water.

Steele was surprised to find that the band numbered more than a hundred, at a quick estimate. Obviously some of Big Bear's strays had returned to the fold. But although he had only five men with him in this advanced patrol, Steele was determined to attack the main body before it could reach the safety of the impregnable peninsula. He accordingly opened fire from the vantage point of a low ridge that overlooked the ford, but the Indians, quickly realizing the small number of their attackers, counter-attacked, attempting to surround the little force. Fortunately for Steele, the remainder of his scouts arrived in the nick of time, and another furious battled raged, with charge and counter-charge up and down the wooded hillside. The intrepid Sergeant Fury was severely wounded leading such a charge, but Steele's hardened veterans, with the advantage of surprise and a commanding ridgetop position, were more than a match for Big Bear's warriors. The Indians eventually melted away to splash across the ford to safety, leaving a dozen dead behind. The scouts ceased firing when they realized that the McLean hostages were being put at risk. One of their shots had narrowly missed Mrs. McLean, who was carrying an Indian child in her arms.

Fearing that Big Bear must now have his back to the wall, Steele determined to parley and sent the Reverend Mr. McKay, his best Indian linguist, down to the shore under a flag of truce. A summons to surrender the prisoners, called out in McKay's great voice, brought only a fusillade of rifle fire. A second attempt brought no better result. McKay then called out asking for McLean to be allowed to speak, but Big Bear himself responded, promising to recross the ford and clear the white men out.

Steele had now done all that could be done with his little force. He collected his three wounded men, burned the Indian encampment on the shore, rounded up half a dozen Indian horses, and withdrew to a safe position twelve miles off, to rest his weary men and played-out horses, which had travelled eighty miles, on very little feed, in two days. He sent an urgent message to Jingo reporting the situation and asking for reinforcements, a request that was passed on to Middleton. Instead of joining Steele, however, Middleton ordered Steele to return and join him, thereby losing all touch with Big Bear and the all-important hostages.

In exasperation, Jingo could only insist that he be allowed to set off instantly for Beaver River, as originally planned, for it might still be possible to head off Big Bear from the vital supplies stored there. In the end, Middleton gave his consent, and Jingo marched at the head of a flying column of infantry, including units of the 65th Voltigeurs and Winnipeg Light Infantry.

Middleton's inability to recognize and exploit opportunity when offered was now demonstrated to the full. Steele's action at Scout Lake, also called Loon Lake, had been the most brilliant battle of the whole campaign, his aggressive pursuit and masterly conduct of the attack nothing short of superb. Jingo, who had recognized his character and ability from the beginning, made a point of turning his brilliant subordinate loose at every opportunity to give full play to his genius. The hard-riding cowboys and constables of Steele's Scouts, all veteran woodsmen and plainsmen, constituted the finest light cavalry in the world, Middleton was assured by a man who ridden with India's Mahrattas and Corps of Guides, as well as Britain's finest mounted regiments. By failing to support this remarkable force and tying it instead to the ponderous progress of his unwieldy army, Middleton abandoned any opportunity of bringing the campaign to a speedy conclusion, and chose instead to plod painfully northwards on Big Bear's long-cold trail. On arrival at Scout Lake, the scene of Steele's remarkable exploit, the general declared the country beyond to be impassable to his troops, and retreated down a road cut previously by Jingo's men. With him went the frustrated horsemen who had once brought Big Bear to bay, and were now compelled to trudge westwards to join the Alberta Field Force at Beaver River. With his voltigeurs and light infantrymen, Jingo had been experiencing the worst conditions and most difficult going of the entire campaign. The marshy lakes and sodden scrubland, now turned into a vast morass of clinging black mud by drenching downpours, was worse than anything they had ever experienced. Swarms of mosquitoes and clouds of persistent horseflies and deerflies drove them nearly mad with their bites. The clammy heat of the days alternated with midnight frosts, for the force was now well to the north of its accustomed prairie climate.

The march was especially hard on the voltigeurs of the 65th, who had marched further than any other unit; more than 500 miles. They also suffered from difficulties unique to their regiment: their boots were inferior to those issued to the Winnipeg infantrymen, and were now quite worn out. Some marched with rags bundled about their feet, others in boots with flapping soles, still others actually barefoot.

Their morale had been weakened by newspaper stories read in Fort Pitt about Ontario Protestants calling them cowards, and Quebec Catholics branding them traitors to the French-Canadian cause. Some of their junior officers had shown themselves to be faint of heart, at best. They were homesick, and could see no point in the eternal plodding through fly-infested bog after an enemy they could never catch.

Their cumulative misery came to a head on June 6, an especially dreary dawn, when they were turned out of their fly-filled tents into a torrential downpour. It was too much, they had had enough, they informed their alarmed officers. They refused to budge another step, and it was no good sending for the old general. They had fought for him and followed him far enough, and now they wanted to go home.

Standing beside them in the pouring rain, Jingo sensed their mood, although none of them spoke. This was no time for appeals to patriotism or reproaches for cowardice. He knew exactly how they felt, huddled in their tattered uniforms, soaked through, their faces swollen with insect bites and far from home and loved ones.

He spoke to them in French, as he always did, and he spoke to them as a father to his family, as he always did.

"My children," he began, "your commander tells me that you want to go home. But I have only one answer, the answer of your grand old song." And then, in a dry, cracked voice, Jingo began to sing, the tune hardly recognizable, but the words familiar as any nursery rhyme:

> Malbrouck s'en va-t-en guerre-a!
> Ne sait quand reviendra.
> (Marlborough has gone a-fighting!
> Who knows when he will return?)

It was simply irresistible. Here was their old general, a gaunt scarecrow in his faded clothes, his black beard bedraggled and his boots spattered with mud, capering in the

rain to the tune of an old folksong they had learned as boys;
a song written by Frenchmen long ago to taunt the soldiers
of an English general. As he jigged about in front of them,
still singing in that awful voice, they roared the refrain back
at him:

> Malbrouck, s'en va-t-en guerre-a!
> Mironton, mironton, mirontaine,
> Malbrouck s'en va-t-en guerre-a!
> Ne sait quand reviendra!

Suddenly the misery, the homesickness, the war-weari-
ness faded. They loved him, just as he loved them, for they
were father and family together, come what may, and they
would follow wherever he led. "Hourra!" they cried.
"Hourra pour le général!" Falling into column of route, they
marched off to shouts of "En avant! Toujours en avant!" and
waved their hats as they passed their Buckskin Brigadier.
That day they not only kept up with the fresher, better-shod
Winnipeg Light Infantry, but they pulled the nine-
pounder—gun, limber, horses and all—out of a deep morass where it had bogged down axle-deep.

While still thirty miles from his objective, Jingo learned
from scouts that Indians, probably hostile Chipewyans allied to Big Bear, had been seen near one of the two HBC
stores at Beaver River. It would be disastrous to lose the race
now, after such long and hard marching. With fifteen
mounted men—all that could be scraped together from his
little force—Jingo rode breakneck for Beaver River. After an
exhausting all-day ride, the little party arrived at the first
HBC post at dusk. There was just enough light to make out
a party of Indians on horses on a distant hilltop, who stood,
observing the post, before withdrawing into the woods.
They were undoubtedly the advance guard of Big Bear's war
band and had arrived less than an hour too late. By the
narrowest of margins, Jingo had won his race!

At dusk next day the infantry arrived, having marched all through the previous night. The weary soldiers, famished after days of light marching rations, were permitted to gorge themselves on the plentiful supplies of bacon and flour in the post, supplies which they had worked so hard to deny to Big Bear's hungry warriors. Stuffed with flapjacks and bacon, Jingo fell asleep on the store's bare wooden floor with his pipe still in his mouth. He was rudely awakened by a bucket of cold water in his face. He had managed to set himself, and his son Harry sleeping beside him, on fire with his burning tobacco.

In the morning, a working party visited the other HBC post, situated at the Roman Catholic mission settlement downriver, and returned with its supplies, amounting to some one hundred bags of flour. They also brought two boats found concealed nearby, which might have been useful to the enemy.

Father LeGoff, the mission's priest, who had been carried off prisoner by the Chipewyans, arrived in camp. His captors had released him but had resisted his pleas to surrender themselves to the soldiers. Jingo sent him back to tell the Chipewyans that unless they surrendered themselves and their arms to him within twenty-four hours, he would burn every longhouse in the settlement. He was determined to make the most of this rare military presence in this remote, and rebellious, area. The Chipewyans, knowing the formidable black-bearded general to be a man of his word, immediately arrived en masse, laying down their arms—some of them pilfered from Fort Pitt, Jingo noted—and surrendering themselves to the mercy of the Great White Queen. All were duly pardoned, having taken up arms in fear of Big Bear and for the sake of the plunder at the abandoned Fort Pitt.

All efforts were now concentrated on securing the release of the McLean family, the last of the prisoners still being held by Woods Crees who had separated from Big Bear and were believed to be anxious to surrender. After Middleton's arrival in camp some three days later, Jingo made preparations to send a detachment to Cold Lake and another to Lac des Iles, both considered to be possible objectives of the Woods Crees. The expeditions were forestalled when the McLeans themselves, escorted by some of their former captors, were encountered en route to Beaver River. They were welcomed into the camp with much jubilation on both sides.

The liberation of the last of the hostages, for which the men of the Alberta Field Force had fought and laboured so painfully and for so long, brought to a joyous conclusion one of its primary objectives. The other, the hunt for Big Bear, ended in anti-climax when the great chief, hunted by hundreds of armed men over a vast stretch of difficult country, gave himself up peaceably to an astonished Sergeant Smart, a mounted policeman left to guard the ferry crossing at Fort Carlton.

The Alberta Field Force, its work done, was now dispersed. Some of the troops were returning to Edmonton, others heading for Battleford for onward routing, but all were homeward bound. Jingo joined with them in their celebrations, but as a man who detested emotional scenes, he could not trust himself to conduct a formal leavetaking. Instead, he slipped quietly away one morning, bound downriver in the unaccustomed luxury of a river steamer for Winnipeg and later Ottawa, to placate the bureaucrats already baying on his trail. The fighting war was over, but the paper war had just begun.

EIGHTEEN

Aftermath

When Jingo interrupted his eastward journey at Battleford to meet the captive Big Bear whom he had pursued so long and so far, he noted in his journal that he felt no animosity towards his old antagonist. Indeed, as he was later to note, both of them had suffered as a result of their actions during the late rebellion. For Big Bear, the sentence was life imprisonment, although he was released after serving only a token term. For Jingo, victory brought more complex penalties. He was informed by the British government that, having been employed by a colonial government during the rebellion, he had forfeited his British Army pension. In other words, having answered his Queen's call to take up arms against rebels, he was deprived of a pension won by thirty years of faithful service to that same queen. It would take three years of intensive lobbying by Jingo, and especially by an old friend and former governor general of Canada, the Marquis of Lorne, before the pension was restored, and he was never repaid for the intervening three-year period.

A longer-lasting penalty was the ordeal of coping with the swarms of civil servants who now bedevilled him. By answering his country's call to "raise a force," he had been forced to seek equipment and supplies, as best he could, on the spot. There were no government forms, in the required number of copies, available on the western frontier. Jingo had signed vouchers for what he needed on the basis of telegraphed authorization from his chief, the Minister of Militia in Ottawa.

These vouchers, now coming home to roost, scandalized the tidy world of the Ottawa civil service. There was no precedent for them, no authorization, no due process, no proper channels. Which department was to pay for these twenty saddles or those three dozen pairs of boots? For the rest of a long life Jingo was to be dunned by pertinacious bureaucrats who would give him no peace, and badgered by reams of paper containing requests, threats, or summonses.

One can understand and even sympathize with the attitude of the government bureaucrats faced with a seemingly unending stream of demands for payment for all sorts of goods and services, all without any sort of proper authorization. Given the tiny federal budgets of the times, the cost of all the supplies and equipment necessary to put some hundreds of men into the field and maintain them there represented a very considerable outlay, just over $4 million, most of it payable to the Canadian Pacific Railway and the Hudson's Bay Company. Certainly the government's claims commission required some pretty convincing answers from the leader of what officialdom saw as little more than a band of brigands. Yet even conceding the need for searching questions, there was clearly a failure on the part of official Ottawa to grasp both the urgency of the situation, with the entire white population of Northwest Canada on the brink of panic in the face of massacre, and the difficulty of securing arms and supplies through regular channels in frontier country cut off from any direct connection with a remote east.

There was something worse than mere incomprehension; there was a certain meanness of spirit in some official attitudes. Steele's scouts, for example, were to be paid a few cents a day above their regular soldiers' pay as a sort of "danger money," since they were expected to operate, far from support, in the very face of the enemy. They had pressed hard on the heels of a retreating but dangerous enemy right up to the final surrender, and they expected to be paid for this period. Some bureaucrat, however, with the benefit of hindsight, ruled that the action fought at Scout, or Loon, Lake had proved to be the final battle of the campaign. He therefore set that date, June 3, as the cutoff date for danger money and ruled that the scouts' subsequent shadowing and harrying of Big Bear's band did not rate as being "in the face of the enemy." This petty-minded penny-pinching infuriated the men who had been in the forefront of the campaign, and saved the government a mere couple of hundred dollars.

On a more personal level, Jingo was dismayed to learn that Middleton, whom he had regarded as a friend since their service together in India, had proved to be a jealous dissembler. Behind his back, Middleton had denigrated him to fellow officers and political superiors as a crank, a fanatic, an unstable and unreliable eccentric unsuited for command. Even worse, Middleton had suppressed Jingo's reports to his political superiors, forwarded through Middleton as his commanding officer, so that as far as official Ottawa was concerned, the trials and achievements of the Alberta Field Force were largely unknown. Certainly they were unknown to the public at large, for the majority of newspaper correspondents naturally travelled with Middleton's column, along with the top brass and the fashionable regiments. The result of this anonymity was that no official recognition was ever made of the force or its achievements, and the endurance and bravery of its individual soldiers went unrewarded.

Jingo had recommended decorations for a number of his men, especially for Steele, the war's most brilliant soldier. In an official despatch, forwarded to Middleton, he had written:

> Major Steele and his cavalry were the eyes, ears and feelers of the force, and their spirited pursuit of Big Bear crowned with success the long and weary march which they had protected and, to a certain extent, guided. The Reverend John MacDougall and Canon McKay, from their large and intimate knowledge of the country, were successfully connected with the force.

In a special recommendation of Steele for the award of the Order of St. Michael and St. George (CMG) he wrote:

> I have the honour to submit for your favourable consideration the name of Major Samuel Steele, Superintendent of the North West Mounted Police, who commanded the cavalry of the Alberta Field Force under my command during the late campaign. I need not detail to you the eminent services he rendered, as already mentioned in my despatches, as well as in that forwarded by him when sent forward by me with my cavalry in pursuit of Big Bear's band; also the details of organization he carried out in raising scouts under my command. I beg respectfully to submit that he has earned the distinction of a C.M.G., usually bestowed for military services to the empire in connection with the colonies.

This request, and others made by Jingo on behalf of other soldiers in his command and, indeed, by other commanders on behalf of their officers and men, went unheeded. No such awards were to be given lest they detract from the glory of the commander-in-chief. The resultant bitterness was best expressed by Steele himself:

It did not matter, however, who was mentioned in despatches; no one but the G.O.C. received any award. He was voted in parliament the sum of $20,000 and was knighted, but there was nothing for General Strange after all his hard work. He had saved Alberta, had rescued captives who had been in Big Bear's hands; not one shot had been fired against the chief or his murderous tribe and their allies, the Wood Crees, except by Strange's men, and he should certainly have been granted the K.C.M.G.

After much lobbying by soldiers involved, a campaign medal for the suppression of the Northwest Rebellion was authorized. A suitable design was chosen and the medal was struck in Britain, to be bestowed by the Queen. The Canadian government was expected, of course, to bear the cost involved, a trifling £1,500, but was reluctant to do so, and so it was the British government that paid the bill.

But the matter was not resolved even then. Regiments taking part in the actual fighting wished to have some mark to distinguish themselves from the much greater number who had been mobilized but had played no active part. Accordingly, a clasp bearing the word "Saskatchewan" was duly authorized and issued to 2,250 soldiers. Once again, the trifling expense was borne by the British taxpayer, so that the Canadian government was able to distribute medals at no cost to itself. Pensions for soldiers disabled for life in the campaign were equally meagre—forty to sixty cents a day, and no hospital care. Active service veterans were given eighty dollars cash or a grant of a patch of bald prairie, as they chose.

Much greater gifts were in store for the commander-in-chief. In addition to his knighthood and cash gift, and confirmation of his rank as major-general, Middleton was also offered the presidency of a large life insurance company on retirement. The offer was subsequently withdrawn after he became involved in a squalid affair arising from an attempt to bring east, as souvenirs, a few bundles of furs that he had "liberated."

It was not only the Alberta Field Force which felt slighted by their commander-in-chief. Middleton had made little mention of the activities of any column other than his own, and had mostly confined himself to an account of his own progress and plans. His final report to the government made scant mention of individual officers or units. This failure to award praise, let alone decorations, brought a storm of criticism from returned militia officers, hungry for at least favourable mention after all the hardships they had endured. In the end, he was forced to resign, and bundled himself and his family back to England in a huff, where he was mollified by being appointed Keeper of the Crown Jewels.

The general air of disappointment in the aftermath of hostilities extended to the vanquished as well as the victors. Riel was denied the state show trial where he hoped to appear centre stage and capture the admiration of the world with his eloquence. Instead, he was put on trial for his life in the grubby little courtroom at Regina. He stubbornly disdained the obvious plea of insanity which his defence lawyers sought to make, and which a government desperate to avoid hanging him hopefully offered. Inevitably, he was found guilty of treason and was duly hanged in the Regina jailyard, together with half a dozen convicted murderers from Big Bear's band.

Wandering Spirit, the war chief who had instigated the slaughter at Frog Lake and had so capably organized the defence of Frenchman's Butte, had sought to escape capture by suicide. Proud and brave to the last, he had plunged a knife into his chest, but he managed to inflict only a flesh wound and was duly executed with the others.

The prevailing air of discontent was felt especially keenly by Jingo, let down by his former comrade-in-arms and disillusioned by official response. In particular, the disregard of his warm recommendation of the men under him—"I have never commanded better soldiers"—and of individuals, including the militant men of the cloth, left him feeling that he had somehow failed them. He was therefore gratified by the presentation of a gold-headed ebony cane subscribed for by members of his scouts, now disbanded, and of a silver tea service, suitably engraved, paid for by the teamsters and other members of his transport corps. Recognition from such sources, he felt, outweighed any amount of official adulation.

Return to the ranch and the re-uniting of his family did much to improve his spirits. Back in working dress of buckskin jacket and chaps, he set about restoring the fortunes of the Military Colonisation Ranch Company, which had inevitably suffered from the effects of the long period of unrest and neglect.

A welcome visitor was an old friend, Sam Steele; in pursuit of some miscreant, his former comrade-in-arms stopped off for a night at Strangmuir, where, he noted in his journal, "I met with all the usual hospitality."

A family Christmas at the ranch house, run like an old-fashioned English country-house party, complete with games and dances and amateur theatricals, was great fun, especially savoured because all knew that it would be the last such family occasion. The three Strange girls were now of an age where they needed better education than could be provided by a frontier governess, and Mrs. Strange was planning to accompany them to England. The elder son, Harry, restless after his adventures chasing Big Bear, had applied to join Jingo's old corps, the Royal Artillery, and expected a summons at any moment to Woolwich.

Even Jingo, it had to be admitted, was feeling unsettled. The Indians nearby had grown resentful and sullen since the failure of the uprising and had promised to wreak revenge on Jingo, the leader of the force they blamed for its suppression. The prairie fires they set had taken serious toll of ranch livestock, and had even threatened the destruction of the ranch house itself and the lives of everyone in it. Perhaps even more disturbing were the rumbles of discontent among the ranch shareholders back east, grown fractious about company policy and returns on their investment. As the man on the spot, responsible for reconciling policy with reality and coping with the day-by-day problems of running a big mixed-stock ranch in what amounted to hostile country, Jingo found the old ranching life he so enjoyed becoming an increasing trial.

Perhaps its blackest moment occurred on the day Jingo drove young Harry to the Gleichen rail station to catch the train east en route to Woolwich in far-off England. He was entered in a new cadet class and he had to hurry, as postal delays had left him little time if he was to arrive on, or close to, the enrolment date. Halfway to the station, they were dismayed to see the vast pillar of smoke, towering high in the sky, that could only mean another prairie fire; the Indians had been busy again! The two scrambled out of their buckboard, removed their coats—Harry was in his best clothes—and set to work with wetted horse blankets in a desperate attempt to stem the flames. It was backbreaking, hopeless work, and after some twenty minutes Harry, looking at his watch, said: "Father, I must leave you. If I miss this train, I miss the next boat for a week. You know my orders."

"Do you mean to leave me on this burning prairie?" exclaimed an astounded Jingo. "It was you who taught me to obey orders," was young Harry's reply. And he drove away, leaving his father, sick at heart, to battle the flames alone.

Loyalty to the Queen took priority over any claims of the father, Jingo wryly reflected. He was later joined by cowboys from the ranch, and with their help was able to divert the flames away from the threatened house and home pastures. But the incident brought home to him the full impact of the loss of his son, who had been such a support to him in running both ranch and a military campaign.

But the vigorous outdoor life of the Canadian frontier, the happiest way of life he had ever known, he still found attractive. It would take a crippling injury to bring it to an end. As his cowboys customarily enjoyed a day of rest on Sundays, Jingo himself was in the habit of riding patrol on the range, near the native reservation, on the Sabbath. On one of these evening rides, two of the ranch womenfolk accompanied him, with Jingo riding a half-broken "cayuse." Having dismounted to retrieve a whip dropped by one of the ladies, Jingo was violently kicked by his horse. The blow shattered his right leg in two places.

As he lay helpless on the ground, Jingo realized that there was no possibility of climbing back into the saddle; it would require a litter or buckboard to move him. He explained the situation to his companions, who made their own arrangements. One was to stand by the fallen Jingo while the other rode to the ranch for help. Accordingly, one rode off into the gathering dusk—in the wrong direction! Her companion rode after her, but having failed to catch her, and afraid of becoming lost, she returned to the injured man. Jingo sent her off in the direction of the ranch, telling her to keep the Chinook wind that was blowing, on her right cheek, and to return with it on her left. She rode off into the night, and Jingo was left alone with this thoughts, all of them gloomy.

Tobacco was his only consolation, and he smoked pipe after pipe as he watched the stars come out and wheel majestically about the great vault above him. Coyotes could be heard, distant at first, but drawing ever nearer. Soon he could see their eyes, glowing faintly red in the starlight. Jingo had no revolver with him, but by occasional shouts he kept the animals at a respectful distance. The minutes crept by, ever so slowly, as Jingo reflected gloomily on his situation. Here he was, old and helpless on the empty prairie, family and friends all far away, the ranch beset by every sort of difficulty here and in the east, his military service unrecognized, his civilian project profitless. For the first time, life seemed a burden, grown too onerous to be borne—and hour dragged after weary hour for what seemed like eternity.

And yet, it was only four hours—four hours before Jingo could hear, his ear to the ground, the far-off drumming of hooves, the rattle and rumble of wheels. It was a buckboard from the ranch, with three cowboys and his lady messenger driving the horses at breakneck speed.

One of the cowboys, Mexican Pete, pulled off Jingo's boot after expertly slitting it and the breeches up the leg. With deft hands he straightened and bandaged the broken limb, and then, with the help of the others, lifted Jingo onto a litter and thence onto the floor of the buckboard. The jolting ride back to the ranch was sheer agony, but the warm camaraderie and care of the cowboys more than made up for the pain of the passage.

Next day, there was a visit from a real doctor, come all the way from Calgary. The lady messenger who had lost her way had managed to find the railway line and had had the good sense to follow it to Gleichen and send a telegraph.

Recovery was long and tedious. When the splinted bandages were removed for examination, the leg was broken again. It had still not mended when another grass fire, this time started by a cinder from a CPR locomotive, broke out near the ranch. Hobbling about on crutches to help save the house, Jingo again broke the leg, which eventually set, months later, in the form "of a modified letter S," as its owner sourly observed.

Financial troubles made this an especially difficult time. The ranch was being starved of the capital needed to re-stock the cattle herds, and despite an increasingly acrimoni-ous correspondence, none was forthcoming from the east. A company director, Alexander Gunn, a Kingston merchant and politician, was fomenting dissatisfaction with ranch policy and management. It all came to a head at a share-holder's meeting late in 1887. As a result Jingo was voted out and replaced as ranch manager by an American, a gentleman named S. S. Rogers. Jingo duly handed over the control of this magnificent ranch, which he had built from scratch virtually single-handed, to a Yankee without ranch-ing experience, backed by a group of Ontarians who had never been west of the Humber River.

Within months, the whole project came crashing down in ruin. Rogers disappeared along with most of the "capital funds," the herds had to be sold, the company was dissolved, and the ranch house was left derelict. Mr. Rogers might have been inexperienced as a rancher, Jingo noted bitterly, but he was an excellent manager — for himself!

At a loose end for the first time in his life, Jingo hobbled about the streets of Calgary, making full use of the hand-some cane given him by his scouts. He was asked to stand for Parliament, for as Cowboy Tom he was one of the most popular figures in the bustling cowtown. But his maverick politics did not accord with either of the established parties, and he declined. With his family now established in Eng-land, there was nothing to keep him in Canada, but he could not bring himself to leave the open prairie life he had grown to love. He was not really an Englishman, of course; he had been born and had served almost all his life abroad, and had visited England only for short intervals in a busy service career. Life there he found too confined and stultifying for his taste, and he made no bones about his preference for Canada. Having helped found its regular army, establish its ranching industry, and fight its first war, he considered himself a Canadian, proud to be associated with the vigorous young nation.

It was the broken leg that ultimately decided him. It would never again be strong enough for him to be at home on a horse, and he now walked with a pronounced limp. He could no longer get about the wide open spaces he so enjoyed, and his family in far-off England wanted him with them.

At length, in 1889, having wound up his affairs in Canada, Jingo embarked for England. His eighteen years in Canada had been the most fulfilling period of his life. He had left an enduring imprint on his adopted country, and especially on the character of its young men, thousands of whom had served under him in training school or artillery corps, or on campaign. For the rest of this life, he would receive letters or visits from men who cherished their association with him. It was not merely his official accomplishments that were remembered; rather it was his personal associations which were most treasured by the friends of "M. le Commandant," "Cowboy Tom," and "the Buckskin Brigadier."

For his part, Jingo had only good memories of Canada, and the bitterness of the last days was quickly forgotten. He had grown to love the country and its people, and he admired "their manly virtues, their amiability, their clear intellects and honest instincts."

He blamed the British for having foisted a political system on the country which had lumbered it with no fewer than nine "talking shops," far too many parliaments and politicians for so small a population. Moreover, English parliamentary institutions, he felt, did not suit the French Canadians and Irish immigrants who made up so large a part of the country's people.

As his ship sailed down the St. Lawrence, bound for England, Jingo wrote in his journal: "Apart from their politics, there are no pleasanter people to live among than Canadians, and the memory of many kindnesses remains to me."

NINETEEN

Around the World

I cannot rest from travel; I will drink
Life to the lees.
                    Alfred, Lord Tennyson, "Ulysses"

It was in the smoking room of a London club that Jingo received an offer that marked the beginning of a new adventure.

He had arrived in England to find his family comfortably settled in a quiet suburban home, his wife busy with the girls, who were finding life at an English school unlike anything they'd ever experienced in far-off Canada. Jingo had looked up relatives, all of them busy with their own lives, and had mooned about London, occasionally bumping into old friends and acquaintances from army days. He took the train to Woolwich once a week to visit Harry, who was getting along famously in the old corps, and to keep in touch with new developments in the artillery world.

It was there that he had first seen the gun that everyone was talking about, the Maxim-Nordenfeldt automatic, or, as it was more commonly and simply called, the Maxim gun. It was being demonstrated at Woolwich for the benefit of the British Army, which was considering purchasing it, and Jingo watched as the experts put it through its paces. He was astounded by its performance, which was infinitely better than anything the Gatlings could do, with their crank-turned multiple barrels. The single-barrelled Maxim, kept cool by a water-jacket and weighing only forty pounds, had a rate of fire of 600 rounds a minute, its ammunition being fed in on a belt.

But it was its ingenious mechanism that fascinated Jingo. When a round was fired, the recoil of the gun opened the breech, ejected the spent cartridge and accepted a new one, then closed, cocked, and fired itself, all at the pressure of a trigger. This gun would revolutionize warfare, Jingo could see. Infantry would no longer be able to attack in mass formation against weapons like these.

The gun had been invented by an American, soon to become a British citizen and a knight of the realm, but now just plain Mr. Hiram Percy Maxim, and Jingo was introduced to him in a London club by a mutual Woolwich friend. Jingo was intrigued by the inventor's ingenuity, and Maxim, it appeared, had asked to meet him. After listening to Jingo's praise for his invention, Maxim declined further laudatory comment with a modest wave of his cigar and the smug comment: "Guess you couldn't make a gun like that, even though you are a general. But you know how to fight with it. I tell you what I want, General. You write us a chapter on the tactical use of the gun, and then take it around the world for us."

The offer, made in so off-hand a manner, took Jingo's breath away. It was irresistible. He had found himself increasingly bored by life in England in general, and in London in particular. The place was too small, too settled, too smug for his taste; he missed the open spaces and open manners of Canada. To a restless nature like his, a peaceful retirement was anathema, and Maxim's proposition offered just the sort of escape he needed. He knew at once that he would accept, but he listened quietly while the inventor elaborated his proposal.

He had been searching for the right man for the job, Maxim explained. He wanted a distinguished officer of rank, preferably one with an artillery background, and General Strange had been recommended to him. Jingo must have relished the reference to "distinguished officer," for not long before, in a farewell letter to Canada's Prime Minister MacDonald, he had wryly noted that he "must be the most distinguished Imperial officer that ever served Canada—distinguished by not having been given three or four letters" after his name, like every other officer of rank who ever served in Canada. It had reflected a touch of bitterness, felt at the end of long and faithful service unmarked by so much as a note of thanks. He had never hankered after public adulation, but it was only human to yearn for some mark of recognition.

And now he was to receive just such a mark—and from such an unlikely source! By the time the pair had finished their cigars, the thing was done. Jingo was to tour the world with the Maxim, "the gun with a soul," as its enthusiastic inventor termed it.

The adventure began with a two-week stint in the Maxim-Nordenfeldt works, where Jingo learned the details of the inner workings of the gun. If he was to be able to sell the gun and instruct unmechanical people in its operation and maintenance, it was essential that he master the intricacies of assembly and disassembly, but for an old gunner the mechanics of the gun posed no problems. Then he was off, watching without regret the docks of Merseyside fade into the smoky mist. It would be the better part of two years before he would see them again.

His first sale was in the unlikely island of Hawaii which, for all its lovely setting and languid air, had a tradition of bloodshed and revolt. Its rulers, more often than not, were established and overthrown by force. For such a ruler in such a place, Jingo reasoned, his gun could represent stability and security, and so indeed it proved.

When Jingo arrived, in November 1888, the ruler was King Kalakaua, a fat, jolly man who had been chosen for the job when the previous ruling line had died out. Intelligent and well educated, he loved a good party, and threw the best ones himself. He was especially fond of poker, and would sit up night after night playing the game with a mixed group of native islanders and white visitors, winning or losing with equal good nature. He reminded Jingo of Charles II, "Old Rowley," with the same easy-going taste for raffish company, and his court had the same louche air. Now in middle age, he had produced no heir, and was concerned only to maintain a grip on island affairs for the balance of his lifetime. Like a famous French monarch before him, he was a fatalist: "Après moi, le déluge." Jingo liked him, the two enjoyed one another's company, and they hit it off famously from the beginning.

The Hawaiian court was entertaining a touring American baseball team when Jingo arrived, and the first official function he attended was an evening reception and dinner in the visitors' honour. It was a magnificent affair, held in the lovely gardens of the palace, floodlit by electric light and with strings of Chinese paper lanterns glowing among the trees and shrubs. The air was warm and scented with blossom, the atmosphere relaxed and friendly. The orchestra, although in Jingo's opinion too heavily addicted to Offenbach, provided pleasant background music. Jingo was enchanted.

His host presided in a cool suit of white linen, nicely set off by a pale blue silk sash, and his courtiers followed his example. The princesses, by contrast, were dressed in the latest Parisian fashion, a style of dress that did not suit them; but the other ladies present looked charming in white teagowns of classic simplicity, a dress admirably suited to the native colouring and physique.

The banquet itself was held in a huge marquee, the feast being laid out on white cloths spread on the ground, the guests sitting cross-legged on grass matting. Squatting so, with his crippled leg splayed at an awkward angle, Jingo found it all excruciatingly uncomfortable. Garlanded with flowers like a sacrificial victim, he comforted himself with the reflection that he was there "to eat rather than be eaten"—something which, a few years earlier, could not always have been taken for granted.

A beautiful woman servant, clad in white, stood behind him with a long-handled feather fan, gently cooling his bald head. Things could be worse!

The food looked most appealing, although its appearance was better than its taste; he could not help wondering whether he was eating roast pork or roast dog, both of which were on the menu. He learned that it was best to dip one's own finger quickly into the sour-tasting pink "poi" or one would be obligated to lick it from the finger of an obliging neighbour.

At the conclusion of the banquet, the pain of his cramped leg forced Jingo to withdraw before the performance of the traditional island love dance, the hula-hula, first recorded by Captain Cook, who noted dryly that the native women "shook themselves in the most whimsical manner." Jingo comforted himself with the prim observation that the dance would have been "more suggestive than graceful."

Next day, Jingo had his private interview with the king and found a ready response to his pitch. The gun was just what he needed to keep order in his turbulent nation, the king declared, as he could not maintain a large army. The gun would give him "an iron battalion, requiring neither pay, rations, nor uniform, but only cartridges, and one cool head and loyal hand to guide it." In other words, sold!

Having accomplished the purpose of his visit, Jingo had time to wander about the island and savour its charms. He noted the growing influence of the United States in island affairs, and the American interest in these British islands, which contrasted so sharply with official British apathy. Despite the native antipathy to America and Americans, he thought Hawaii must inevitably fall under the sway of the United States.

Like many before him, and many more after him, Jingo left the islands with a real regret and the pleasantest memories of the place and its people. The threat of the Maxim, he hoped, would end the cycle of repression and revolution which had brought so much bloodshed to so lovely a place.

The vastness of the Pacific, the remoteness of its islands, the other-world quality of the Antipodes, with their distinctive flora and fauna, made a great impression on Jingo as his ship steamed westwards. More and more his thoughts turned to the need for better communications than were now provided by the occasional mail steamer, to link this new world with the old European civilization which had so recently discovered it. Surely underwater telegraph cables could link Australia to America, just as they had tied America to Europe? Surely Canada should be connected to its great sister nation of Australia by a regular steamship service, and who better qualified to provide it than the Canadian Pacific Railway, which had just joined Canada's east coast to its west?

> Without such communication, and a Pacific cable, Western Canada is a cul-de-sac [he wrote], for the line from Vancouver to Japan is an outlet to a foreign country, with which the trade of Canada is as nothing compared with what it would be with Anglo-Saxon Australasia.
>
> The commerce of Canada is closed to the south by the hostile tariffs of the United States, as well as by Canadian protective duties, neither likely to be entirely removed. Communication and trade eastward with Australasia, and westward with England, would

give new life to Canada, and make her a long line of
commerce, the longest and strongest link in the chain
of a Federated British Empire—instead of driving her
into annexation with the United States, for the sake of
a commercial outlet.

In these musings, Jingo was anticipating, by only a year or
two, the great network of undersea cables soon to be laid
across the Pacific, and the fleet of graceful white-hulled
Canadian Pacific Empresses which would link Vancouver
with Japan and Australia.

As he made his leisurely way about the world—he would
spend more than a year in Australia, New Zealand, and
Tasmania—he had the time and opportunity to reflect on
the achievements and shortcomings of the British Empire.
The Englishman abroad, he noted, was far superior to the
Englishmen to be met at home, free of the parochial smug-
ness which he so disliked in England. In bringing the rule of
law and civilized standards of care and compassion to primitive societies, the Empire could play a beneficent role in
remote parts of the world, but Jingo considered that it was
not always fulfilling its responsibilities. For one thing, there
seemed no coherent, continuing policy in England for the
Empire it seemed to have acquired more or less by chance.
The British public had only apathy for the far-flung Empire
won for it by the expenditure of so much life and effort, and
left the conduct of its affairs to, as he termed them, "permanent secretaries who govern the empire without responsibility, having no soul to save, no corporate body to be kicked."

But it was the failure to sense the economic benefits that
would be made possible by the development of trade within
the Empire which most angered him. Canada and Australia
in particular could enjoy a vast and varied trade between
them, he was sure, each having products which the other
lacked and needed. Canada made the farm machinery

which Australia wanted; Australian wine could be enjoyed in Canada. Australia had fine quality hardwood, Canada plentiful softwood. As a self-made Canadian, he saw an affinity between the character of the two peoples. He liked the Australians and thought the people of New Zealand "the most kindly, genial and unpretentious society it has been my lot to meet."

En route home, he was less impressed by colonial circumstances in Africa. He did not think it possible for such Anglo-Saxon institutions as parliamentary democracy, with its respect for law and toleration of an official opposition, to be grafted onto primitive societies accustomed over the millennia to tribal despotism. Here, even more than elsewhere, he sensed the growing might of an aggressive new Germany, a looming threat to world peace, and was made gloomy by British apathy in the face of it.

"To the average Englishman, a lamp-post in Piccadilly is more important than half a continent overseas," he wrote in his journal. Only the British Admiralty seemed able to think in global terms, and had acquired a belt of coaling stations and dockyards which encircled the globe, so that a British warship could steam and be maintained indefinitely in any part of the world.

Musings on empire and the growing confrontation of world powers alternated with much reading of philosophy in the long days of peaceful voyaging, so that it was a wiser and certainly more thoughtful Jingo who steamed up the grubby reaches of the Mersey to be greeted by his welcoming family.

TWENTY

Recessional

To follow knowledge, like a sinking star,
Beyond the utmost bound of human thought.
Alfred, Lord Tennyson, "Ulysses"

By the time he was sixty years old, the world had little left to show Jingo, few experiences left for him to savour. He seemed to have been everywhere, met everyone, done everything. Into his lifetime he had crammed wars and wanderings, battle and shipwreck, triumph and terror, the warmth of comradeship and the excruciating loneliness of the solitary wanderer. He had penetrated the mysterious heart of Tibet, had climbed mountains, borne tropic heat and Arctic cold, crossed deserts and oceans, had mingled with men and women of every race in every quarter of the globe, conversed with princes and paupers. On foot, on horseback, on elephant, camel, and yak, and in a dozen man-made conveyances he had explored the limits of the physical world. Now, increasingly, he turned to the world of the intellect. Always an avid and omnivorous reader, he began, at the age of sixty, to write.

A faithful keeper of diaries since boyhood, he had all the minutiae of a long and adventurous life at his fingertips, and he began to sift and collate the accumulated mass of raw material into a coherent and concise account of his experiences over sixty years. The result, representing months of the most concentrated work, was a thick book, published by Remington in London in 1893 and entitled, in typically flamboyant style, *Gunner Jingo's Jubilee*, jubilees being very much in the public mind after the mammoth celebrations for that of the Queen.

Written in Strange's inimitable style, it was a vivid and racy account of soldiering and travelling throughout the Victorian period, when much of the world was still young and unexplored and every sort of adventure beckoned. It was illustrated by Jingo himself with a remarkable series of pen-and-wash drawings, and from the beginning it was a great success, going through three editions.

The favourable reception given his book encouraged further writings, and over the next few years he turned out a series of newspaper and magazine articles, pamphlets and booklets, mostly on military subjects or matters of public moment. While serving in Canada, he had written the first Canadian Artillery Manual, and he now followed this basic work with more refined technical writings, including "Artillery Retrospect," and a broader view of the state of military affairs in Canada, a long article titled "Military Aspects of Canada."

Having been eye-witness to some of the events of the Franco-Prussian war, a milestone in military affairs, he wrote a history, *The Franco-Prussian War, 1870-71*, but by now his interest in purely military affairs had been exhausted and increasingly he turned to more general subjects. Philosophy and religion occupied his attention, and his writing, by the turn of the century, was confined to the carrying on of an enormous correspondence. He was, by now, one of the most widely acquainted men alive, with friends in every walk of life, seemingly in every city and country around the world. He kept in touch by letter with many old comrades-in-arms, and followed their careers with the greatest interest. He was especially pleased with the rapid rise to the post of commissioner of his old Mounted Police friend and cavalry leader, Sam Steele, which endorsed his view of his old comrade as a fine fellow and a born leader of men.

An opportunity to renew this friendship occurred in February 1901, when Steele, en route home from the South African War where he had distinguished himself in command of a Canadian light cavalry regiment, Lord Strathcona's Horse, was honoured in a ceremony at Buckingham Palace. Steele was decorated with the Victorian Order, and later paraded with his regiment to receive the King's Colour from the hands of King Edward VII. But he recorded afterwards that his greatest pleasure on that memorable day was to see "my old friend of the Far West," General Strange, present at the ceremony. Mrs. Strange had been unable to attend, but Miss Strange, their eldest daughter, stood at the general's side.

After fulfilling his official obligations, Steele was free to journey down to Camberley and enjoy a weekend visit "at the hospitable home of General and Mrs. Thomas Strange. It was like old times on the plains of the then Wild West to meet those who had done so much for me, and I was indeed delighted to find the man who 'made' the Canadian Artillery in such splendid health, and taking such a deep interest in the affairs of the country." It was a visit he would repeat later when opportunity offered. Subsequently, he spent a day at Woolwich, where he had the pleasure of being shown around the artillery establishment by "the son of my very best friends," Harry Strange, who had directed the field gun in support of Steele and other members of the Alberta Field Force at Frenchman's Butte. Harry was now a major in his father's old unit.

Many of Jingo's young officers in the Canadian Artillery also rose to high rank, and Strange took great pride in their achievements, especially those of the battery units he had commanded, which played a distinguished part in the South African War.

Finding English life a bit confining, Jingo moved his family to Ireland and settled down in Kerry, where he could enjoy a more active outdoor life, with plenty of fishing and rough shooting. He was appointed a magistrate for the district, and found a new interest in administering the law to a part of the country with its own age-old, if unwritten, code of behaviour.

The subject of tariff reform, especially dear to the heart of a man who believed that the Empire's dominions and colonies suffered through the indifference of a selfish home government, also occupied much of his interest, and he wrote innumerable letters to editors on the subject and played an active part in the formation of the Tariff Reform League.

An ardent patriot, who had always deplored the fact that what in the United States was called patriotism was derided in "the dis-united states of Britain" as jingoism, he took an active part in the organization of the National Service League. With the onset of the Great War in 1914, which he had long foretold as a result of rising German nationalism and militarism, he occupied himself increasingly with the welfare of the families of army casualties.

The outbreak of war with Germany and the onset of "the troubles" in Ireland prompted a return to England, and the Stranges established themselves at Camberley, west of London. Only half an hour from the capital by train, and therefore close enough to keep in touch with friends there and in Woolwich, Camberley still offered the peace and quiet of the countryside, as well as interesting military activity at Sandhurst, the Royal Military College. It was here, in 1918, that the death of Maria brought an end to the Stranges' long and happy marriage.

The old widower found the prospect of a solitary celibate life quite intolerable, and before the year was out he had married again, at the age of eighty-seven. The bride was Janet, daughter of the late Reverend Mr. J. A. Fell and now, in her late sixties, herself the widow of the late Colonel F. C. Roxton of the Worcester Regiment.

The remarkable record of the Canadian Army throughout the Great War, and especially the leading role played by its gunners, "his" gunners, was a source of immense pride to their former commandant, and he maintained a brisk correspondence with his old unit. In 1925, at the age of ninety-three, he contributed an article to a Canadian military journal, and although he was unable to attend, he was greatly pleased to be invited to the fiftieth anniversary of the Royal Canadian Artillery which he had helped to found. As he revealed in a letter to a friend, the distinction of which he was proudest was that conferred on him by his successor, General Luard, as "the father of the Canadian Artillery," and hence the unofficial father of Canada's regular army.

On July 9, 1925, Major-General Thomas Bland Strange, at the age of ninety-three, died peacefully in his sleep at his home in Camberley.

He was buried, as befitted a former commandant, in the cemetery at Woolwich, with all the military pomp and ceremony of a field officer's funeral. Full ceremonial honours were rendered by men of his old corps, the Royal Artillery, complete with band and guard of honour, and to honour the former colonel commandant of the Canadian Royal Artillery, representatives of the Canadian government and military establishment were in attendance. Heading the Dominion delegation was Colonel H. Crerar, DSO; other officers of rank included Major-General A. C. de Lotbinière, CB, CSI, CIE; Major-General S. T. Wood, CMG; Colonel Low, DSO; and Lieutenant Hugonin, RA. Crerar would later rise to high command in another world war,

Lotbinière was a friend from Jingo's early days in Canada, Wood was a former commissioner of the RCMP, and Low was an old friend, late of Hodson's Horse. Hugonin represented the 8th Battery, RA, which Jingo had led when it captured the guns of the Sepoy Black Horse Battery in the great Mutiny.

Standing bareheaded above the grave of their old friend on a windswept cemetery hill, the little group represented the vast range of time and space encompassed by the life of Thomas Bland Strange, Galloping Gunner Jingo.

ENVOI

It is a tiny building, a mere shed, bleached and blasted by more than a century of wild winter winds, its windows boarded over and its weathered door fastened shut with a rusty padlock. It stands in a grove of poplars at the side of an abandoned road, now quite grown over, under the blue dome of prairie sky, the only landmark breaking the featureless sea of waving wheat and grass stretching to the horizon on every side.

This forgotten place, silent save for the whispering of its poplars in the breeze, is all that remains of one of the first and most famous ranches in the Canadian West, whose name, "Strangmuir," is still borne by the locality and its railway siding, although the few scattered residents have long since forgotten why. The main ranch house, a dozen miles from the village of Gleichen, southeast of Calgary, was torn down a few years ago to make way for the present wheat fields, its foundation stones bulldozed into a ditch. Now only this little outbuilding, preserved for use as a granary, survives as a memorial to the man who once lived here.

On the Blackfoot Indian reserve to the east, an impressive monument and a national historical plaque preserve the memory of Crowfoot, the wise old chief, but of his friend and frequent host, "Cowboy Tom" Strange, who helped build both the Canadian West and Canada itself, no other trace remains.

It is curious how little recognition has been accorded Jingo's contributions to Canada, then or now. In the United States, his feats would have made him a folk hero, an Ethan Allen or a Davy Crockett, but in Canada such heroes gain little fame. There is a monument to the Alberta Field Force on the riverbank at Edmonton that acknowledges the Force's leader. Fort Normandeau, built by the voltigeurs of the 65th, still stands on the riverbank west of Red Deer, where Strange put it to defend the ford. With its timber towers, its ramparts, and its ditch, it is a tiny gem of nine-teenth-century frontier fortification, and the site has been made into a provincial park. Fort Ethier, a loopholed block-house, also dating from the troubled times of the 1885 rebellion, is on private property, standing in the Lucas farm five miles north of Wetaskiwin.

Fort Saskatchewan, a pivotal point in Strange's cam-paign, is incorporated into the jail of the settlement of that name, twenty miles northeast of Edmonton. Further down the river route followed by the Alberta Field Force, Fort Victoria, whose picturesque setting Strange so admired, still preserves part of its Hudson's Bay Company establish-ment.

In Saskatchewan, Frenchman's Butte and Loon Lake, the sites of the last battles fought on Canadian soil, are now identified by cairns and plaques marking points of interest. Each remains today much as it was in 1885, and the site of Steele's action, on a narrows joining two beautiful lakes, is a provincial historic park, seven miles north of Loon Lake village. At Frenchman's Butte, reached by a short gravel road off Highway 3 north of Lloydminster, some of the rifle pits dug along the hill can be seen, and the strength of the site of Wandering Spirit's last stand still impresses the visitor.

Fort Carlton has been restored as a tourist attraction. The nearby scene of its police force's humiliation at Duck Lake is marked with a cairn and a plaque, but the restored village, now part of a historic park, was actually built as a movie set for the filming of a period western.

Fort Pitt, with its sad memories of Dickens and his detachment, has been partly restored and its historic cemetery is well looked after.

In the military base at Shilo, Manitoba, stands Strange Hall. Built in 1960, it is the recreation centre for the camp, a huge complex housing a swimming pool, gymnasium, theatre, bowling alley, and other facilities. In the officers' mess a portrait of Gunner Jingo looks down approvingly on a new generation of Canadian gunners, trained in the traditions established more than a hundred years ago by the great man himself.

Beyond this, no memorial remains, no recognition of the remarkable contribution made by Strange during the formative years of this country. In part, this may be due to his long life, which saw him survive, like some prehistoric dinosaur, from one age into another. As a young soldier he fought with cannon that had fired at Waterloo, yet he lived on into the age of the aeroplane. He arrived in a frontier Canada where a man might lose his scalp in an Indian raid, but was still living when Canada entered the Jazz Age, Mary Pickford rose to become America's Sweetheart, and at the old Hanlan's Point ballpark in Toronto, someone called Babe Ruth hit his first professional home run.

In part, too, his obscurity was brought about by his failure to court higher authority, military or political, on whom recognition depends. Bureaucracy has little regard for mavericks, and Strange had no patience with the petty proprieties of officialdom.

Yet when all has been said, Strange's obscurity probably stems most from the circumstances of time and place. The hard-working artisans and subsistence farmers of newly confederated Canada had neither the time nor the inclination to pay much regard to its soldiers, however heroic.

Generals have never cut much ice in this most prosaic of nations. Wolfe, the most famous of them all, has not a single statue to his memory in the country he wrested from imperial France.

In the rapidly developing Canada of the twentieth century, there could be even less place for an unrepentant adventurer, an ardent imperialist who had once blown men from guns, an outspoken maverick whose views would ruffle the most complacent and brand him as a hopelessly Victorian chauvinist.

Strange has suffered also from having been caught in the parochial politics of a Canada divided into two racial solitudes, a divide he was never able to bridge, despite his best efforts. As an English-speaker who often commanded French-speaking troops, he was suspect on both sides of the divide, his leadership forgotten by both. Yet it is surely ironic that Riel, a deluded visionary who gave his life attempting to destroy a nation he despised, should be remembered and revered by the people of that nation, whereas Strange, who gave so much of his life in that nation's service, should be forgotten. A very Canadian paradox.

Strange indeed!

BIBLIOGRAPHY

Deane, R., *Mounted Police Life in Canada*, London, Cassell, 1916.

James, W.M., *The British in India,* London, Macmillan, 1883.

McCourt, E., *The Buckskin Brigadier*, Toronto, Macmillan, 1955.

Mitchell, G., *RCHA: Right of the Line*, Ottawa, RCHA, 1986.

Morton, D., *The Last War Drum*, Toronto, Hakkert, 1972.

Mulvaney, C., *The North-West Rebellion*, Toronto, Hovery, 1885.

Russell, W.H., *My Diary in India,* London, Routledge, 1860.

Sergeant Pearman's Memoirs, London, Jonathan Cape, 1968.

Steele, S.B., *Forty Years in Canada*, Toronto, Jenkins, no date.

Stewart, R., *Sam Steele, Lion of the Frontier*, Toronto, Nelson, 1981.

Strange, T.B., *Gunner Jingo's Jubilee*, Edmonton, University of Alberta Press, 1988.

Turner, J., *The North-West Mounted Police*, vol. 2, Ottawa,   King's Printer, 1950.

Note: The archives of the Royal Canadian Military Institute have the Northwest Rebellion reports and diaries of J.P.A. Caron, Minister of Militia; Major General F.O. Middleton; Lt.-Col. James Mason, commanding officer of the Royal Grenadiers; R.S. Cassels of the Queen's Own Rifles of Canada; and the personal diary of a militia private, identity unknown. All are of great interest.

INDEX